THE KINGDOM OF SAUDI ARABIA

Architecturally, the University of Petroleum and Minerals at Dhahran, the world's largest university of oil technology, triumphantly exemplifies the Arab features of low closed masses and one vertical element (the water tower).

THE KINGDOM OF SAUDI ARABIA

STACEY INTERNATIONAL   LONDON

Principal contributors

Principal contributors were attached to the organizations and institutions listed when their contributions were written.

Editorial Direction and Research
Robin Dunipace
Rhona Hanbury
Anthony Lejeune
Rosamund McDougall
Angela Milburn
Charlotte Odgers
Jane Rawlinson
T. C. G. Stacey
Hilary Wilton-Steer

Art Director
Anthony Nelthorpe MSIAD
Assisted by Tod Slaughter

Arabic usages
E. F. Haddad
Ahmed Mostafa
Greg Shapland

Indexer
Michèle Clarke

Professor Sir Norman Anderson
Institute of Advanced Legal Studies,
University of London
H. St. John Armitage, O.B.E.
Dr. Randall Baker
University of East Anglia
Jeremy Barnett
British Council, Riyadh
Dr. Richard A. Chapman
University of Durham
Hajj D. Cowan
School of Oriental and African Studies,
University of London
Peter Duncan
Stanford Research Institute, Riyadh
Dr. Abdullah S. El-Banyan
Ministry of Labour and Social Affairs, Riyadh
Professor William Fisher
University of Durham
Dr. Hassan H. Hajrah
King Abdul Aziz University, Jiddah
G. R. Hawting
School of Oriental and African Studies,
University of London
Dr. Abbas Khalidar
School of Oriental and African Studies,
University of London

Professor T. M. Johnstone
School of Oriental and African Studies,
University of London
Dr. Fadil K. Kabbani
Deputy Minister for Mineral Resources,
Saudi Arabia
Geoffrey King
School of Oriental and African Studies,
University of London
James P. Mandaville
Arabian American Oil Company, Dhahran
Elizabeth Monroe, C.M.G.
St. Antony's College, University of Oxford
Dr. Theodore Prochazka
University of Riyadh
Dr. Fazlur Rahman
University of Chicago
Dr. George Rentz
Hoover Institution, Stanford, California
Cécile Rouchdy
Dar el-Hanan School, Jiddah
Dr. Mahmoud Esma'il Sieny
The Arabic Language Institute,
University of Riyadh
Dr. Ibrahim Zaid
General Organization for Social Insurance,
Saudi Arabia

Principal photographer: Peter Carmichael

All photographs in this volume were specially commissioned from Peter Carmichael, except for those listed below. Page numbers and quantity of photographs, if more than one, follow the photographer's name.

S. M. Al-Ghamdi, Aramco 20(2), 28, 156; Al-Khalifa, Aramco 36, 89, 97, 99(3), 102, 105, 106(4), 117, 145, 159, 163, 176–7, 182, 192, 197, 210–11, 213, 221(2), 222–3, 233, 234; Al-Yousif, Aramco 42–3, 85, 156–7; S. M. Amin, Aramco 86, 87, 100, 100–1, 107(2), 141(2), 175, 177, 179, 180, 212; Aramco 12–13, 13, 28, 34, 68, 80–1, 85, 105, 138, 141(3), 157, 166(2), 166–7, 167(2), 174(2), 174–5, 183, 186, 188–9, 198, 233, 236; Azad Boyadjan 10, 11; Cusdin, Burden and Howitt 242–3; D. Hadley 24(2), 40; Dr. David Harrison 20, 21(2), 22; Keystone Press Agency Ltd. 87, 131; T. H. Kiilsgaard 24(2); Geoffrey King 36(4);

Chris Kutschera 54, 63, 65, 68, 85, 96, 138–9, 148, 214; James P. Mandaville Jr. 20(4), 21, 22; Middle East Archives 65, 70(2), 94–5, 108, 109, 160–1, 187, 221, 225; Ministry of Information, Riyadh 10, 11, 70, 71, 91, 96(2), 140, 141, 147(2), 188(3); B. H. Moody, Aramco 69(2), 84(2), 132–3, 143, 174–5, 176, 204–5, 209; Safour Naamani 96, 103, 105, 106, 107(2), 109; Mathias Oppersdorf 13, 36–7, 49, 52–3, 58–9, 63; Dr. Angelo Pesce (Ministry of Information, Riyadh) 50–1; Woody Pridgeon 22(2); Ralph Roberts 24; Royal Geographical Society 78(6); Saudia 13, 19, 20(5), 33(2), 121, 138–9, 142, 145(2), 163, 167.

The Kingdom of Saudi Arabia
Stacey International
128 Kensington Church Street, London W8 4BH

© 1977 Stacey International

ISBN 0 905743 04 0

Maps and diagrams specially prepared by
Arka Cartographics Limited, London
Designer Le Roy-Chen
Cartographers Peter Arnold, Roger Bourne,
Bob Brett, Lee Brooks, Kevin Diaper,
Paul Draper, Allan Rees

Set in Monophoto Century by
Tradespools Limited, Frome, England
Colour origination by
Culver Graphics, High Wycombe, England
Printed and bound in Japan by
Dai Nippon Printing Company Limited, Tokyo

The publishers gratefully acknowledge help from the following organizations and individuals:

Fuad al-Angawi; Abdul Rahman al-Ansari; Mohammed El Aqeel, Ministry of Communications, Riyadh; Aramco World Magazine, Beirut; Aramco Public Relations Photography Unit, Dhahran, and Burnett Moody; H. St. J. Armitage, O.B.E.; Tarif Asad; Majid El-Ass; Salem Azzam, C.V.O.; British Council, Riyadh, and Jeremy Barnett; British Embassy, Jiddah; British Library, London; British Museum (Natural History); Central Planning Organization; Riccardo Cesati, Milan; Cusdin, Burden and Howitt, Chartered Architects, London; Ghaleb Abul-Faraj; Mohammed Said Farsy, Town Planning Office, Riyadh; Fauna Preservation Society, London; Nassir Haidary; Dr. David Harrison; David Howard, Robert Matthew & Co.; Abdulla Al-Ibrahim, General Organization for Social Insurance, Riyadh; Robert Irving; Abdul Karim Jamal; Mohammed

Khayyat; Stuart Laing; Ministry of Information, Riyadh, and H. E. Dr. Abdul Aziz M. Khoja; National Geographic Society, Washington, D.C.; Reda Nazer; Bob Nordberg, Aramco; E. D. O'Brien Organization; Izzidin Ali Osman; Dr. Angelo Pesce, Naples; Fuad al-Rayis; Michael Rice & Co. Limited; Alan Rothnie, C.M.G.; Royal Geographical Society, London; Royal Institute of International Affairs, London; Saudia, Jiddah: Public Affairs Division and Yarub A. Balkhair; Saudi Arabian Embassy, London; Saudi Arabian Monetary Agency, Jiddah; St. Antony's College, Oxford; School of Oriental and African Studies, University of London; H. E. Sheikh Fahd K. al-Sedayri; Said Sieny; Stanford Research Institute, Riyadh, and Peter Duncan; University of Durham; Dr. Abdullah al-Wohaibi; World Wildlife Fund, London; H. E. Dr. Mohammed Abdu Yamani.

Maps   Diagrams

Charts, diagrams and maps are based on the latest facts available at the time of their preparation, but subsequent developments may have superseded information contained therein.

Contents

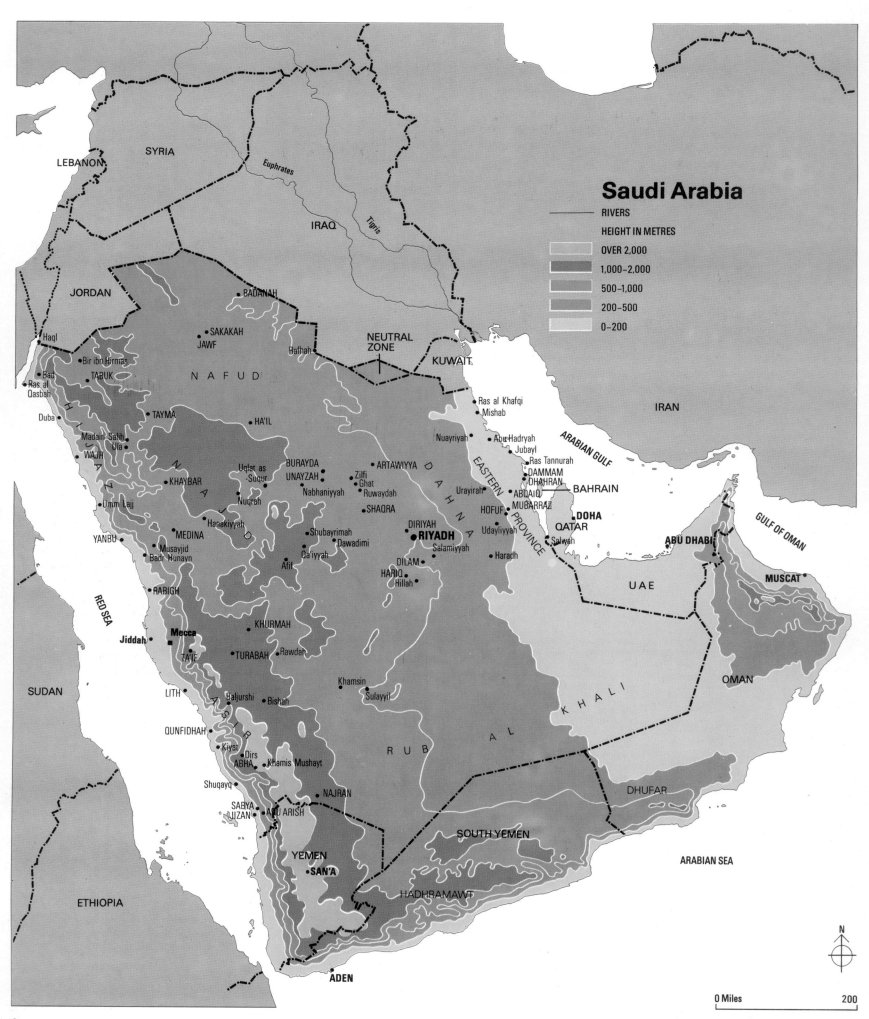

Saudi Arabia

— RIVERS

HEIGHT IN METRES

OVER 2,000
1,000–2,000
500–1,000
200–500
0–200

LEBANON
SYRIA
IRAQ
Euphrates
Tigris
JORDAN
BADANAH
NEUTRAL ZONE
KUWAIT
Haql
Bir ibn Hirmas
SAKAKAH
JAWF
Rafhah
Ras al Khafgi
Mishab
IRAN
Bad
Ras al Qasbah
TABUK
N A F U D
Nuayriyah
Abu Hadryah
Jubayl
Ras Tannurah
ARABIAN GULF
Duba
TAYMA
HA'IL
Madain Salih
Ula
WAJH
Uqlat as -Suqur
BURAYDA
UNAYZAH
ARTAWIYYA
D A H N A
DAMMAM
DHAHRAN
BAHRAIN
KHAYBAR
Nabhaniyyah
Zilfi
Ghat
Ruwaydah
Urayirah
ABQAIQ
MUBARRAZ
Umm Lajj
Nuqrah
SHAQRA
HOFUF
DOHA
QATAR
Hanakiyyah
Shubayrimah
DIRIYAH
RIYADH
Udayliyyah
Salwah
ABU DHABI
GULF OF OMAN
YANBU
MEDINA
Qa'iyyah
Dawadimi
Salamiyyah
Musayjid
Badr Hunayn
Afif
DILAM
HARIQ
Hillah
Haradh
EASTERN PROVINCE
MUSCAT
RED SEA
RABIGH
KHURMAH
UAE
Mecca
Rawdah
Jiddah
TA'IF
TURABAH
Khamsin
R U B   A L   K H A L I
OMAN
LITH
A S I R
Baljurshi
Bishah
Sulayyil
SUDAN
QUNFIDHAH
Kiyat
Dirs
ABHA
Khamis Mushayt
DHUFAR
Shuqayq
NAJRAN
SABYA
UIZAN
ABU ARISH
SOUTH YEMEN
ARABIAN SEA
YEMEN
SAN'A
ETHIOPIA
HADHRAMAWT

ADEN

N

0 Miles   200

8

The Islamic calendar

Comparative Tables of AH and CE Dates

The Islamic era is based on the Hijrah, the migration of the Prophet Muhammad from Mecca to Medina, which took place on 16 July 622 CE. The Islamic year is lunar, and has 354 days. There are approximately 103 Hijri years to a Gregorian century; AH stands for Anno Hegirae (hegira being the Latinized form of Hijrah), and CE for Christian Era. The Hijri year begins on the day of the month indicated.

AH	CE	
1	*622*	16 July
10	*631*	9 April
20	*640*	21 December
30	*650*	4 September
40	*660*	17 May
50	*670*	29 January
60	*679*	13 October
70	*689*	25 June
80	*699*	9 March
90	*708*	20 November
100	*718*	3 August
110	*728*	16 April
120	*737*	29 December
130	*747*	11 September
140	*757*	25 May
150	*767*	6 February
160	*776*	19 October
170	*786*	3 July
180	*796*	16 March
190	*805*	27 November
200	*815*	11 August
210	*825*	24 April
220	*835*	5 January
230	*844*	18 September
240	*854*	2 June
250	*864*	13 February
260	*873*	27 October
270	*883*	11 July
280	*893*	23 March
290	*902*	5 December
300	*912*	18 August
310	*922*	1 May
320	*932*	13 January
330	*941*	26 September
340	*951*	9 June
350	*961*	20 February
360	*970*	4 November
370	*980*	17 July
380	*990*	31 March
390	*999*	13 December
400	*1009*	25 August
410	*1019*	9 May
420	*1029*	20 January
430	*1038*	3 October
440	*1048*	16 June
450	*1058*	28 February
460	*1067*	11 November
470	*1077*	25 July
480	*1087*	8 April
490	*1096*	19 December
500	*1106*	2 September
510	*1116*	16 May
520	*1126*	27 January
530	*1135*	11 October
540	*1145*	24 June
550	*1155*	7 March
560	*1164*	18 November
570	*1174*	2 August
580	*1184*	14 April
590	*1193*	27 December

AH	CE	
600	*1203*	10 September
610	*1213*	23 May
620	*1223*	4 February
630	*1232*	18 October
640	*1242*	1 July
650	*1252*	14 March
660	*1261*	26 November
670	*1271*	9 August
680	*1281*	22 April
690	*1291*	4 January
700	*1300*	16 September
710	*1310*	31 May
720	*1320*	12 February
730	*1329*	25 October
740	*1339*	9 July
750	*1349*	22 March
760	*1358*	3 December
770	*1368*	16 August
780	*1378*	30 April
790	*1388*	11 January
800	*1397*	24 September
810	*1407*	8 June
820	*1417*	18 February
830	*1426*	2 November
840	*1436*	16 July
850	*1446*	29 March
860	*1455*	11 December
870	*1465*	24 August
880	*1475*	7 May
890	*1485*	18 January
900	*1494*	2 October
910	*1504*	14 June
920	*1514*	26 February
930	*1523*	10 November
940	*1533*	23 July
950	*1543*	6 April
960	*1552*	18 December
970	*1562*	31 August
980	*1572*	14 May
990	*1582*	26 January

Transfer from Julian to Gregorian calendar

AH	CE	
1000	*1591*	19 October
1010	*1601*	2 July
1020	*1611*	16 March
1030	*1620*	26 November
1040	*1630*	10 August
1050	*1640*	23 April
1060	*1650*	4 January
1070	*1659*	18 September
1080	*1669*	1 June
1090	*1679*	12 February
1100	*1688*	26 October
1110	*1698*	10 July
1120	*1708*	23 March
1130	*1717*	5 December
1140	*1727*	19 August
1150	*1737*	1 May

AH	CE	
1160	*1747*	13 January
1170	*1756*	26 September
1180	*1766*	9 June
1190	*1776*	21 February
1200	*1785*	4 November
1210	*1795*	18 July
1220	*1805*	1 April
1230	*1814*	14 December
1240	*1824*	26 August
1250	*1834*	10 May
1260	*1844*	22 January
1270	*1853*	4 October
1280	*1863*	18 June
1290	*1873*	1 March
1300	*1882*	12 November
1310	*1892*	26 July
1318	*1900*	1 May
1319	*1901*	20 April
1320	*1902*	10 April
1321	*1903*	30 March
1322	*1904*	18 March
1323	*1905*	8 March
1324	*1906*	25 February
1325	*1907*	14 February
1326	*1908*	4 February
1327	*1909*	23 January
1328	*1910*	13 January
1329	*1911*	2 January
1330	*1911*	22 December
1331	*1912*	11 December
1332	*1913*	30 November
1333	*1914*	19 November
1334	*1915*	9 November
1335	*1916*	28 October
1336	*1917*	17 October
1337	*1918*	7 October
1338	*1919*	26 September
1339	*1920*	15 September
1340	*1921*	4 September
1341	*1922*	24 August
1342	*1923*	14 August
1343	*1924*	2 August
1344	*1925*	22 July
1345	*1926*	12 July
1346	*1927*	1 July
1347	*1928*	20 June
1348	*1929*	9 June
1349	*1930*	29 May
1350	*1931*	19 May
1351	*1932*	7 May
1352	*1933*	26 April
1353	*1934*	16 April
1354	*1935*	5 April
1355	*1936*	24 March
1356	*1937*	14 March
1357	*1938*	3 March
1358	*1939*	21 February
1359	*1940*	10 February
1360	*1941*	29 January
1361	*1942*	19 January

AH	CE	
1362	*1943*	8 January
1363	*1943*	28 December
1364	*1944*	17 December
1365	*1945*	6 December
1366	*1946*	25 November
1367	*1947*	15 November
1368	*1948*	3 November
1369	*1949*	24 October
1370	*1950*	13 October
1371	*1951*	2 October
1372	*1952*	21 September
1373	*1953*	10 September
1374	*1954*	30 August
1375	*1955*	20 August
1376	*1956*	8 August
1377	*1957*	29 July
1378	*1958*	18 July
1379	*1959*	7 July
1380	*1960*	26 June
1381	*1961*	15 June
1382	*1962*	4 June
1383	*1963*	25 May
1384	*1964*	13 May
1385	*1965*	2 May
1386	*1966*	22 April
1387	*1967*	11 April
1388	*1968*	31 March
1389	*1969*	20 March
1390	*1970*	9 March
1391	*1971*	27 February
1392	*1972*	16 February
1393	*1973*	4 February
1394	*1974*	25 January
1395	*1975*	14 January
1396	*1976*	3 January
1397	*1976*	23 December
1398	*1977*	12 December
1399	*1978*	2 December
1400	*1979*	21 November
1401	*1980*	9 November
1402	*1981*	30 October
1403	*1982*	19 October
1404	*1983*	8 October
1405	*1984*	27 September
1406	*1985*	16 September
1407	*1986*	6 September
1408	*1987*	26 August
1409	*1988*	14 August
1410	*1989*	4 August
1411	*1990*	24 July
1412	*1991*	13 July
1413	*1992*	2 July
1414	*1993*	21 June
1415	*1994*	10 June
1416	*1995*	31 May
1417	*1996*	19 May
1418	*1997*	9 May
1419	*1998*	28 April
1420	*1999*	17 April
1421	*2000*	6 April

Introduction

HM King Khalid of Saudi Arabia.

This comprehensive work is launched at a seminal period in the history of Saudi Arabia, as one of the most exceptional countries in the world emerges into modern statehood.

As the extent of the bounty of its natural resources became apparent, the ancient land of Arabia, under Saudi leadership, had various options. That it chose firmly to seize its opportunities and accept its full responsibilities both to itself, now and in the future, and in the Islamic, Arab and world communities, is a

*measure of the quality of the Saudi Arabian
people and the leadership they have enjoyed.
    When King Faisal died a martyr's death on
March 15, 1975, King Khalid took over established
policies in both domestic and foreign fields. Under
King Khalid's guidance, the country has forged
ahead on its predicted course. It was on behalf of
the King that Crown Prince Fahd emphasized the
unwavering commitment to Islam "from which
emanate all our ideals". In the context of Islam
the Five Year Plans have evolved, bringing radical
changes to the standard of living of Saudi
Arabians, their welfare and social security, their
education and personal expectations. In industry
and agriculture, self-sufficiency had become the
goal, securing the future with sound husbandry of
today's resources.
    A similar continuity prevails in foreign policy,
rooted in the reign of the late King Abdul Aziz ibn
Saud. Put simply, it is one of peace and Islamic
solidarity – a policy proven actively to contribute
to good sense and stability. A comparable
commitment has guided the country in its
commercial policy, since Saudi Arabia's financial
weight today is such as to affect the free world's
economy.*

*   King Khalid has summed up his country's role:
"The interests of the world are intermingled, and
because of this interdependence the world looks
to a new and co-operative spirit. We, as a Muslim
state, draw this spirit from our Qur'anic
constitution. The Holy Qur'an says, 'O People, we
have created you of male and female and make out
of you nations and tribes in order for you to know
each other. The most deserving before God is the
most pious among you.' So it is the duty of all of
us to act for understanding among nations to
achieve a better life, worthy of human dignity. We
pray that Arabs and Muslims carry the torch of
this human spirit for the whole human spirit in the
world at large."*

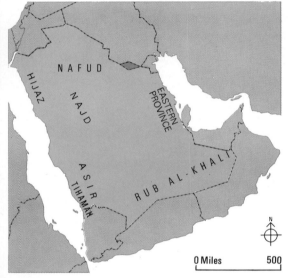

1 The Country

The heat is often forbidding, the face of the landscape often cruelly dry. And yet temperatures and seasons vary greatly, and parts of Saudi Arabia's vast area enjoy dependable rains. Underground water from past geological eras can be tapped to make the rich powdery loess bloom. The great sand deserts alone must always defy the ingenuity of man to make them bring forth. But they too can be made to yield their mineral wealth.

In contrast to Saudi Arabia's familiar image, the green uplands of Asir, in the south-west (far left), are well watered and have sustained a settled population from ancient times. Given regular water supply, much of the dun landscape of loess scrub desert (top picture) would bring forth plentifully. The second picture (above) shows the typical sabkhah territory of the Gulf coast and islets. The only regions condemned to barrenness are the great deserts of Nafud in the north, and the Rub al-Khali, or Empty Quarter (bottom picture), in the south.

Geography and Climate

THE Arabian peninsula, of which the Saudi Arabian state forms by far the largest part, covers well over three million square kilometres (Saudi Arabia itself comprises 2,300,000 square kilometres – nearly 900,000 square miles). The whole area is thought to be a detached fragment of an even larger continental mass which included Africa (*see also* page 20). Large rifts (it is suggested) developed because of thermal currents in the lower mantle of the earth, forcing apart surface masses or "plates". The Arabian plate is held to have drifted northwards, impelled by the opening of the Red Sea and Gulf of Aden, and by subsequent spreading of the sea floors – a movement that may well be continuing.

As it moved, the Arabian plate tilted, with the western side upraised and the eastern side lowered, so that the east became covered by layers of younger, sedimentary rocks. In the west, disturbance associated with the opening of the Red Sea led to much upwelling of magma, which has produced the extensive lava fields (*harrah*) that occur all along the west side of the country, especially in the Mecca-Jiddah-Medina area. Because of this geographical origin, with ancient resistant rocks in the west, capped here and there with very recent lava, and progressively younger rocks towards the east, Saudi Arabia exhibits in its geography, very broadly speaking, a north-south running "grain". In the extreme west, along the Red Sea, there is a coastal plain (Tihamah), flat and usually very narrow, except in the Jiddah area where it offers a small but useful lowland gap giving access to Mecca and the interior. Then immediately to the east is a formidable succession of high plateaux with steep scarp edges dominating the Tihamah below. Here occur the highest peaks in Saudi Arabia; particularly south of Mecca, where heights of over 8,200 feet are reached. East again of this highland zone is an extensive region of irregular plateaux and upland basins, the largest of which are those of Medina and Rakbah,

The mountains of the south-west plunge from plateaux of 8,000 ft and peaks of 10,000 ft to lowland valleys, where regular crops are grown.

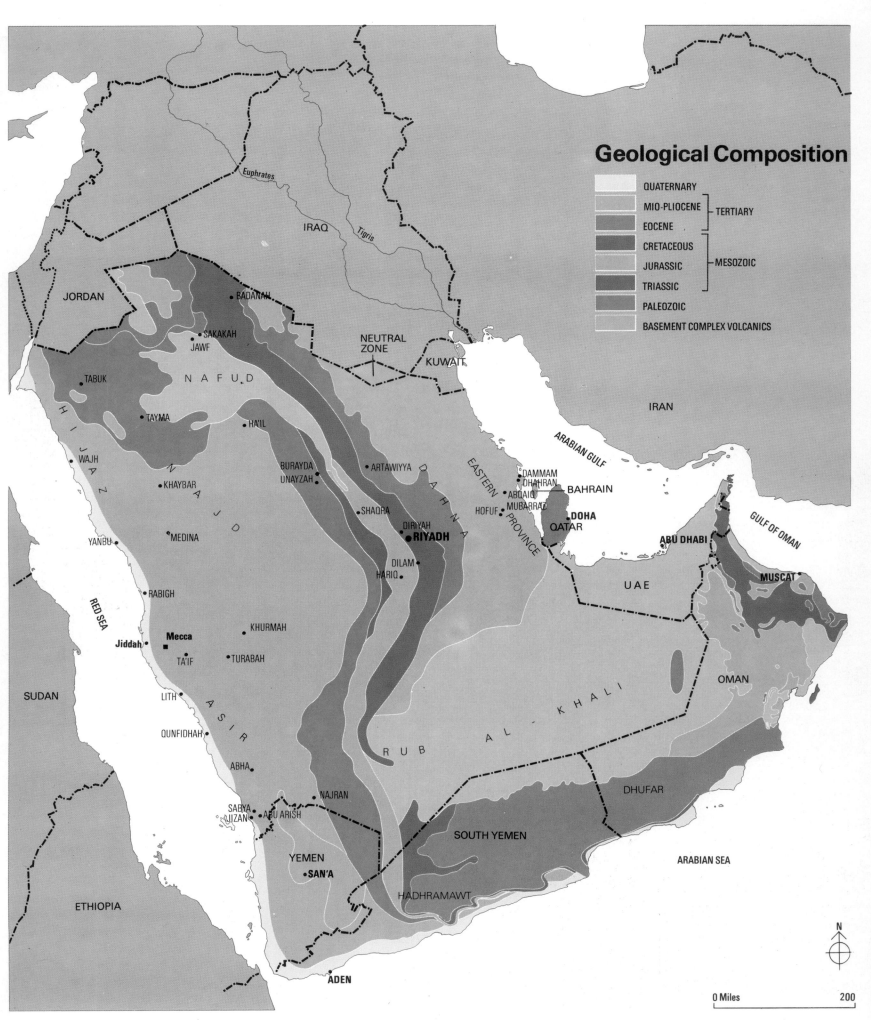

Geological Composition

- QUATERNARY
- MIO-PLIOCENE ⎤ TERTIARY
- EOCENE ⎦
- CRETACEOUS ⎤
- JURASSIC ⎥ MESOZOIC
- TRIASSIC ⎦
- PALEOZOIC
- BASEMENT COMPLEX VOLCANICS

JORDAN

IRAQ

Euphrates

Tigris

NEUTRAL ZONE

KUWAIT

BADANAH

SAKAKAH

JAWF

TABUK

N A F U D

TAYMA

HA'IL

IRAN

ARABIAN GULF

WAJH

KHAYBAR

BURAYDA

UNAYZAH

ARTAWIYYA

DAMMAM
DHAHRAN
ABQAIQ
MUBARRAZ
HOFUF

BAHRAIN

EASTERN PROVINCE

DOHA
QATAR

MEDINA

SHAQRA

DIRIYAH

RIYADH

ABU DHABI

GULF OF OMAN

YANBU

DILAM
HARIQ

UAE

MUSCAT

RABIGH

RED SEA

KHURMAH

Mecca

Jiddah

TA'IF

TURABAH

RUB   AL - KHALI

OMAN

SUDAN

LITH

A S I R

QUNFIDHAH

ABHA

NAJRAN

DHUFAR

SABYA
JIZAN
ABU ARISH

SOUTH YEMEN

ARABIAN SEA

YEMEN

SAN'A

HADHRAMAWT

ETHIOPIA

ADEN

H I J A Z

N A J D

D A H N A

0 Miles   200

N

where collection of sub-surface water allows human settlement on a larger scale.

Further east, altitude gradually declines, but then occurs a whole succession of younger, sedimentary rocks – sandstones, limestones and marls. The harder series stand out as scarps or isolated ridges, with lower, flatter valleys formed in the less resistant strata between. The most imposing of these scarps is the Jabal Tuwayq, a limestone ridge that attains 3,200 feet and extends in a sinuous curve north-west and south-west of Riyadh, which lies in a gap breaking through the Jabal. Gradually, altitude diminishes eastwards, until one of the last of these scarps occurs near Hofuf, after which the surface drops to form the low-lying coastal plain of Hasa.

Although some lowland areas or basins consist of bare rock pavement, most tend to be covered in loose rock deposits eroded by wind, by shattering due to temperature contrasts and, in the recent geological past, by water action. Near hill or plateau bases are stony areas of larger rock fragments; further away are outwash gravels, while in areas of low relief sand predominates, with silts in valley bottoms. Sand covers large areas. In the north, the Great Nafud is an expanse of sand dunes (*uruq*), often reddish in colour, interspersed with areas of bare rock pavement. A narrower zone of sand, ad Dahma, links the Nafud to an even larger expanse of sand, indeed the largest sand desert in the world – the Rub al-Khali (Abode of Emptiness), which occupies much of the south of Saudi Arabia. In the extreme west the Rub al-Khali is a "sand sea" (Bahr es Safi) surrounded by gravel plains: in the east, there are massive dunes with salt basins (*sabkhah*). The whole area was for long an extreme barrier to human movement, but oil prospecting and the discovery of artesian water have reduced its difficulty.

Of all the sizeable countries on earth, Saudi Arabia is probably the driest. It derives its weather mainly from the north and west: climatically it is linked to the eastern Mediterranean and adjacent lands, in that it has a long, hot and almost totally dry summer, with a short cool winter season during which a little rain occurs. This is because air masses reaching Arabia have been largely exhausted of their moisture. Although Arabia is surrounded on three sides by sea, aridity is the dominant feature.

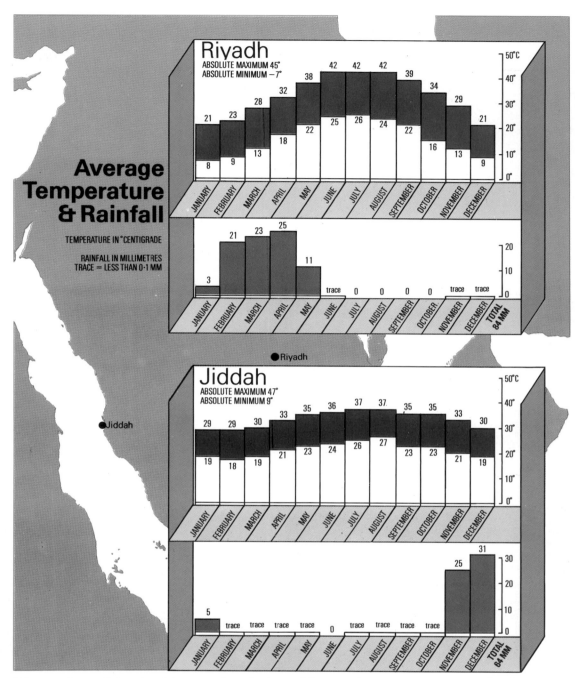

Average Temperature & Rainfall

TEMPERATURE IN °CENTIGRADE

RAINFALL IN MILLIMETRES
TRACE = LESS THAN 0·1 MM

The surface of the Arabian peninsula is slightly on the tilt – higher in the west, and dropping gently from the geologically very ancient Western Plateau towards the Gulf.

The sea keeps temperatures fairly constant in the coastal regions; in the interior day/night and summer/winter temperatures vary sharply. Rain, though scarce, can cause flooding.

With the sole exception of Asir in the extreme south-west, any influences from the southern tropical zones are excluded by the highland rim that runs from Oman through the Hadhramawt to the Yemens.

Because of the dryness of the air reaching Saudi Arabia, and the consequent lack of cloud, insolation is considerable, producing very high summer temperatures – up to 45 or 50°C, and sometimes even more in the southern deserts. But the cloudlessness also allows heat to escape from the surface at night, especially in winter; so temperatures

drop quite markedly between day and night, and between summer and winter. The night coolness, with a 10 to 22°C drop at both seasons, is a boon in summer but leads to sporadic frost in the interior of the centre and north during winter; –7°C has been recorded at Riyadh.

Rainfall is scanty, irregular and unreliable, occurring mostly during the months from October to April. Except along the Red Sea coast, and inland over the mountains of Asir, summers are practically rainless, and in the interior several years may elapse without rain. The extreme south of Saudi Arabia, the

While Saudi Arabia has no permanent rivers reaching the sea, a dependable flow of water nourishes the deep wadis of the south-west in winter months.

virtually uninhabited Rub al-Khali, is almost entirely without rain – one of the driest areas on earth; but over the rest of the country (Asir excepted) annual totals amount to about 100 mm, though 150 mm have been known to fall locally within twenty-four hours. Because of temperature contrasts, winds can be strong, even violent, raising dust storms from time to time. On the coasts relative humidity is high, due to sea breezes that bring in moisture; this effect is, however, local, and most of the interior is extremely dry. The mean figures given on page 17 for Jiddah and Riyadh illustrate the principal features of the Saudi Arabian climate, as well as the contrasts between coast and interior. The hills of Asir, however, do participate in the marked summer rainfall which benefits the Yemen plateau.

Until recently the difficulty of the terrain, its aridity and the consequent scarcity of good soil sharply controlled the ways of life within Saudi Arabia. Apart from a few fishermen and traders, Saudi Arabia was able to support only a small population, estimated at 1.5 to 2 million in the 1930s. Possibly half of this could be regarded as "rural settled" – cultivators, village craftsmen and shepherds moving locally over short distances with their animals. At least a quarter of the population was wholly nomadic, following a regular pattern of rough grazing of sheep, goats and camels, which involved considerable annual movement. Both ways of life depended upon the use of wells which tapped water-tables at moderate or shallow depth; for there is no perennial river.

In some cases, catchment of water is local, from rapid percolation of rainfall, but over many parts of Saudi Arabia there is a much larger series of water-tables that allow "creep" of water underground from the better watered south-west through to the east coast. Some of the wells which tap this kind of water-table are large; Mecca and Medina have a number, and others occur, for example, at Mudawwara, Tabuk and Ula. Some of this underground water is from wetter climatic phases of an earlier geological time, and is not replaced by present-day rainfall when drawn off.

Today, with the advent of planned irrigation and exploitation of underground water resources, four or five times the former population is supported, and major cities have rapidly evolved at Riyadh, Jiddah and Mecca.

*The giant groundsels and bearded
lichen on evergreen trees* (seen on the
right) *characterize the sub-tropical
Alpine vegetation of highland Asir.*

Flora and Fauna

The remarkable variety of Saudi Arabia's flora is due to the country's range of climate and soils. In some areas a sudden rainfall will make an apparent desert bloom in a matter of hours. Many other "garden" species only survive if regularly watered.

The yellow cassia

A young pomegranate

The spiny sea holly

A flowering hibiscus

Centaurea sinaica (thistle)

Acacia ehrenbergiana

Anthemis deserti

Rumex vesicarius

Cistanche Tubulosa

Echinots

Opuntia

The Tamarisk survives the fiercest droughts.

Calatropis Procera

MAPS and geography books make Arabia a part of Asia, but plant and animal life clearly bear out the theory that it is really an extension of Africa. The desert steppes which now link the peninsula with Asia are the bottom of an ancient sea which once divided the continents. The Red Sea is a rift through a single mass of igneous rock, the Arabian-African Shield.

Saudi Arabia's wildlife is thus an African complex of species, evolving and mingling with invaders from the Asian mainland.

The animals and plants of northern and north-eastern Saudi Arabia are generally closely related to or identical with Saharan species. To the south and the west, wildlife assumes its older, tropical African character. Only in the Oman mountains, known to be geologically related to the highlands across the Gulf, do we find strong Asiatic elements.

Plant Life

Except in parts of the Asir highlands, where the juniper, the wild olive, and some other larger trees grow together over large areas, there are no forests in Saudi Arabia. In some parts, scattered small acacia trees are common. Further east and north the vegetation is typical of arid steppes – hundreds of square kilometres of small, drought-adapted shrubs, a metre or less high. Often one species, such as the *rimth* saltbush or the yellow-flowered *arfaj* shrublet, dominates the landscape. The ground between these shrublets is green for only two to three months of the year, when winter rains bring forth a host of herbs. Among these annuals, known collectively as *usht* by the Beduin, are the desert *Anthemis* or camomile, many species of the mustard family, and a striking iris.

Only the salt-impregnated bottoms of *sabkhahs*, small areas of rock-floored desert, and a few fields of actively moving dunes do not support any plants. Even most parts of the Rub al-Khali have scattered shrublets of the prickly *hadh* saltbush, a *Tribulus*, or the scarlet-fruited *abal*.

Arabia's famous hunting dog, the saluki.

Mammals

The largest wild mammal of Saudi Arabia is the Arabian oryx. This one hundred-kilogram antelope with long, straight horns, which was known in this area in Biblical times now sadly appears to be almost extinct; this is mainly the result of over-hunting. Until recently there was some hope that small groups might still exist in the wild, particularly in the Rub al-Khali in the south-east, but recent reports have not been encouraging.

Also much diminished is the gazelle, which was common over most of Arabia until it was slaughtered by motorized hunting parties in the 1930s and 1940s. Gazelles of various kinds used to be common, such as the Saudi Arabian Dorcas Gazelle, which was found in south-east Arabia, and the Sand Gazelle which ranged throughout the country, but they are now rarely seen except in remote areas of the south and in some hill tracts. Like the oryx, they have adapted to desert life, obtaining much of their water needs from the scanty vegetation.

The mountain goat, or ibex, is found in high country in the far north-west, the Hijaz mountains, and the south-west.

The cheetah was seen sometimes on the broad plains of the far north and south, but now may well be extinct. The caracal probably still exists in the north, while the leopard has been reported from the highlands of Asir. The rare Arabian sand cat, amazingly like a domestic cat in appearance, inhabits some of the most barren sand country.

The wolf, the jackal, foxes, and the striped hyena are found in Arabia, as are the hedgehog, the porcupine and the ratel, or honey badger. More common rodents are the small Arabian hare and the jerboa, or kangaroo rat. The rat-like jerd and mouse-sized gerbil burrow beneath desert shrubs. Baboons are not unusual in the central Hijaz and Asir highlands, where they raid terraced croplands.

Birds

The ostrich is now extinct in Arabia,

although it has figured in Arabic poetry since pre-Islamic times. One of the last on record was seen near the Iraqi border in 1938, and caches of complete egg shells are still sometimes found by Beduin under drifting sands.

Game birds in Saudi Arabia include the *hubara* bustard, the sand grouse, quail, partridges, doves, the stone curlew, and the courser.

Many European birds pass through Arabia on spring and autumn migrations – flamingoes, storks, swallows, wagtails, warblers, and many others. Among the few true desert residents are several larks, including the sweet-voiced hoopoe lark, known to the desert Arab as *Umm Salim*, "Salim's mother". Another songbird, the bulbul, is an oasis resident.

Reptiles

The water-conserving body structure of reptiles makes them well adapted for life in arid lands, but many cannot endure extremes of heat and must lead nocturnal or subterranean lives. Thus, although some fourteen species of snake have been reported from Saudi Arabia, few are seen. One of these might be the small, thick-bodied sand viper, a venomous but seldom lethal creature that moves like the sidewinder of the American South-West. More dangerous, but fortunately very rare, are the Arabian hooded cobra, found in well-vegetated areas of the mountainous west, and the all-black hoodless cobra in the central and north-eastern deserts. Harmless snakes are more common, among them the *malpolon*, which spreads its neck into a hood when cornered and is often mistaken for a cobra. Potentially dangerous, but shy, sea snakes are found in the Arabian Gulf.

There are no poisonous lizards in Arabia, although two species are imposingly large: the sixty-centimetre long, plant-eating *dabb*, and the even longer, whip-tailed *waral*, or monitor lizard. The sand skink is found beneath dune slip faces; its smooth submarine-like form is well adapted to life in sand.

Marine Life

The former Gulf pearl fisheries have

A kitten of Arabia's rare sand cat.

The Oryx may now be extinct in Arabia.

The spiny hedgehog is well defended.

Many species of reptiles are found in Saudi Arabia – most remarkable of the lizards being, perhaps, the dabb *(right), which can absorb its moisture by breathing (the only animal in the world to do so), allowing it to live in a waterless desert.*

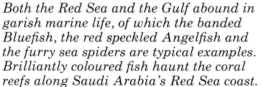

Both the Red Sea and the Gulf abound in garish marine life, of which the banded Bluefish, the red speckled Angelfish and the furry sea spiders are typical examples. Brilliantly coloured fish haunt the coral reefs along Saudi Arabia's Red Sea coast.

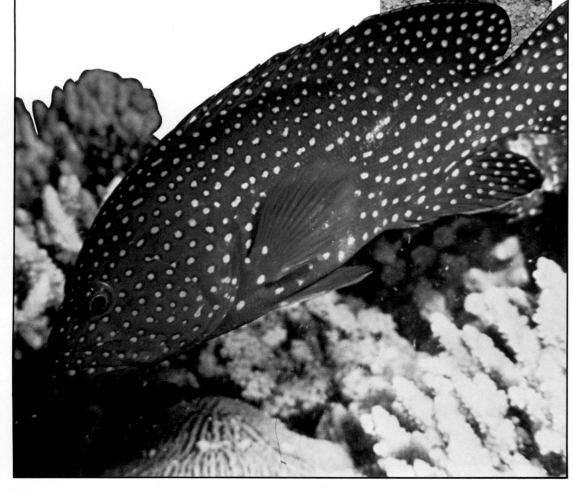

An eleventh hour rescue operation has saved the Arabian oryx from certain extinction at the hand of man.

almost disappeared since cultured pearls flooded the markets, but the development of commercial fishing, particularly for shrimp, has provided a substitute industry. Sea turtles nest on the low-lying Gulf islands but are threatened by over-hunting.

Sharks are common in the Gulf but are not a threat to bathers. The deeper waters of the Red Sea are better shark territory. Sea mammals include the porpoise, occasional whales, and the dugong.

Insects
Saudi Arabia is remarkably free of insect pests. Mosquitoes and malaria have been wiped out by Government campaigns in most districts.

Among the more common desert insects are the dark-hued ground beetle and the scarab beetle. Not strictly insects, but arachnids, are the scorpion, the large, non-venomous camel spider, and the crimson velvet mite seen on the sands after rain.

Conservation
The Saudi Arabian Government, realizing that many of Arabia's animals are near extinction, has now outlawed hunting except under strict conditions; a few years ago "Operation Oryx" was launched by the Fauna Preservation Society, the World Wildlife Fund, and various other international organizations for nature conservation, and two males and a female were taken to the United States of America. They were successfully settled in Arizona, and there are now eighty-two of these rare animals in various American zoos; the long-term aim is that the oryx will eventually be reintroduced into its original habitat. The Saudi Arabian Government contributed to this remarkable rescue; the next step is to be the restocking of animals in their former natural ranges and the development of such herds to ecologically balanced sizes; King Khalid's interest in conservation is well known. The gazelle may yet roam the central and northern plains again; the ostrich and cheetah resume their ancient habitat.

Arabia's larger mammals now protected by conservation policies include (left to right, from the top): *the Arabian ibex, believed to be the progenitor of the domestic goat; the Arabian gazelle, found in the mountains and foothills of the west and south; the caracal lynx, still to be seen in remoter corners of the country; and the fleet-footed cheetah, whose speed over short distances of semi-desert can reach 60 mph. Two other species of gazelle are also very rare – the Saudi Arabian dorcas gazelle and the slender-horned gazelle. The Arabian tahr is known to survive in the mountains of Oman. The World Wildlife Fund and other societies have ensured the survival of the Arabian oryx by establishing a herd in Arizona from animals captured in Saudi Arabia. The oryx is probably extinct in the wild. Until the middle of this century the ostrich was still seen in Arabia.*

Mineral Wealth

Blessed with a vast land area, and in most areas relatively easy overland communications, Saudi Arabia is well placed to exploit a wide range of minerals – which include gold, iron and asbestos.

AS the existence of ancient mineworkings have hinted, Saudi Arabia is proving to be naturally rich in much more than oil. A programme of intensified prospecting is being carried out by the Directorate General of Mineral Resources. Through agreements with the Government of Saudi Arabia, the US Geological

The top picture *shows complex folding of pre-Cambrian shield rock in the south-west. Nickel gossan, and gossan from pyrite* (above right and right) *of the Arabian shield point to exploitable deposits; copper mining has already begun at Ma'had Dhahab* (above).

Survey, the French Bureau de Recherches Géologiques et Minières, and the Japanese Geological Mission are studying many mining districts in the Kingdom in order to determine the geologic and tectonic position of metallic and non-metallic deposits.

Most of the modern discoveries have been in central and western Saudi Arabia in rocks of the Precambrian Arabian Shield, although some finds have also been made in the much younger rocks along the Red Sea coast. Palaeozoic rocks which overlap the Shield in the north and east are also being investigated.

The Precambrian metallic mineral deposits fall into four major types: stratiform iron-nickel deposits; massive polymetallic base-metal deposits; gold-silver deposits; and disseminated molybdenum-tungsten deposits. Other metal deposits

occur on the Red Sea coastal plain, and in hot brines and sediments of the deeps in the axial trough of the Red Sea.

Known occurrences of metal deposits form regional belts of mineralization which relate closely to structural rock formation. Seven principal mineral belts and/or zones have been delineated in the Precambrian rocks of the Arabian Shield. These include the Bidah, Sabya, Nuqrah and Al Amar copper-zinc belts; the Salwah copper-zinc zone; and the Hijaz and Najd gold-silver belts. Recent exploration has also indicated several massive sulphide deposits, although the main economic metal is copper, with lesser amounts of zinc, gold and silver.

Many of the reported gold-silver deposits in the Shield appear to form belts that parallel the dominant northwest trend of the Najd fault system or trends of related subsidiary shears. Hundreds of ancient gold-silver prospects have been located and examined, and current exploration suggests that these mines have future potential.

Important iron deposits, large massive and disseminated strata-bound pyrite deposits and massive stratiform nickel-bearing sulphide deposits discovered in the Arabian Shield approach economic size, grade and access requirements.

Of the economically significant non-metallic mineral resources to be found, phosphate, magnesite, glass sand, gypsum, salt, and structural and cement materials are all being mined in increasing quantities.

Structural materials including clays, shales and perlite are being investigated for the production of light weight aggregates. Marble in pleasing colours and patterns is quarried from many localities in the Arabian Shield and three cement plants in Saudi Arabia are utilizing the abundant cement materials indigenous to the country.

So far, all estimates of the size, quality and variety of metallic and non-metallic mineral resources suggest that Saudi Arabia's natural reserves can be relied upon to provide much future wealth.

Mounded basalt characterizes the surface of part of the Jabal Hashahish Quadrangle (immediately above).

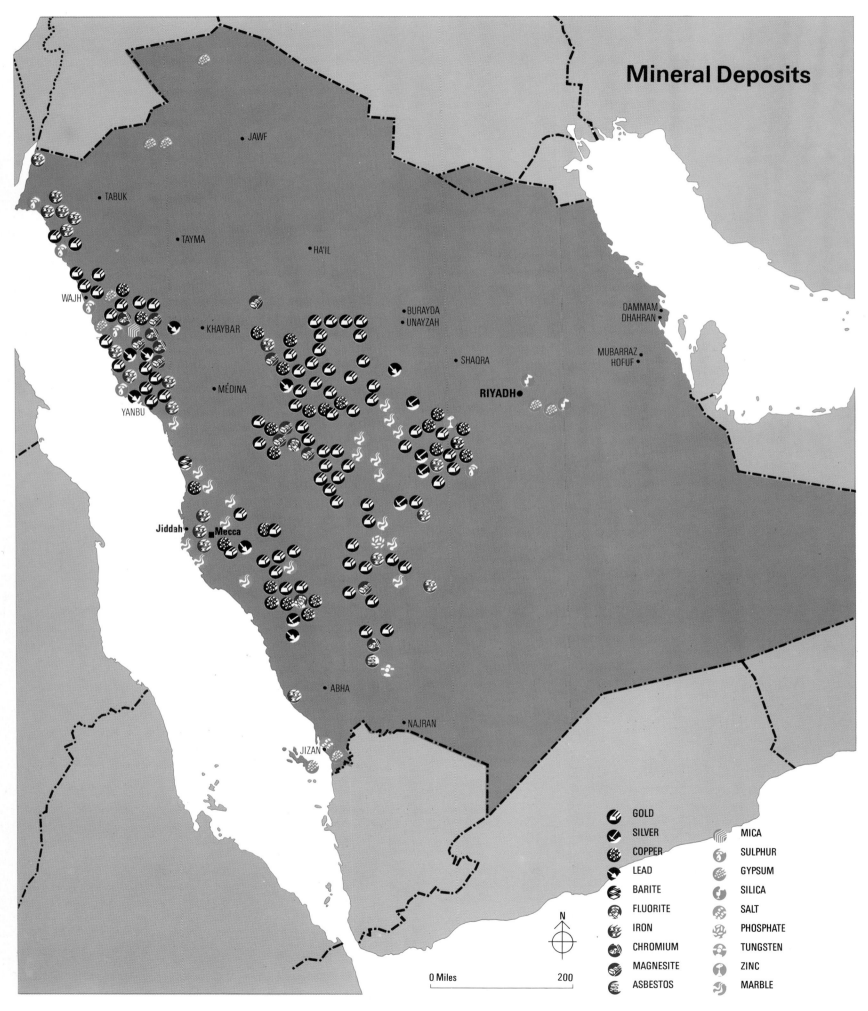

Mineral Deposits

JAWF

TABUK

TAYMA

HA'IL

WAJH

KHAYBAR

BURAYDA
UNAYZAH

DAMMAM
DHAHRAN

MÉDINA

SHAQRA

MUBARRAZ
HOFUF

YANBU

RIYADH

Jiddah • ■Mecca

ABHA

NAJRAN

JIZAN

GOLD		MICA	
SILVER		SULPHUR	
COPPER		GYPSUM	
LEAD		SILICA	
BARITE		SALT	
FLUORITE		PHOSPHATE	
IRON		TUNGSTEN	
CHROMIUM		ZINC	
MAGNESITE		MARBLE	
ASBESTOS			

N

0 Miles   200

2
The Cities

The cities into which people are flocking today may be modern but are seldom new. Settled people have for centuries outnumbered nomadic.
Mecca's and Medina's scholastic pre-eminence has at times been rivalled by Jerusalem or Damascus, Baghdad or Cairo, but never their spiritual role.

Despite the many massive modern buildings that dominate the skyline of Riyadh, the fastest growing city in the Middle East, the blend of the traditional with the new has been preserved. Certain historic buildings, such as the palace in the foreground, survived for a while the surge of modern development, but most such relics of the era of Abdul Aziz have disappeared. Yet several new Government buildings have kept architectural faith with traditional Arab designs. The map (below) shows the sites of major cities.

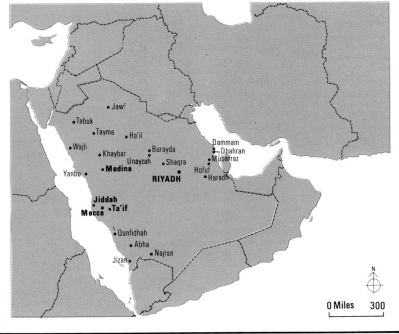

Cities~an Introduction

SURPRISINGLY – in the light of popular belief – the greater part of the people of Saudi Arabia have lived the settled life, rather than the nomadic one, at least over recent centuries. Many of these, it is true, have lived in villages, whose size would be determined by the quantity of fresh water available. On the other hand, links with and awareness of their major cities have since ancient days belonged deeply to the patterns of thought and life in the Arabian hinterland.

The first city of Saudi Arabia must always be the Holy City of Mecca, spiritual capital of all Islam. Though

Mecca's permanent population is much less than that of modern Riyadh (growing towards one million) or Jiddah (already over half a million), at the height of the annual pilgrimage of Muslims to Holy Mecca it contains over a million people. Mecca's founding is attributed to the presence of the well opened in the desert by God to save the lives of Hagar and her son, Isma'il, from whom – with his father Abraham – the Arab race traces its descent. Other stories tell of Abraham labouring with his son Isma'il to rebuild the Holy Ka'bah as a stone structure and site of worship. The Ka'bah, of course, remains,

though it has been reconstructed from time to time throughout the centuries.

Although Mecca boasts many fine modern buildings, including its splendid Islamic conference centre, determined efforts have been made to preserve its traditional Arabian character. The same is true of Arabia's other Holy City of Medina, the "shining city", which to the delight of the pilgrim or Muslim visitor has remained a small city of some one hundred thousand souls and whose life centres round its magnificent green-domed mosque and famous library and its Islamic University.

By contrast, Riyadh is today very

On an approach to Mecca, lively oriental imagination is displayed (below), *while in Riyadh* (bottom) *Najdi features prevail in Government offices.*

The fortified wall of old Jiddah – captured by the forces of Abdul Aziz in 1925 – is still visible (below) *in an aerial photograph taken in the 1930s. It had already been pulled down by 1950, to allow Jiddah to*

largely a modern city, spaciously laid out, graced with several fine ministerial buildings, and growing fast on the basis of imaginative city planning. It was restored by King Abdul Aziz as the site of the Saudi capital. With its plentiful water and its site by the Wadi Hanifah, Riyadh's history is ancient. As the historic city of Hajr it was the oldest capital of the Yamamah region. It is the centre of a relatively fertile area.

Jiddah – the Bride of the Red Sea – founded by Caliph 'Uthman ibn 'Affan in 647 CE, but certainly a fishing settlement before that – is today the largest port on the Red Sea, with a magnificent modern harbour. Much of the picturesque Jiddah of traditional Arab architecture has been pulled down to make way for modern office blocks, banks, apartment blocks and the like. But an old quarter preserves the grace and intimacy of an Arabian city. As the diplomatic capital of the Kingdom it is the site of over fifty embassies.

While Saudi Arabians watch the towns of Yanbu and Jubayl expand dramatically as major industrial centres, several other cities are developing fast – in every case under town plans which control the use of land for residential, industrial or agricultural purposes, the development of public utilities, population density and road and traffic systems. They include Burayda and Unayzah, in the Qasim area, and Ha'il further north; in the east Dammam and its neighbours al-Khubar, Saihat, Ras Tannurah and Abqaiq; and in the south-west Jizan, Najran and Khamis Mushayt.

The two beautiful cities of Ta'if and Abha play an increasing role as summer resorts, both being set among mountains. It is to Ta'if that the Royal Family moves during the hot months. Stone-built Ta'if is cool at all times of the year.

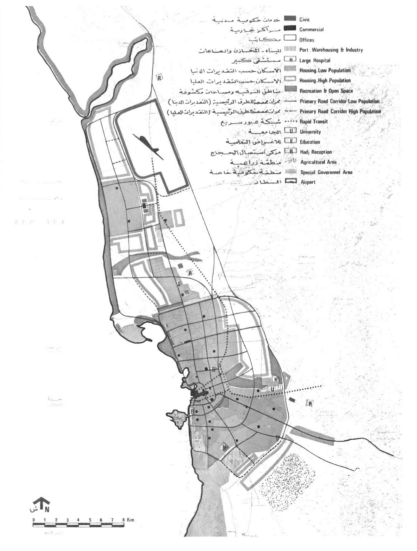

begin its expansion (bottom left). *The spacious planning of today's Jiddah is already just visible in the aerial shot taken in 1968* (below), *showing the first version of the main roundabout, and the edge of the* lagoon. *But by the mid-seventies* (bottom) *the heart of Jiddah was that of a noisy, gleaming international city. Jiddah's development today is masterminded by a City Planning Office which has brought the air*port (circled in red) close to the city centre and has designated open spaces for recreation (green) (below).

Reference Example:
Numbered Site 51 Grid Ref 5E

9	3A	Agriculture and Commerce College
26	4C	Agriculture and Water Department
62	6E	Agriculture and Water Ministry
88	11E	Airport
86	10E	American Military Mission
6	2E	Arabic Language College
82	7E	British Council

67	6F	Central Planning Organisation
13	3D	Commerce, Chamber of
51	5E	Commerce and Industry Ministry
71	6F	Commercial College
63	6E	Communications Ministry
8	2E	City Hall (Baladia)
12	3B	Civil Defence
81	7B/C	Convention Centre and Hotel
18	4C	Customs Office
21	4C	Education College

61	6E	Education Ministry
4	2D	Emirate
38	4/5F	Employment Office
15	3/4B	Engineering College
50	5E	English Language Centre USIS
60	6B	English Language Institute, British Council
49	5E	Faisal Secondary School
53	5E	Finance Ministry
58	6B	Fine Arts Institute

11	3B	Foreign Affairs Department
66	6F	General Control Bureau
44	5C	General Personnel Bureau
1	1F	Girls Education College
42	5A	Girls Secondary School
73	6F	Girls Secondary School
25	4C	Government Department
32	4D	Grievance Board (Ombudsman)
87	11E	Health Institute

52	5/6E	Health Ministry
72	6F	Income Tax Department
19	4C	Information Ministry
16	3/4B	Intelligence Department, General
47	5D	Interior Department
64	6E	Interior Ministry
17	4B	Municipalities Department
48	5D	Training Institute

10	3B	Justice Ministry
68	6F	Justice Ministry
54	5F	Labour and Social Affairs Ministry
39	4F	Labour Office, Central
35	4E	Library
77	6G	Library
84	9E	Military Guest House
59	6B	Model Capital School

Riyadh

22	4C	Municipalities Department (Technical)	70	6F	Public Administration Institute	56	6A	Royal Palace	29	4D T.V. Station
			45	5D	Public Works Department	41	4F	Royal Technical College	75	6F University
46	5D	Passport Office	30	6/7G	Race Course and Sports Stadium	7	2E	Shari'al Sciences College	65	6E Vocational Training Institute
57	5/6B	P.E. Institute	79	6G	Racing Club	36	4E	Social Affairs Department		
44	5C	Pensions Department	78	6/7F/G	Racing Club Garden	74	6F	Social Security Office	24	4C Water Department
85	9E	Petroleum and Natural Resources Ministry	76	6G	Racing Club H.Q.				33	4D Water Tower
			69	6F	Radio Station	3	2B	Teachers Upgrading Centre	30	4D Yamama Secondary School
43	5C	Pilgrimage and Waqfs Ministry	20	4C	Radio Station	5	2E	Telegraph Office		
40	4F	Police College	55	5G	Railway Station	23	4C	Town Planning Office	83	7/8G Zoological Gardens
29	4D	Police Secretariat	14	3F	Riyadh Secondary School	27	4C	Traffic Police Office		
34	4E	Post Office, Central								
28	4D	Post Office, General								
2	2B	Primary Teachers Training College								

Riyadh's most familiar landmark has become its central water tower.

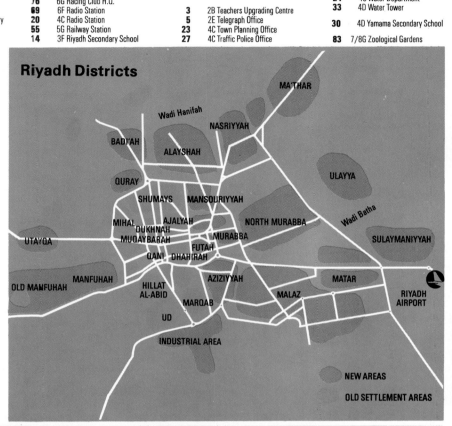

Riyadh Districts

MA'THAR
Wadi Hanifah
NASRIYYAH
BADI'AH
ALAYSHAH
QURAY
ULAYYA
SHUMAYS MANSOURIYYAH
MIHAL AJALYAH
DUKHNAH NORTH MURABBA Wadi Batha
UTAYQA MUQAYBARAH MURABBA SULAYMANIYYAH
FUTAH
QANI DHAHIRAH
OLD MANFUHAH MANFUHAH AZIZIYYAH MATAR
HILLAT MALAZ RIYADH AIRPORT
AL-ABID
MARQAB
UD
INDUSTRIAL AREA
NEW AREAS
OLD SETTLEMENT AREAS

Key:
- MINISTRIES & GOVERNMENT DEPARTMENTS
- FURTHER EDUCATION & CULTURAL CENTRES
- BANKS
- FIRE STATIONS
- HOSPITALS
- HOTELS
- MAIN MOSQUES
- MAIN SOUKS
- PUBLIC GARDENS
- RED CRESCENT

King Abdul Aziz' favourite Palace was the Qasr al-Murabba, built in 1936.

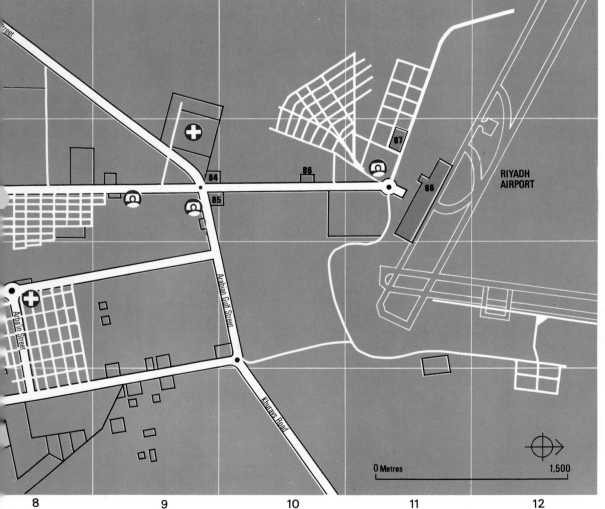

RIYADH AIRPORT

87
86
84
88
85

Arabian Gulf Street
Arbain Street
Khurais Road

0 Metres   1,500

8   9   10   11   12

Alongside Riyadh's Post Office was the satellite tracker, linked to Telstar.

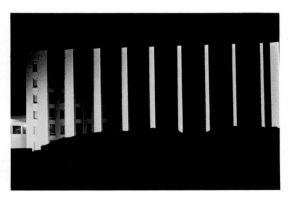

Imaginative lighting illuminates the side of the Intercontinental Hotel.

1 3D Ashur House

2 4C/D Bayshan House
3 6D Bayt Zainal
4 4B Building on the spot of
    Bayt al-Baghdadi

5 3B Clock Tower

6 6C Former Aramco Residence
7 7C Former British Consular Chancery
8 5B Former British Legation
9 6C Former Dutch Legation
10 6D Former Egyptian Legation
11 6D Former Qaymaqamat
12 5C Former Russian Legation

13 4B Jafali Building

14 5B Municipality

15 3D Nasif House
16 5C New al-Falah School
17 5E Old al-Falah School
    (green dome)

18 5B Police
19 2B Post Office
20 2B Prince Newaf Building

21 2B Saudia Town Office
22 3C Shurbati Building
23 4E Suq al-Badu
24 3C Suq an-Nada (Main Suq)

25 3/4C Urban and Residential Centre
    (Queen's building)

BANKS

HOSPITALS

HOTELS

MAIN MOSQUES

Fish Quay

RED SEA

MANQABAH

Fish Market

Old Quarantine Pier

Port Street

King Abdul Aziz Square

King Abdul Aziz Street

King Faisal Street

Bab Sharif

Bab Medina

Coronation Square

Medina Road

Ministry of Foreign Affairs

Qashla

Muhammad Abd Al Wahhab Street

Bab Mecca

Baghdadiyyah Street

Eve's Tomb Cemetery

Asad Cemetery

Al-Sahla Street

Saudia Building

Jiddah

Jiddah's 14-foot monument to man's space endeavour has a touch of Brasilia.

The Queen's Building is one of modern Jiddah's most successful structures.

Saudia's headquarters control the nation's fast expanding airline.

Traditional Architecture

In Mecca, a determination to preserve the ancient character of the spiritual centre of the world of Islam has dampened tendencies to tear down the glories and intimacies of the past. Only Muslims are allowed to enter holy Mecca, whose foundation dates from God's miraculous provision of a well for Isma'il, son of Abraham, and his mother, Hagar.

URBAN communities are nothing new in Saudi Arabia; in certain areas they have existed for centuries. Between them is desert inhabited by a now dwindling number of tent-dwelling Beduin. Isolated by great distances and with different social conditions, climates and building materials, these settled areas have evolved distinct regional styles of architecture.

Extant buildings in a traditional style are rarely more than two hundred years old: but until the recent and almost total transformation of Saudi Arabia by determined modernization there was no stimulus to change the indigenous styles, so that buildings erected not long ago adhered completely to the old techniques and designs.

Four main Saudi Arabian architectural styles are characteristic of four regions – eastern Najd, central Hijaz, southern Hijaz and Asir, and the Arabian Gulf coast.

Eastern Najd

The main building material is unfired mud-brick; the completed wall is made smooth by the application of mud-plaster. These walls are very thick, and provide insulation against the extremities of the local climate. The roofing consists of wooden beams, usually of tamarisk, with palm matting or twigs spread above. This is covered with a layer of mud. Stone is used only as the foundation of a house or in fortifications.

The Najdi mosque consists of a walled enclosure around an open courtyard, with a covered sanctuary built against the *qibla* wall. Cut into this wall is the *mihrab* niche, which projects beyond the back wall of the mosque; an arrangement common in both ancient and modern mosques in Saudi Arabia. The roof of the sanctuary rests on colonnades with keel-arches, the number of colonnades depending on the mosque's size and im-

The startlingly unique traditional architecture of the mountainous south-west is best seen in the province's capital of Abha. Official encouragement is given to the preservation of ancient architectural techniques, with the characteristic louvred house walls – so designed to protect the clay-built structures from winter rains.

wooden doors, and the windows by wooden shutters. Both shutters and doors are decorated with incised geometric patterns picked out in colour, or by geometrics burned into the pale wooden surface. The only other external decorations are rows of V-shaped mouldings on the walls, and crenellations which vary in design from area to area.

local conformity is attributable to common influences brought about in the area by the *hajj*, by trade and by trading connections further afield, particularly with Egypt.

The buildings common to all these cities are two, three or more storeys high, with level roofs. The entrance is often vaulted by a round-headed or

portance. Some mosques have underground prayer-chambers for use in winter. In Arid and further south, one or two staircases nearly always give access to the roof; in this area the mosques are either without minarets, or have only a diminutive tower over the staircase to the roof. In Sudayr and Qasim, however, minarets are tall and cylindrical.

Najdi houses are often built around a central courtyard, with only a few openings on to the street, thus maintaining the privacy of family life. The buildings have one, two or three storeys depending on their importance. The entrances to the houses are closed by large rectangular

Elaborately shaped mud finials stand at the corners.

The position of the reception rooms varies. In most larger houses the lower rooms are used for storage, and visitors are received upstairs. However, rooms designed to receive guests appear in Sadus and Unayzah on both the ground floor and the upper storey. In a corner of these reception rooms there is usually a small hearth for coffee-making, with shelves above.

The Central Hijaz and its Coast
Mecca, Medina, Ta'if and Jiddah all have a similar type of architecture. This

pointed arch, and the wooden doors are decorated with rather stiff and stylized carving. The outer walls are frequently, but not always, whitewashed.

Decoration is concentrated in the elaborate wooden screens which face the upper storeys of the building around windows and balconies, with an effect recalling the *mashrabiyya* screens of Cairo. These screens guard from view people standing at windows or on balconies. They are arranged on the façade of the building in various ways; in some houses they occupy the whole of the upper area, while in others, two very high screens are set to right and left of a

The tremendous impact of the petroleum industry has by no means destroyed the traditional character of all ancient towns of Arabia's eastern region – as witness the view of Qatif (below). *Like Hofuf, it was the site of a Turkish fortress until captured by Abdul Aziz in 1913, in the drive for unity. The map indicates architectural areas.*

Traditional architectural techniques are illustrated by (from the top) a typical village of the south-east (Ghamid), palaces and houses in Riyadh, Jiddah houses with slatted balconies, and a pavilion-style house in Tarut, eastern Saudi Arabia.
(Drawings are by Geoffrey King)

The unique charm of Saudi Arabia's Red Sea coast is illustrated by such fishing settlements of Wajh (below), where peaceful communities linking Red Sea trade and fishing with the interior have survived for centuries. Offshore, parts of this coast are skirted by coral reefs, breeding grounds of many varieties of brilliantly coloured fish.

tecture. These have inward-sloping walls, slight crenellations and small apertures, but they vary in height and proportion.

The houses of the Abha area are built of mud or stone or a combination of both. In those buildings constructed of mud, layers are applied successively and each layer is left to dry before another is added. Horizontal rows of protruding stone

Although there is no single local form of building, technical and decorative devices recur in structures otherwise quite different. All of these eastern buildings, however, are distinguished by fine proportions, both in dimensions and decoration.

The wind-towers of Bahrain and Dubai do not appear on the Saudi coast. In-

small central screen. Yet other houses have much smaller screens around the windows alone, occupying a lesser area of the whole façade.

Southern Hijaz and Asir
From Bilad Zahran and through Bilad Ghamid, north of Abha, the standard building material is rough-cut stone. These villages are often defensively positioned on hilltops, especially in Bilad Zahran, and the continuous faces presented by the outermost houses give the effect of a fortified wall. Elsewhere, in valleys and plains, the villages are in less defensible positions. In both regions one or two rectangular towers are a constant feature of the village archi-

slabs are placed between each mud-layer to break up the flow of rainwater, which would otherwise dissolve it. The mud areas of the houses are often white-washed, thus emphasizing the horizontal division of these tower-like structures.

The Arabian Gulf coast
The eastern towns of Saudi Arabia are situated between the desert and the Gulf. The climate is similar to that of the Red Sea shore, with a high rate of humidity and persistent uncomfortable heat in summer. Also as on the Red Sea coast, the building material is coral aggregate and wood. The walls are made smooth with plaster. The roofing system employs palm thatch and wooden beams.

stead, on the Saudi shore, certain rooms are arranged to benefit from the slightest breeze, while other rooms are better suited to cooler winter conditions. Thus in the centre of Qatif the houses are of several storeys. The lower rooms have small windows, whereas the uppermost storey has large arched openings piercing the walls for ventilation. On the out-skirts of the town two-storey kiosk-like buildings once existed, with walls pierced by large arches. They appear to have been summer pavilions.

This eastern architecture bears no significant relationship to buildings inland, but has a marked similarity to those found in Bahrain, Qatar and Dubai and its neighbours.

3 The People, their habitat & way of life

The interplay of the hard, disciplined, wandering life of the desert and the settled life of farmers, craftsmen, merchants and teachers in the scattered towns has for countless centuries formed the character of the people. Today, well tested values stand remarkably firm among the challenges of modern city life.

A boy from Diriyah demonstrates his desert heritage no less by his fine clear-cut features than by his characteristic red headdress, the ghotra. *Fundamentally of Armenoid stock, Saudi Arabians have nonetheless effortlessly accepted intermingling of stock from elsewhere – from Africa, for example, and from Iran and Baluchistan.*

Arabian Faces

Variety in apparel and headdress can indicate the influence of locality, profession, or social standing. The red and white check *ghotra* (as below) is as a rule worn in winter months, for it is warmer, and the *ghotra* of light white cotton (*top row*) in summer.

Top row, left to right: *Saudis from the south-west, east coast, and Qasim.* Centre: *A coppersmith, and an oilworker.* Below: *While the majority of Saudi Arabia's traditionally nomadic population has now chosen to settle, desert disciplines and the lifestyle that accounts for the dignity and serenity of the Saudi character still prevail among a substantial minority.*

The Unity of the Saudi Arabian People

IT is the town culture – markedly Islamic – which brings together the various strands in Arabian society, to form a complex but harmonious whole, combining the virtues of Beduin life with merchanting acumen and a high standard of literacy and education.

The ancient records of Arabia show a society simultaneously at many distinct but interdependent stages of development. Beside the high civilization of the ancient South there is mention of Beduin, who do not, however, seem to play a role of any great importance. In early Islamic times, the interrelationship between nomads and townsmen is closer, each depending on the other for essential goods and services.

Although the early towns were organized in quarters corresponding to the tribal origins of their inhabitants, the conditions of settled life produced a culture superior to that of the tribes in the desert. One aspect of the rise of Islam can be seen as a clash between the aspirations of the town and the customs of the desert, where animism had been the principal religion. Many of the most important historical events during the first centuries of Islam must be interpreted to some extent in tribal terms, but there was a strong reaction by those who thought of the Islamic community as a whole.

The old poetry gives a good account of Arab life in pre-Islamic times. It describes a heroic society demanding heroic virtues. The heroes are the symbol, the poets the voice, of their tribes.

It was the task of the poet, and of the invisible being who whispered inspiration into his ear, to act for the tribe in diplomatic negotiations, and to vanquish the opposing poet's familiar spirit. Before a battle he had to create martial ardour in his own people and weakness in the enemy. These incantatory poets verged on sorcery, which is doubtless why they are condemned in the Qur'an.

Some of the customs of early tribal society – such as the habit of exposing unwanted female children – were banned by Islam. Gambling and the drinking of wine were also forbidden, warfare between Muslims was condemned and revenge discouraged.

The old way of life still persisted to some extent, however. The Qur'an complains that the Beduin sometimes put tribal obligations above their duty to Islam. Over the centuries, urban society continued to develop while Beduin society altered very little. The economic changes of the twentieth century have now intervened. The motor car spelt the end of Beduin wealth based on camel and horse breeding, and the rise of the oil industry has forced them into new occupations.

There have always been differences between the southern and northern Beduin. Those of the south dress differently, and in their migrations do not live in tents, but merely hang a sunshade from a tree, or go between mountain caves and camps.

The Beduin of the north ride their camels on saddles, while the southerners ride without saddles and much further back. The northern Arabs are believed to have adopted the saddle for use in war against their powerful neighbours, because it allows another warrior to be mounted behind the rider.

The aristocracy of the desert are the camel-rearing tribes. The sheep-rearing tribes were thought to be of lower social standing but, as the nomadic way of life has been eroded, any social disadvantage has now virtually disappeared.

Individuals or groups have always attached themselves to powerful persons or groups to obtain protection and the sheep-rearing tribes may have been clients who were not granted full right of membership in the more powerful tribes with which they had associated themselves for protection.

The economic basis of nomadic life lay in the utilization of resources difficult to exploit. Many scholars believe that it was not the weaker members of the tribe who were forced out of the oases and and fertile areas, but rather the strongest who launched themselves into the hostile desert.

It is clear that there are not and never were, nomads in Arabia who have had complete economic independence. They have always relied on the settled areas

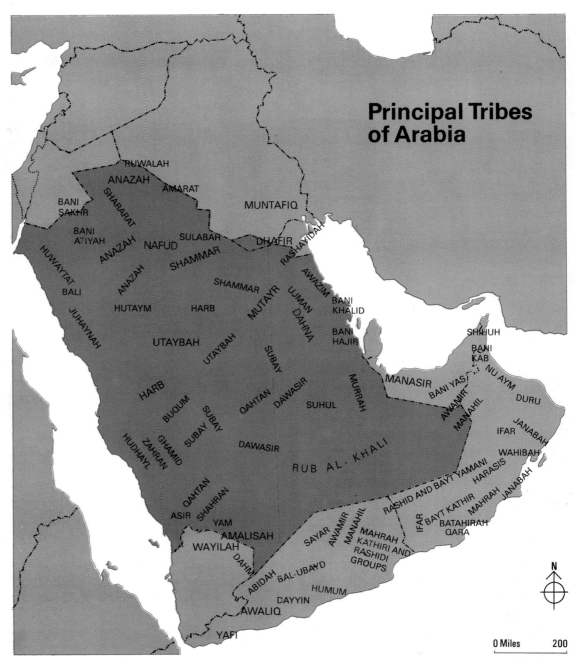

Principal Tribes of Arabia

O Miles   200

Tribal allegiance gives both character and meaning to life among Saudi Arabians, ensuring a sustained loyalty to locality, while allowing for the prevailing national unity.

for an important proportion of their food.

H. St. John Philby has written of the unifying achievement of King ibn Saud by the mid-1920s: "The Arabia over which he was to rule for nearly three more decades was united as never before: . . . and the realm which he had carved out with his sword and his faith would descend intact to his successor. The vital factor . . . was his reputation for justice and resolution, which was seldom put to the test, and always vindicated when the rare need arose. For the first time in human memory Arabia had a single ruler whom all could, and did, respect."

"The Arabia over which King Abdul Aziz ruled was united as never before . . . The vital factor was his reputation for justice and resolution, always vindicated when the need arose."

41

The People of the Central Province

THE inhabitants of Central Arabia – the Najdis – are a gifted and remarkable people. Adapting easily to the furious rate of change which prevails in Saudi Arabia today, they have proved their aptitude for jobs which were completely beyond the purview of their ancestors. Yet their basic conservatism and their attachment to traditional ways and ideals remain strong; they believe in treasuring the fundamental principles they have inherited, knowing that if they fail to do so, they will be left rootless. They cling to the flowing robes and headgear of their forefathers as an outward manifestation of this belief. Family allegiances are as strong as ever. Marriages arranged by parents for their offspring prove more durable and contented than marriages in the West. The spirit of Islam continues to permeate thinking.

Fully to appreciate their charm and strength of character, an outsider must visit them in Najd, and see how they rejoice in, and delight to share, the simple pleasures of life – love of the desert and the exhilaration of the chase, with falcons flashing down on the prey; horse races and camel races, the sword dance exalting the old martial prowess of the Arabs; the flow of conversation, spiced with cardamom-flavoured coffee and sweet tea; the banquet spread on a rug, with succulent mutton crowning a mound of rice, the poet reciting his rhymes; and the passing around of the incense burner when the time has come for guests to take their leave.

Najd (that is, "highland") has never been easy to reach from the outside. The mountain barrier of the Hijaz towered above the land to the west, and on the other three sides lay a wilderness of sand. But trails did thread their way into the interior, and resolute men followed them. Members of tribes calling themselves sons of Qahtan or southern Arabs moved northwards and intermingled with the sons of Adnan or northern Arabs they found there. The chiefs of Kindah, a southern tribe, founded a kingdom in the late fourth century of the Christian era, the first organized state known to have existed in Najd, but it was doomed to fall after only a few decades. Men of Tayy,

another southern tribe, went even further north to what is now called Jabal Shammar. The Najdis of today are in the main the offspring of these northern and southern stocks. In other parts of the Arab world Arabs have blended themselves with the indigenous peoples, but in Najd they have maintained a thorough Arabness which is perhaps their most distinguishing characteristic. In a sense they are Arab aristocrats, though their pride in this respect is tempered by the Islamic doctrine which proclaims piety rather than blood to be the true touchstone of nobility.

Najd had little to offer beyond the bracing air of the uplands, the stark beauty of landscapes, pastures for the grazing of herds of camels and flocks of sheep and goats, and scattered springs and wells. The pastures and the watering places helped to bring about the age-old dichotomy of Arabian society between the nomads and the settled folk. The nomads roamed from pasture to pasture and from source to source, while the denizens of the oases clustered together in spots where water flowed abundantly enough to irrigate their date palms and other plants. Neither element had much understanding of or sympathy for the

other, and brawling often broke out between them.

The people of Najd have always loved eloquence, especially when cast in the form of poetry. During the century before Islam, there was an outpouring of magnificent verse in classical Arabic, much of it composed by men and women of Najd. This literature resembles a gorgeous tapestry depicting the life of that time and the ideals of Arab society. The poets held manliness and fortitude and honour to be supreme virtues. Men showed tenderness towards women, whom they pledged to protect with their lives. Frequent wars and feuds called for courage on the field of battle; death was never to be feared. Leaders and elders deserved respect, but could not and did not act autocratically. The harshness of existence in a largely barren land and the need of wanderers for food and shelter fostered the traditions of hospitality and generosity. Hatim, a poet of the tribe of Tayy, is still the paragon of open-handed giving throughout the Arab world.

As the new religion of Islam advanced in the Arabian peninsula, it met resistance in central Najd where, soon after the death of Muhammad the Prophet, a false prophet, Musaylimah the Liar, preached a heretical creed. To overcome him, Abu Bakr, the first Caliph, had to call upon his finest general, Khalid ibn al-Walid, the Sword of God. Once the Najdis came to understand the spiritual message and values of Islam, however,

The map shows, in black, the areas of central Arabia. The black tents (right) *are woven of goat hair.* Far right: *Najdi craftsmanship is worked into the hilt of this National Guardsman's* khanjar.

they devoted themselves enthusiastically to its cause. As warriors and missionaries, countless Najdis left their homeland, many never to return. Carrying the gospel as far east as China and as far west as the Atlantic, these Najdis contributed largely to the expansion of the faith. Their old pagan fearlessness was now reinforced by the promise of eternal life in Paradise for those martyred in the path of God.

Najd, relatively secure in its geographical isolation and possessing few riches to be plundered, was not a strong magnet for foreign invaders. The bane of the region, however, remained for centuries civil strife and almost incessant feuding, town against town, tribe against tribe, nomadic bands against settled communities. This feuding militated against the formation of a powerful and durable state, and the absence of such a state meant that there was no authority to enforce effectively the Sacred Law of Islam and hold the people of Najd to orthodoxy. As time went by, backsliding became common. Many Najdis embraced innovations and beliefs abhorrent to the true spirit of Islam.

In the eighteenth century a religious scholar of central Najd, Sheikh Muhammad ibn Abd al-Wahhab, determined to bring Najd and the rest of Arabia back to the original and undefiled form of Islam as revealed through the Prophet Muhammad and upheld by the first generations of pious believers. To achieve this purpose he allied himself with Muhammad

ibn Saud, the ruler of the oasis of Diriyah not far from Riyadh. This alliance survived in the person of the late King Faisal, who was descended on the paternal side from the ruler and on the maternal side from the Sheikh.

The reform movement inaugurated by the Sheikh relied for support principally on the townsmen. Contrary to the misconception common in the West, the townsmen in Najd far outnumber the Beduin; this appears to have been true during the past several centuries at least. Despite some checks in the nineteenth century, the reform movement is still alive and vigorous, commanding the allegiance of the people of Najd, who thus stand out in the Islamic world as

The ancient skills of falconry represent one of the most sophisticated sporting activities in the world. Skilled falconers are to be found among all communities in the country outside the major cities. The game most often sought is Mac-Queen's bustard (hubara), *sand grouse and stone curlew, dove, quail and courser. Falcons are kept hooded unless they are being worked. A skilled man will train a falcon in under three weeks. Of several varieties of falcon, the peregrine – shahin – is probably commonest: they are swift, bold and persevering. The saker falcon – hurr – is also favoured.*

Men of Unayzah gather for a dignified but spirited traditional dance, com- *bining skilful sword play with complex drumming.*

The desert air is sweetest to many a Najdi. Watchtowers dot the landscape, sited on high ground, and built of clay and stone or a combination of both. Towns were once walled, and reinforced with towers: the bigger towns possessed administrative citadels, some of which remain. Inside homes have plastered walls, often with stylized floral decorations and geometric patterns carved in the plaster. Small niches for storage are cut into the walls of even the smallest houses.

being among the foremost champions of conservative fundamentalism.

In the twentieth century the late King Abdul Aziz, popularly known as ibn Saud, found himself confronted with a problem of far-reaching implications. The reform movement, of which he was a devoted proponent, had as a cardinal objective the weeding out of all reprehensible innovations from Islamic society. So which new things were acceptable and which were not? Ibn

Saud took the liberal view that modern devices such as the automobile and the telephone, as long as they were useful to the community and not harmful to its religious beliefs, were acceptable. Various fanatical tribal chiefs rejected this view. They also chafed under the restraints ibn Saud placed on their raids against those Arabs they regarded as infidels in the neighbouring states of Transjordan and Iraq. Finally, they rose in revolt against their sovereign. After

much bitter fighting ibn Saud, who secured an even larger measure of help from the townsmen of Najd as the revolt went on, succeeded in crushing the rebellion. Since then tribalism has died out as a political force.

Today the loyalty of the Najdis to the House of Saud, a house sprung from the heart of their own region, is unswerving. At the same time, the old provincialism of the different parts of the Kingdom has been steadily waning. In the past Najdis

45

Traditional House Styles

Traditional methods of building in
Saudi Arabia are highly efficient. The
unfired clay bricks, finished in plaster,
which provide the basic material, give
excellent insulation against the heat
of the sun. Roof structures are usually
of tamarisk. Mouldings, crenellations
and finials beautify the exteriors,
executed with grace and restraint.

*An instinctive sense of design prevails
among the country's builders of traditional
houses – as these examples from Burayda
in the Qasim area indicate. Crenellations
and rooftop edges are picked out in white.
The windows and air vents, peepholes and
hatches, by which occupants of houses can
look out or inspect the arrival of visitors,
are unfailingly worked into the overall
design with confidence and panache.
The triangular decorations of the
doorway* (centre picture) *are widely
found throughout the country.
Family and social life may proceed at
three levels – in the street, within the
house itself, and on the level of the
complex of roofs, parapets, and* alfresco
stairways.

and Hijazis often looked at each other with a jaundiced eye, and Sunnite Najdis tended to disdain their Shi-ite neighbours in Hasa and Qatif to the east. Now they are all coming to think of themselves primarily as Saudi Arabs, fellow citizens of a state created, held together, and built up by two families of genius, the House of the Sheikh and the House of Saud.

The prevailing of ibn Saud's liberal view meant an era of great changes in Saudi Arabian society. The pace was slow at first. In the 1940s, two decades after the suppression of the recalcitrant chiefs, Riyadh was still a walled town built of mud-brick. The country had only a handful of paved roads, and modern airports were just beginning to be constructed. Since the 1950s the rising production of oil has helped to make the pace increasingly rapid and in recent years almost impossible to catalogue.

Yet life among today's people of the Central Province does retain its profundity and society its balance. The impact of modernism, the explosion of opportunities, the infusion of new wealth, have created strains, but manageable strains. Whereas in former times illiteracy was widespread in Najd, with the only formal instruction being in the religious sciences and the ancillary discipline of the Arabic language, the government now wages an anti-illiteracy campaign. Primary and secondary schools abound in the towns and villages, and in Riyadh, universities for both men and women with their *curricula* largely shaped on Western models, win the commendation of visiting Western academics. Young Najdis in growing numbers go abroad for postgraduate work and demonstrate their ability to hold their own with students from all parts of the world.

Not only in the sphere of education but in other spheres as well, modern Najdis are mastering new techniques and acquiring new outlooks. In the government of Saudi Arabia and in private business Najdis are proving their aptitude for callings, some of them highly technical, which a generation or two ago would have been unthinkable. All this pays tribute to the intelligence, innate skills, and versatility of this people who for long were cut off from the mainstream of modern industrial civilization.

(*See also* Sections 8 and 9)

The Arabian Horse

The legendary Arabian horse originated in the deserts of Saudi Arabia and through the centuries has been highly regarded for its extraordinary stamina and endurance.

The Najd pure-bred Arabian horse variously coloured bay, chestnut, grey or brown, stands from fourteen to fifteen hands in height. The head is larger in proportion than that of the English thoroughbred, the chief difference lying in the depth of the jowl. The ears are quite large but beautifully shaped, the eyes large and mild, the forehead wide and prominent, and the muzzle fine, sometimes almost pinched. The crest is slightly arched and the neck strong; the head is held high, the shoulders oblique, and the hoofs are round, large and very hard. The back is short and the croup longer and typically more level, with the tail set higher than in most other saddle breeds; indeed, Arabs have boasted that they could use them to hang their cloaks on.

For cross-breeding, the Arab stallion is notable for the transmission, to inferior stocks, of constitution, quality, intelligence and style.

It is written in the Qur'an that every man shall love his horse, while according to the *Hadith* the Prophet is said to have owned fifteen mares in his lifetime and to have quoted the following about them: "After woman came the horse, for the enjoyment and happiness of man."

The People of the Western Province

Traditionally, the people of western Arabia have linked the world of Red Sea and Mediterranean with the interior.

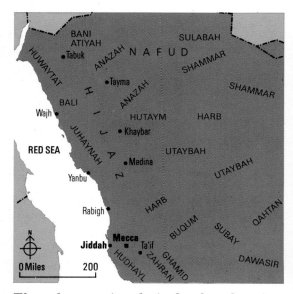

Though water is relatively abundant in the mountainous west, the lore of the desert prevails among the tribesmen and makes men hardy and devout.

OF all the natural divisions into which the Kingdom may be reduced, the Western Province is the most diverse. It approximately corresponds to the region known immemorially as the Hijaz. It is an area of about 80,000 square miles extending approximately 200 miles inland from Haql in the north to Qunfidhah in the south.

It is a land of great variety where cultivated hilltops give way to seemingly endless desert, where steamy heat yields to bracing winds and frosts, and where townsmen live cheek by jowl with nomads. Over the whole area, the ebb and flow of many civilizations has left its impress on the people. Yet, out of all this diversity it is possible to identify a Hijazi, not by physical appearance or by way of life, but by a bond of historical and cultural associations. For centuries, the settlements have been linked by the passage of caravans bearing precious cargoes and communities of the devout performing the *hajj*, the years spent as an outlying province of the Ottoman Empire and fourteen centuries of pro-

visioning and serving the *Ḥaramayn*, or Holy Cities.

The origins and distribution of the Hijazi peoples have been strongly influenced by geography. North of a line from Jiddah to Ta'if is a land of deserts: arid mineralized mountains or great sweeps of sand and stone. Where the fortunes of geology have yielded water near the coast or at a few points inland, settled communities of farmers, traders, fishermen or sailors have formed. But where aridity prevails then man has adapted to a way of life based on movement. In consequence, the northern Hijaz has never been able to support significant densities of population, with the one striking exception of Medina, where water gushes out from beneath the great lava field of the Harrat ar-Rahah.

To the south of the Jiddah-Ta'if line is another world entirely. There, high above the foetid heat of the Tihamah, the ascending winds of the summer monsoon bring regular rains which have permitted the development of many hun-

dreds of tiny farming hamlets. Outward and downward from the mountains aridity prevails, and settlements become fewer until the wandering way of life prevails once more.

Although the word "Hijaz" means "barrier", the history of the area and its peoples belies the term. The barrier referred to is the Great Escarpment which runs along, rather than across, the Hijaz, dividing it only from the interior plateaux. This same escarpment transforms the arid Hijaz into a natural corridor between the frankincense and myrrh country of Arabia Felix and the rich markets of the Fertile Crescent. Along this route a number of resting places and trading centres developed such as Mecca, Medina, Khaybar, Tayma and Tabuk, where water was available to sustain a settled population. Into these settlements came the merchant adventurers of the past: the Nabataeans in their troglodyte city of Madain Salih; the Jews in their fortress towns of Yathrib and Khaybar; the Babylonians with their palace gardens at Tayma.

From pre-Islamic times the city of Mecca held a special place as a centre of pilgrimage and culture: a role which was greatly emphasized after the *hajj* brought new racial and cultural strains into the Hijaz and, as the word of the Prophet spread, so the diversity increased. Many who came stayed, while others brought their skills to the service of the pilgrimage: from India came the grain merchants to Jiddah; from the Hadhramawt, the traders and importers; from Java the descendants of Muslim missionaries, and, from Turkey and Egypt, the soldiers to police the desert trails. Sometimes, as in Mecca and Jiddah, the ethnic types congregated into district *haras* or

quarters of the city such as the Nusla Yamaniyya of Jiddah. Often, however, the individual groups were absorbed into the cosmopolitan embrace of the Hijazi way of life, only their names distinguishing their origins: the al-Tunsis (Tunisia), the Daghestanis, the Yamanis (Yemen) and the al-Misris (Egypt).

Such are the demographic origins of the cities such as Jiddah, Mecca, Medina, Ta'if and Yanbu. In the smaller towns and oases of the north, a lasting symbiosis developed between, on the one hand, the itinerant Bedu such as the Bili, Huwaytat, Juhayna and the Harb, and on the other hand, the settled farmers of the agricultural oases. Very often the

oases were dependencies of one or other Bedu group and were peopled by slaves and their descendants brought from Somalia, Eritrea and the *Suahil* (coast) of East Africa. This introduced a negroid trait into the ethnic diversity which already existed, but, in general, brought none of the more pernicious aspects which accompanied slavery in the European Empires and Dominions.

In the south, along the coast, the African strain is strong and the Takarinah retain their distinctive thatched dwellings and racial features, though their African dialects have yielded to a universal use of Arabic. In the stone hamlets of the highlands, however, a

Semitic homogeneity prevails, possibly because the farmers, pressed hard upon their pocket-handkerchief-sized farms, could neither use nor support a slave population.

The variety of landscape and habitat is reflected in the traditional social organization of the peoples. The Bedu form a complex skein of relationships based on common ancestry, so that lineage is not only a matter of great pride, and prodigious feats of memory, but also an entrée into a system of territorial rights, privileges and obligations. Binding this loose hegemony is a structure of, often hereditary, sheikhs wielding an even looser form of control. The villagers,

on the other hand, may have some form of affinity by residence, but, in general, they belong to a wider community such as the Ghamid or Zahran tribes south of Ta'if. In the cities the situation is much more fluid. Some traditional sheikhly families are afforded their customary respect, but now they must compete with the great businessmen and traders, and an emerging group of technical and professional men.

Recent trends have accelerated many of the forces which shaped the population of the province. Most significant is the wealth created by the oil industry and the economic impetus it has given to the Hijaz, traditionally the commercial heart

of the country. Following the boom years of the 1960s, increasing numbers of people began to flow into the Hijaz in several well-defined streams. At the same time, a clearly differentiated pattern of internal movement established and reinforced itself.

From Syria, Palestine, Egypt, Pakistan, Lebanon and Iraq have come the skilled and semi-skilled workers needed to fill the gaps left by sudden and rapid growth. They have concentrated mostly in the cities and towns, but some, notably doctors and teachers, have been sent into rural areas. This is seen by the Saudis as a stop-gap measure while the country trains its own qualified staff.

The glittering western Arabian city of Jiddah (left) has immemorially been the country's commercial centre, and has acted as the principal reception for pilgrims, particularly, in the past, for those arriving by sea from Islamic Africa and, latterly, through its airport, for pilgrims bound for Mecca from all over the world. By the late 1970s it was still diplomatic centre and headquarters of the Saudi Arabian Monetary Agency. Intricate latticing and wood carving pay tribute to the skills developed over centuries of settled life in the western highland city of Ta'if (above).

Unskilled Yemenis have poured north to work on the building sites. Women from Ethiopia and Somalia have come seeking domestic employment.

Within the Hijaz the economic take-off has had no less an impact on the indigenous population. The Bedu have been fast quitting their traditional pastoral wanderings: exchanging the camel caravan for the Mercedes truck, the goathair tent for a breeze-block house on the outskirts of a town or city. Here too, job and origin are closely allied: find a taxi driver and you have found a Bedu.

The hill villages are just about holding their own and the cities continue to burgeon. The built-up area of Jiddah, for instance, expanded by 300 per cent between 1964 and 1971, and some 30 per cent of the city's population has moved in since 1970. Of the total Hijaz population of, perhaps 1,500,000, over 60 per cent are resident in the five main historic towns and there seems little doubt that the urban population is increasing both absolutely and relatively every year. The romance of the desert, if it ever existed, has yielded to the opportunities of the town. The rigours of subsistence farming in the mountains must now compete with the security of paid employment and an urban environment.

Yet all of the five major cities of the Western Province are of ancient foundation. Jiddah, commercial and industrial focus of the Western Province, has been an active port, certainly for 1,200 years, probably much longer. It is increasingly cosmopolitan. The other port of the region, Yanbu, until recently much sleepier than Jiddah, is also featured on the earliest maps and records of the west Arabian coast. Already, by the mid-1970s, it was beginning to take in new population in anticipation of the vital role planned for it in the country's economic blueprint.

Mecca, "the Blessed", lying at 2,000 feet in its hollow among the hills, is

The hill villages hold their own while the cities continue to burgeon.

truly of the area, yet as the most venerated shrine in all Islam, is cosmopolitan in its spiritual role. So, too, Medina, also at 2,000 feet, centre of religious learning and site of the Islamic University's three colleges of Basic Religion, *Shari'ah* (Law), and Missions. The abundant wells of both cities have secured their survival over the centuries: both are growing fast today.

Lastly, Ta'if, by virtue of its high elevation (5,000 feet), became increasingly the annual refuge of those trying to escape the stifling summer heat of the lowland. Monarch, court and cabinet move to Ta'if in summer, making it for these months the second capital. For centuries Ta'if and its fine surrounding uplands have been the provider of fruit for the Hijaz, and of rosewater (*attar*), distilled from its vast acres of rose gardens, for the whole of Arabia, and, indeed, for Europe too. Today, with its magnificent road leading from the coast, and its spacious villas, it is the resort of the Western Province.

(*See also* Sections 8 and 9)

For the traveller in the great northern desert of the Nafud, the wells and comforts of Tayma (far left) were always a symbol of contentment and restoration. Today, with modern irrigation, indigenous food crops (centre) abound in the Western Province, whose traditional name of Hijaz means "barrier". Yet the land is a barrier no longer, for with its ports and roads and expanding cities, and many of its citizens turning to technical and engineering professions like the crane operator (below), it is more of a gateway.

The People of the South-West

The monsoon and rugged highlands bring a different appearance, custom and temperament.

THE traditional name for the south-west, Asir, means "the difficult region" – and so indeed it is, for the outsider. The range which, as one moves southwards, becomes the south-western massif of peaks and terraced valleys and plateaux at over 6,500 feet actually begins with the hills to the north of Ta'if and includes the hill of Arafat, known to all pilgrims to Mecca. But the route southwards through the foothills was indeed a difficult one, until the building of today's highway, and more difficult still from the west, where the great block of mountain rises precipitously from the low coastal plain, the Tihamah.

To the east, the Asir slopes more gently down into the largest sand-sea in the world, the Rub al-Khali. Southwards, these highlands of Saudi Arabia are

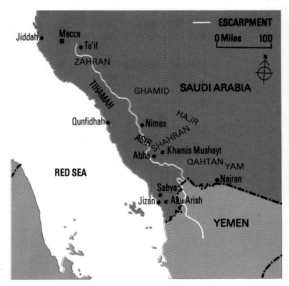

In the settled and agricultural south-west, traditional veiling of women has not taken hold, and vivid colours and jewellery characterize the apparel. Right: a similarly vigorous sense of colour is exploited in the interiors of lowland homes.

separated by deep valleys and a rugged causeway of uplands from the mountains of northern Yemen. The people south of the border are different in appearance, custom, temperament and religious attitude from their Saudi neighbours. But both regions catch the monsoon rains.

The south-west is the one well-watered region of Saudi Arabia. The annual rains have cut deep gorges beneath the high peaks and valley walls. To hold the soil from the ferocity of the rains, the farmers have – for thousands of years – turned the valleys and bowls into beautifully contoured walled steps. In this ancient terrain grow every manner of cereals, fodder crops and fruit.

Likewise, to protect their dwellings, the people have evolved the unique practice of mortaring into the outer walls row upon row of shale louvres. In so fine a natural setting, a sense of design prevails. Homes are washed outside with colours that intensify the upland sunlight. Smithing abounds, as does the wearing of jewellery. Strong colours prevail among the women's dress. There is a celebrated grace and confidence among the highland people.

The south-west is not all highland. To the west, beneath the steep, sometimes vertical escarpment, lies the lowland Tihamah. And the Tihamah in turn presents two different aspects, the valleys, and a sandy plain stretching towards the Red Sea. Generally speaking, the people in the highlands are taller than those in the lowlands.

The heavier and relatively dependable rainfall has allowed south-westerners, for the most part, to live a settled life as cultivators of the soil and as herdsmen. The different regions are identified according to the tribal groups which inhabit them. The most important groups, from north to south, are Zahran, Ghamid, Hajr, Asir, Shahran, and Qahtan. When referring to a particular area one says for example, Bilad Zahran, "the land of Zahran", or Bilad Asir, "the land of Asir".

In the highlands, villages are found in clusters and the appearance of these differs often significantly from area to area. Thus between Bilad Dhahran and Bilad Hajr, the houses are built of stone, while southwards towards Asir, both stone and mud houses are found, the latter being more numerous. Before the expedition of the late King Faisal (then a Prince) some two generations ago, which brought it into the Kingdom of Saudi Arabia, this south-western area was a warlike region where feuds between villages were commonplace. The disused watchtowers which dot the landscape everywhere are witnesses of that period.

Because of their altitude the highlands are cool in the summer with plentiful rain. This makes it a good region for agriculture. Indeed, the highlanders are an agricultural people, growing barley, millet, vegetables and fruit, but the date palm is not grown in the highlands. The terraced field, to be seen everywhere on the mountain slopes, is

The influence of Africa is seen in the conical homes of the southern Tihamah coast of the south-west (left and below), while characteristic Yemeni features are found in the south-western villages (far left) bordering on Saudi Arabia's mountainous neighbour.

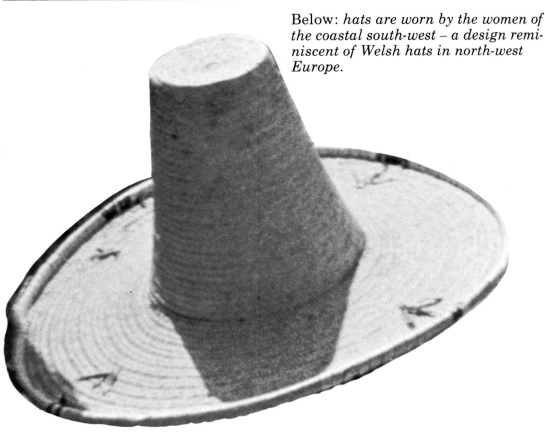

Below: *hats are worn by the women of the coastal south-west – a design reminiscent of Welsh hats in north-west Europe.*

The highland farms are compact, orderly and highly productive, assured of an adequate rainfall.

commonest of all. To ensure a better yield, irrigation is used in both orchards and non-terraced fields generally found in the drier and flatter areas. The water may come either from a water course swelled by rain, or from a well. In many areas where irrigation is mechanized, wells are drilled directly on the farm land, and pumps are placed in the old wells to replace muscle power.

The highland farms are compact, orderly and highly productive. Sophisticated marketing and excellent road and air communications today enable produce from the high Asir to reach Jiddah, Riyadh and the Gulf coast. The farmers enjoy a high standard of living, many of them owning cars or trucks or mechanized agricultural equipment. Yet, as is refreshingly true elsewhere in Saudi Arabia, new techniques and rising expectations and the advent of schools, hospitals, modern roads and dams, have not destroyed respect for traditional values and styles. For example, while some "functional" modern buildings have gone up in Abha, in the Asir as a whole homes are built in the highly distinctive, time-tested styles, with the encouragement of an enlightened regional administration.

Inevitably – and desirably – the highland people will be brought increasingly into contact with the "outside" world as a result of the certain growth in the tourist trade. Now that major roads have been opened from both north and south, and with the expansion of already efficient airline services to Khamis Mushayt, the flow of visitors escaping the summer heat of the lowland plateaux will swell year by year, affecting both the economy and the outlook of the indigenous people.

At the southern end of the south-west region lies the oasis of Najran, below the highland chain. Although linguistically it must be considered part of Najd, geographically it is part of the south-west. The architecture, of mud and straw, belongs to the south-west and not to central Najd. Furthermore, the half-moon shaped windows of tinted glass above the main windows of the houses in Najran are Yemeni in style.

The oasis of Najran lies in sandy desert and in summer the temperatures are high. Since it is the sand desert in particular which supports nomadic life,

Beduin come into close contact with the settled elements of the population of Najran. The main agricultural products are dates, as the climate allows the growth of the date palm, and grapes, which are famous in the south.

The clothing of the men consists of long shirt-like robes, like those of their counterparts in Najd; but here the width of the lower edge of the garment is greater. They may be white, blue or olive in colour. The headgear is usually a red and white checkered headcloth. The women wear long, waisted, colourful dresses, often heavily embroidered. Stress is on individuality. In the Asir region the peasant women wear broad brimmed sombrero-type hats. Women rarely veil the face.

In the Tihamah the population is of two types, sedentary people living in villages, and nomads. The sedentary population of the valleys is in close contact with the highlanders. There are dirt roads winding up the steep mountain passes separating the two regions. Today, the impressive Jizan highway is the most used link between these valleys and the flatter lands bordering the Red Sea.

A good example of a village of the valleys, the Tihamah, is Rijal, west of Abha. The village is of stone and built on two sides of a narrow valley. The way the houses rise on the slopes gives the impression of skyscrapers. Rijal used to be a trade centre, but the shops are now closed down as the Abha-Jizan road has diverted their trade. But the village is still renowned in the region for goldsmithing.

The interiors of the houses in Rijal are attractive. Even more than in Abha the walls are decorated with gay stylized designs painted by the women. For more decoration colourful imported enamelware adorns the shelves on the walls.

In the Rijal area agriculture is restricted to the sides of the valley. There is little terracing. The fields in the bottom of the valley have high retaining walls to protect them from the violence of flash floods. Higher up the slopes towards the highlands, where the climate is cooler, coffee has become a successful crop.

The other type of population found in the valley are the nomads who raise sheep and goats. They are unlike the Beduin of central Arabia. The men often

Traditional Trades along the Coast

Areas of the south-west have escaped the intrusive hand of modern development, and a content and self-sufficient life survives in the towns and villages along the coast, which draw their prosperity mainly from rich fishing grounds of the Red Sea. Much fishing takes place by night. The catch is landed at dawn, and in such centres as Jizan and Sabya sold at once at the waterside market. The boats are motor-powered.

Sesame oil is patiently crushed from the seed in a revolving mortar worked by camel power (right). Today, the ancient techniques are rapidly disappearing with the spread of electric power and modern machinery. While local needs are well supplied by fishermen working small boats (below), a modern, deep-water fishing industry is developing based on the bigger ports. Below, right: local cloth is dyed a rich saffron in a sabya workshop.

go bare-chested, wearing a length of colourful cloth around their waists. Their side-arm is a sword-like curved dagger just under a metre long, a protection against leopards. Often their headgear is a tall, black, brimless hat with a flattish backward-sloping top. The women wear tall straw hats with brims, similar to the hats worn by South American Indians.

Coastal Tihamah is flat and sandy. The majority of the population is agricultural, growing mostly millet. In Wadi Baysh, about forty miles north-east of Jizan, is a vast expanse of millet covering about six hundred square miles. Much of this region is newly watered by rain floods stored in the massive Jizan dam, which is transforming a former wilderness into a significant grain-producing area, including an extensive experimental farm run by the Government. The visual impression of so much millet is strongly reminiscent of the endless maize fields of the American Mid-West.

Southwards down from the Red Sea coast, the influence of Africa is clearly to be seen among the people and their style of life. Conical houses are built in clusters behind high reed palisades. On the flats inland from Jizan, these villages present remarkable toothed silhouettes on the horizon. The single-chamber houses, lined with mud, are brilliantly painted inside with imaginative designs that reach to the pinnacle of the underroof. Fishing is a major local industry, the Spanish mackerel being a principal source of protein food. The traditions of seamanship have maintained links with the Eritrean coasts across the Red Sea.

In the extreme south-west where the mountains rise sharply out of the plains, the lowland markets on the Saudi side of the frontier are frequently thronged with Yemenis with produce to sell. Higher Saudi standards of living bring higher prices.

In both the highlands and the lowlands the many markets constitute an important part of the people's life. The market in a village may be open every day or only once a week. If the latter is the case, market day is on a fixed day of the week, and, like anywhere else, that day is a social occasion for the people of the neighbouring villages. Often the name of the village incorporates the name of the day on which the market was customarily held. Thus: Khamis Mushayt, "the Thursday of Mushayt", Ahad Rufaydah, "the Sunday of Rufaydah", Sabt Tanumah, "the Saturday of Tanumah". Such places are usually referred to by the people of the region only by the name of their market day: Khamis, Ahad, Sabt. In some towns, where the market nowadays is open all week, as in Abha and Khamis Mushayt, market day sees more wares on display than other days of the week. On market day one may find nomads coming up from the

Tihamah to trade with the highlanders. In the markets, in addition to food and modern goods, one finds local products, such as straw baskets and hats, keys and nails made of locally mined iron, or, as in Najran, salt mined in the Empty Quarter.

The people of the south-west pride themselves on their hospitality. When a guest arrives, he is feasted by his host and various other members of the family who, on a more prolonged visit, take turns to entertain the guest. Besides the standard fare of lamb and rice, a dish offered to the guest is *arikah*, half-baked bread dough served in a big circular dish covered in brown honey. The guest fashions pieces of dough between his fingers into the shape of a spoon which he then dips into a side dish filled with white honey.

Weddings are a most important social occasion. Guests come, often from far away, to participate in the festivities.

There is dancing and singing on two separate days, one day for the men, and the following day for the women. On the men's day the guests dance in public in lines or circles, singing to the accompaniment of drums. There are also dagger dances.

On the women's day there are similar songs and dances performed in a marquee to the accompaniment of drums and pestle and mortar which serve as a percussion instrument. The women put on all their jewellery on such an occasion. Such ceremonial reflects the rich oral traditions of song and poetry of the people of the south-west.

(*See also* Sections 8 and 9)

The highland south-west is today a sought-after resort during the heat of the lowland summer. A bluish wash gives a jewel-like quality to an Abha farmstead. The slate louvres ensure weather-proofing (left).

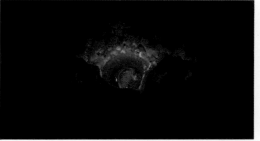

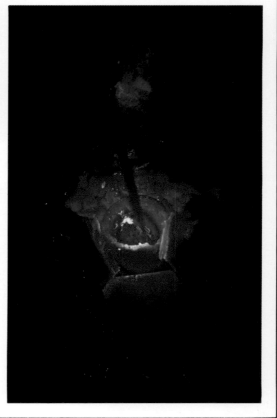

Metalcraft

The skills of silver-smithing (*right*) are not lost, nor the sense of design in, for example, these door handles (*left*). *Above:* an elder of the Asir region today wears his dagger for cere-monial purposes and (*far left*) intricate workmanship is evidenced in an elaborate sheath.

The People of the Eastern Province

THE coastal strip of the Eastern Province is low with relatively plentiful water; it was here that oil was first discovered. The shore is sandy, with salt flats occurring in depressions. Sandy plains from Jubayl to Kuwait Bay, drifting sand and dunes from Jubayl southward, a great belt of sand known as the ad-Dahna and a rock plateau called the Summan are the region's other main features. The Eastern Province also includes large sections of the Rub al-Khali – the Empty Quarter.

For many years communication with other provinces in Saudi Arabia was negligible, apart from a rare caravan along the coast; but despite its reputation for bleakness and ferocity there was a steady movement of people into the region from the sea. Enterprising individuals came wherever social conditions allowed travel routes to develop, thus adding non-tribal sectors to the population and building up coastal centres. This polyglot population became socially integrated with other groups but remained politically subordinate to the tribal factions of the interior.

There the balance between desert and oasis displayed almost polarized contrasts. The nomad's environment is one of inescapable heat and shortage, alleviated by space and freedom of movement. Such a life is led by the al-Murrah tribe along the northern edge of the Empty Quarter. These tribesmen move their entire household in pursuit of grazing for their animals every few days throughout most of the year. They live largely on their animals' milk products and to a lesser extent on their meat, on dates and on small amounts of rice or unleavened bread. Their inherited independence makes it difficult for them to fit into schemes of modern development.

The agriculturalist is generally better fed and better sheltered. The tribes of Bani Khalid and Bani Hajir live in the Haradh and Hofuf oases. The area in which Hofuf is situated bears the name Hasa, which signifies the "murmuring" of streams. The gardens of Hasa are magnificent, well tended groves amid colonnades of great palms.

The oil industry has brought increasing prosperity to the whole province. Even deep in the hinterland tribesmen dress better and live more safely and satisfactorily than their grandfathers did. Oil turned the port of Dammam into the thriving centre of the region, and its neighbour al-Khubar – once a fishing village whose inhabitants supplemented their living with pearling – into the expanding centre of business. A few miles inland, dominated by the rocky spur on which stands its University of Oil and Mineral Technology, lies Dhahran, nerve centre of the oil industry. Copious underground water sustains the swiftly growing city population.
(*See also* Sections 8 and 9)

Farmers have always worked the ground in the oases of Qatif and al-Hasa, growing dates, squash, watermelons and the long, thin "snake" cucumbers. Nowadays, the farms yield crops of beans and peas, maize, carrots, cauliflower and celery, and a poultry industry thrives, providing eggs and chicken both for the Eastern and Central Provinces.

The sea, Gulf trading, fishing and (up to the present century) pearl fishing, have pervaded the lives of the people of the Eastern Province. Inland, Hofuf (above) remains as a typical traditional stronghold. Eastern Saudi Arabia has played a key part in the history of the area for 7,000 years.

Extent of Arab Empire
in Second Islamic Century
(8th Century CE)

- ISLAMIC THROUGHOUT THE CENTURY
- CHRISTIAN OR OTHER THROUGHOUT THE CENTURY
- GAINED BY ISLAM FROM CHRISTIANS
- GAINED BY ISLAM FROM OTHERS
- GAINED AND LOST BY ISLAM TO CHRISTIANS
- LOST AND REGAINED BY ISLAM FROM CHRISTIANS (CYPRUS)

London

KINGDOM OF
THE FRANKS

Paris

Tours

Bordeaux

AVARS

Venice

ASTURIAS

Toulouse

KINGDOM OF
THE LOMBARDS

SLAVS

ANDALUSIA

Rome

Seville · Cordova

Tangiers

MAGHRIB

BERBERS

TRIPOLI

Tripoli

BARCA

MALTA

CRETE

MEDITERRANEAN SEA

Palermo

EAST ROMAN BYZANTINE EMPIRE

Constantinople

KHAZARS

MAGYARS

BLACK SEA

CASPIAN
SEA

IBERIA

ARMENIA

Aleppo

SYRIA

Damascus

Alexandria

Jerusalem

Fustat
(Cairo)

EGYPT

FEZZAN

Nile

RED SEA

HIJAZ

Medina

Mecca

ARABIA

NAJD

YAMAMAH

YEMEN

San'a

HADHRAMAWT

DHUFAR

Mosul

Euphrates

Tigris

Baghdad · Ctesiphon

Karbala

Najaf · Kufa

Qadisiyah

Hamadan

Susa

Basra

Qadisiyah

BAHRAIN

Qatif

KERMAN

Persepolis

PERSIA

KHORASAN

Sarmarqand

SIND

MEKRAN

Indus

OMAN

Muscat

ARABIAN SEA

64

PUNJAB

4
History

From a pre-historic past whose civilizations are only today being revealed by archaeologists, the country became the illumined focus of countless people, from Spain to India, as the centre of swiftly expanding Islam. But a firmly unified Saudi Arabia was forged only on the third attempt, by the audacity and vision of King Abdul Aziz.

Liths bearing Aramaic inscriptions were found in Tayma (left). Scripts excavated in various parts of Arabia, as that in Himyaritic and Lithianic from the south and north (above), yield evidence of sophisticated civilizations reaching back some three millennia. The function of these fragments, which tell of priests and kings, was votive.

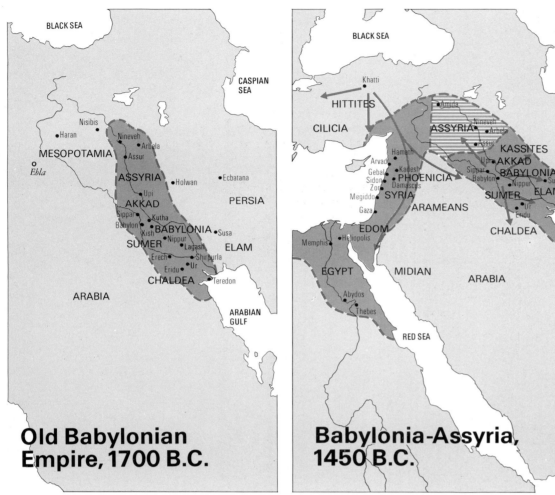

Old Babylonian Empire, 1700 B.C.

Babylonia-Assyria, 1450 B.C.

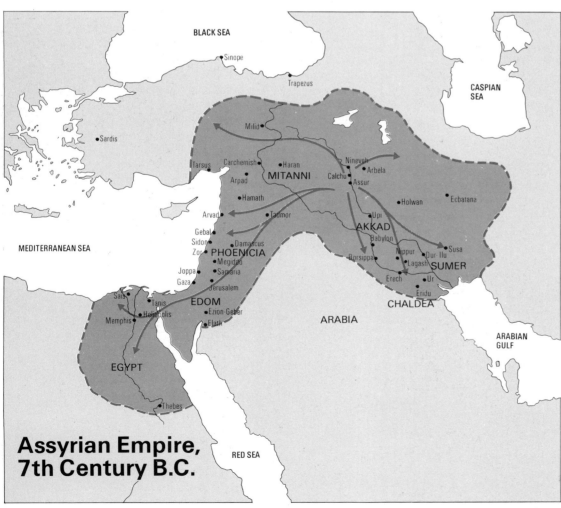

Assyrian Empire, 7th Century B.C.

Pre-Islamic Datelist

Involving Arabs and Related Peoples of the Near and Middle East

BC

2350	Sargon builds Akkad
2300	Ascendancy of Ebla (Tell Mardikh)
2270–2233	Reign of Naram-Sin of Sumeria
2200	Decline of Pharaonic Old Kingdom
2000	Zenith of civilization of Dilmun
1991–1792	12th dynasty of Middle Kingdom of Pharaohs
1728–1686	Hammurabi reigns (founder of Babylon)
1700	Abraham leads migration to Palestine from Ur
1570–1545	18th Egyptian dynasty founded in Thebes by Ahmose
1545–1525	Amenhotep of Egypt moves capital to Akhetaton (Tell al-Amarna)
1530	Hittites sack Babylon. End of first Amorite dynasty
1502–1448	Egyptian conquest of North Nubia and neighbouring Mediterranean coast under Thutmose III
1361–1352	Tutankhamun reigns
1300–1200	Rise of Sabaeans under the Queen of Sheba in South Arabia
1280	Treaty signed. North Syria recognized as Hittite, South Syria (Palestine) as Egyptian
1234–1215	Hebrews' exodus from Egypt
1200	Damascus gained by Aramaeans
1100–888	Rise of Sidonian state
1020	Saul anointed. First King of the Hebrews
945	Shishak of Libya ousts Pharaohs
936–923	Reign of Solomon
900–842	Rise of Damascus
884–859	Rise of Ashur-nasir-pal and an initial Assyrian conquest successful
875	Israel becomes a vassal of Damascus
814	Carthage founded by Phoenicians
806–732	Decline of Aramaean Damascus
733	Tiglath-Pileser of Assyria defeats Israel
732	Tiglath-Pileser overthrows Damascus, centre of Aramaean power
727–722	Shalmanese V of Assyria conquers Tyre
722–705	Sargonid dynasty. Ascendancy of Assyria
705–681	Sennacherib destroys Babylon
671	Tirhaka of Ethiopian dynasty in Egypt defeated by Assyrians under Esarhaddon
600–593	Phoenicians under Pharaoh Necho circumnavigate Africa
605–562	Reign of Nebuchadnezzar II. Restoration of Babylon and creation of the Hanging Gardens.
586	Nebuchadnezzar destroys Jerusalem, capital of Judah
572	Nebuchadnezzar conquers Tyre
550–529	Cyrus of Anshan in Elam founds Achaemenid dynasty in Persia
546	Cyrus overthrows Croesus and seizes Sardis

539 Babylonians under Belshazzar defeated by Persians
539–332 Phoenicia under Persian rule
529–521 Cambises of Persia conquers Egypt
521–485 Darius I establishes Persepolis
490 Darius loses Battle of Marathon to Athenians
480 Spartans defeat Persians at Thermopylae
480 Xerxes of Persia routed by Greeks at sea battle of Salamis
446 Artaxerxes I makes peace treaty with Greeks
330 Alexander the Great burns Persepolis
323 Alexander the Great conquers Babylon and dies there
312–280 Seleucus I founds the Syrian Kingdom
300 Petra becomes Nabataean capital
226 Parthians defeated by Sassanids
218 Hannibal of Phoenicia crosses the Alps
202 Hannibal defeated by Romans
133 Attilid Kingdom creates extensive province of Asia
169 Antiochus IV of Syria defeats Ptolemy IV of Egypt
85 Nabateans take Coele-Syria from Seleucids
69–83 Tigranes of Armenia makes conquests in Macedonian Kingdom
64 Romans conquer Syria
51–30 Rule of Cleopatra in Egypt
48 Julius Caesar conquers Pompey at Zela
44 Caesar murdered
30 Roman annexation of Egypt
37–4 Rule of Herod the Great of Judaea
6 Birth of Jesus (as calculated by scholars)

CE
0–100 Himyarites migrate to Axum (Abyssinia)
27 Death of Jesus
70 Titus, Roman Emperor, starves Jerusalem into surrender
106 Romans destroy Nabataean Petra
114–116 Rome at war with Parthia
123 Hadrian renounces Euphrates territory
195–199 Severus conquers Mesopotamia
226 Foundation of the new Persian Empire
268–273 Palmyra conquers Syria, Mesopotamia and parts of Egypt
330 Constantinople becomes seat of Eastern half of Roman Empire
354–430 Life of Augustine
433–453 Attila, ruler of the Huns
525 Abyssinians conquer Yemen
568–572 Fall of Rome
571 Birth of Muhammad
575 Khosran I of the Sassanids expels Abyssinians from the Yemen
586 Muhammad marries Khadijah of the Quraysh tribe
610 Muhammad's first revelation outside Mecca
614 Persians conquer Damascus, Jerusalem and Egypt
622 Muhammad flees from Mecca to Medina, the *hijrah* and official beginning of the Moslem era
632 Death of Muhammad

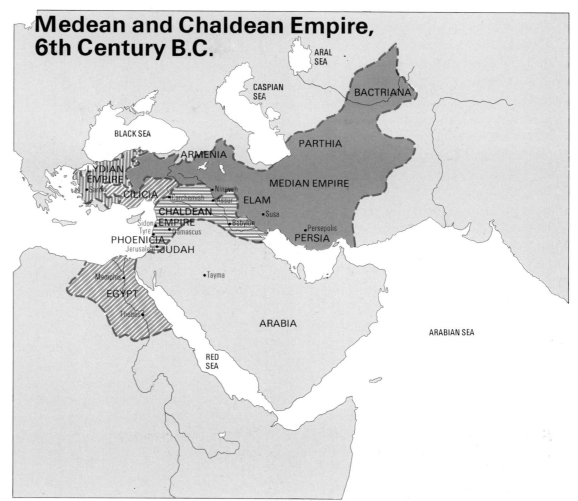

Medean and Chaldean Empire, 6th Century B.C.

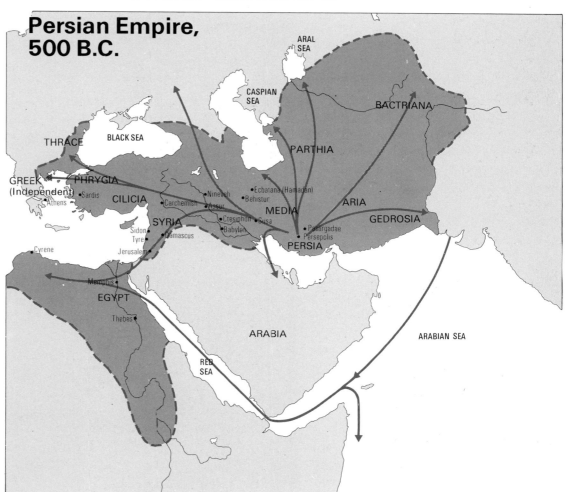

Persian Empire, 500 B.C.

The "Age of Darkness" to the Coming of the Prophet

SCHOLARS may disagree about the location of the cradle of the human race, but about the cradle of civilization there is no disagreement. It lies in the area called the "Near East" and is composed of the Fertile Crescent – Mesopotamia (modern Iraq), Syria, Palestine, Egypt, Anatolia (Asia Minor, Turkey) and Persia (Iran). At one time most of Europe and much of the Middle East was covered in ice, but to the south of this ice-sheet, Africa and Arabia were fertile with grass and streams flowing in what are nowadays dry *wadis*. The climate gradually changed, the ice-sheet retreated and the grasslands advanced.

International highways have always

linked Africa, Europe and Asia, and these continents provided the stage not only for the world's three great monotheistic religions but also for some of the earliest, most spectacular and enduring discoveries and achievements of man. The civilizations which developed in this area passed on to later generations a matchlessly rich heritage of science, art, literature and philosophy.

Civilization as we recognise it probably began in the vicinity of the basins of the Rivers Tigris and Euphrates in Mesopotamia, the River Nile in Egypt and the River Indus valley. From here it spread over the Middle East, while men in the rest of the world still lived in a primitive state. The area of the Middle East, originally a European geographical term loosely used to designate that part of south-western Asia nearest Europe, has a recorded history filled with drama – the rise and fall of empires, the growth and decline of great cities, the ascendancy and decline of great peoples, wars, invasions and deportations, kings and emperors, treachery, intrigue and disasters.

Long before written records existed

the people of the Middle East had developed urban life, with ordered governments, religions, and social and economic institutions. Earlier still, those who occupied the Fertile Crescent had discovered metal, realized its potential and worked it into tools and weapons which replaced the more primitive stone implements of preceding generations. Civilization first developed where it did because this was the one area of the globe which provided the climate, vegetation, and fauna necessary for the transition from a life of nomadic grazing and hunting to a settled existence. Through migration, invasion or cultural osmosis these remarkable accomplishments eventually found their way into the Eastern Mediterranean and the Aegean islands, and thence to the European mainland where they formed a prelude to the classical civilizations of Greece and Rome, parents to all Western civilizations. The full extent of the debt that Greece and Rome owed this area was hardly appreciated until recently, a debt which does not make the glory that was Greece less glorious, or the grandeur that was Rome less grand. In fact, it was not until the early nineteenth century that scholars began to rediscover the empires of Egypt, Babylonia and Assyria and to reconstruct their cultural institutions. As for the Hittites and their empire in Anatolia, the rediscovery began as late as the twentieth century. Historians and archaeologists disagree about some of the detail of pre-Islamic history but during the last century a great deal has been ascertained by exploration and excavation. Only since the 1960s has the role of what today is Saudi Arabia begun to be revealed by the discoveries of archaeologists.

The Sumerians created one of the earliest civilizations in an area adjoining Arabia. By 3000 BC they occupied their new homeland of Sumer at the head of the Arabian Gulf, at the watershed of the Tigris and Euphrates rivers. The principal city was Ur. Other cities founded then were Erech, Lagash and Nippur. Eridu was a burgeoning port on the coast, although its site is now some 130 miles inland, and the other cities are just mounds in the desert. Irrigation, trade, the use of money and codes of laws were all developed by the Sumerians, and their clay tablets of pictorial and syllabic writing became the cuneiform script widely used in the ancient Middle East. Our modern science of astronomy is derived from their advanced knowledge of the stars, supplemented by Babylonian, Greek and Islamic influences. They used wheeled vehicles, and built beautiful and imposing arches with dried bricks as a feature of their tower temples, known as *ziggurats*. Archaeologists have found good examples of utensils, sculpture and other remnants of the Sumerian way of life in the tombs which were con-

structed for each dead leader, and which habitually included all the men and women who had been his close servants in his lifetime.

But contacts between the rich lands of Mesopotamia and the coast of eastern Saudi Arabia were already vigorous during the preceding two millennia, the earliest traces beginning in 5500 BC and continuing through the rise of Dilmun (today's Bahrein and neighbouring mainland) during the third millennium, when the Arabian Gulf ports were of great importance, as excavations inland from Abqaiq have proved.

Traditionally the people known as the

Semites are thought to be descended from Shem, the eldest son of Noah. Their language was closely related to that of the Sumerians and they lived a nomadic existence north of Sumer, eventually filtering into central and northern Mesopotamia. Gradually they built up their own city states such as Kish and Mari, having for many years plundered their more advanced neighbours, the Sumerians. About 2360 BC the first empire of recorded history emerged, that of Akkad, in the area which became known as Babylonia. Akkadian influence spread beyond Mesopotamia to Arabia. This empire was destroyed after a couple of centuries, and, although Akkadian Sem-

The exceptionally well-preserved rock tombs and dwellings of Madain Salih in north-western Saudi Arabia give vivid evidence of the civilization of the

Nabataeans who flourished two thousand years ago on the rich trade in frankincense and myrrh – the same Arab stock that built Petra, in Jordan. The

finely decorated façades and shrines carved out of the living rock show the unmistakable influence of Greece (opposite above).

69

Nabataean life was strictly controlled by an elaborate priesthood, occasionally depicted in stone relief (far right); temples served also as palaces. The Nabataean ancestors of today's Arabs were masters at extracting water from precipitation in the most forbidding of arid territories, and preserving it in underground cisterns hewn out of the rock. Pinnacles of soft rock (opposite) became natural citadels.

ites continued to be one of the main elements in the population, other Semitic powers gained ascendancy, notably the invaders of Mesopotamia, the Amorites, who came from the present area of Syria.

The ancient city of Babylon was ruled in the eighteenth century BC by the Amorite, King Hammurabi. Basic laws were formalized and great progress was made in the fields of scholarship and science, especially mathematics and astronomy. The Hittites overwhelmed the Amorites in approximately 1600 BC. These tribes from Asia Minor absorbed Syria and made treaties with the Egyptians before they too were overcome by an invasion of barbarians from Europe in 1200 BC. The Kassite dynasty ruled Babylonia successfully for four hundred

years. Thereafter it came to be ruled by Assyria.

The Assyrians had settled in northern Mesopotamia; their capital was Assur on the Tigris, named after their national god. Nineveh later became the imperial capital, and the cultural ideas of the Babylonians and the Sumerians were developed by the Assyrians with their own characteristic variations. Very active commercially, they used stamped silver bars for money, employed letters of credit and originated the practice of lending money to neighbouring people at an interest rate of twenty or thirty per cent. They constructed huge libraries for cuneiform documents and great palaces and temples. From the tenth to the seventh centuries they remained

Madain Salih, though built by Nabataean Arabs, was strongly influenced by the architecture of Greece. This north-western Arabian twin of Petra was built to forestall the Romans in their attempt to take over the spice and frankincense trade, which the Nabataeans controlled until 106 CE.

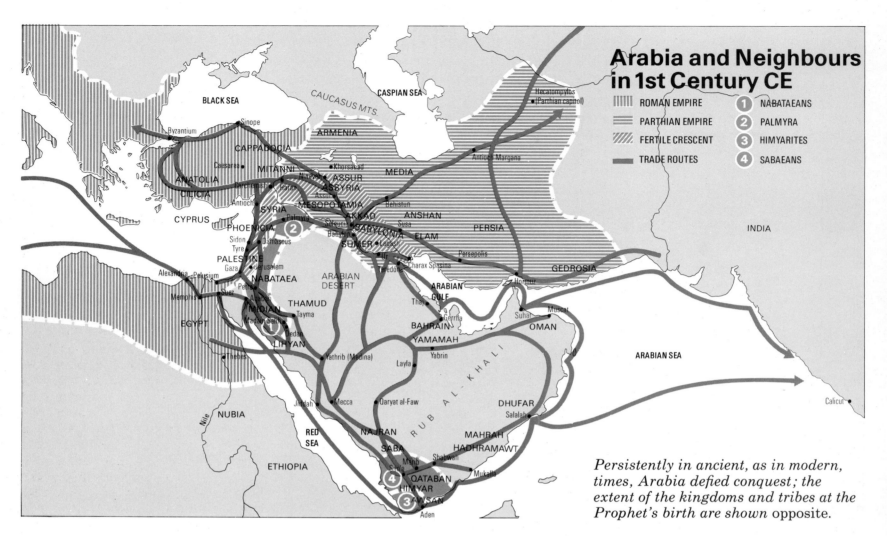

Arabia and Neighbours in 1st Century CE

ROMAN EMPIRE		①	NABATAEANS
PARTHIAN EMPIRE		②	PALMYRA
FERTILE CRESCENT		③	HIMYARITES
TRADE ROUTES		④	SABAEANS

Persistently in ancient, as in modern, times, Arabia defied conquest; the extent of the kingdoms and tribes at the Prophet's birth are shown opposite.

powerful, employing iron weapons to arm their bellicose formations of infantry, cavalry and archers. Eventually in 612 BC the Assyrians were overthrown by a combination of Medes, Babylonians and Persians, and Nineveh was destroyed.

Babylon continued to be powerful and remained a centre of scholarship. The city was destroyed by the Assyrian conqueror Sennacherib as a punishment for rebellion, but was rebuilt by his heir, Esarhaddon. It later became the capital of an empire known as Babylonia, which was created by the Chaldeans, who included both Aramaeans and Arabians. Nebuchadnezzar was the greatest of its kings; he conquered a reviving Egypt, destroyed Jerusalem in 586 BC and rebuilt Babylon with greater grandeur. The famous Hanging Gardens became one of the seven wonders of the world. Two chariots could race abreast on the city walls. Palaces and temples combined to make Chaldean Babylon one of the most remarkable capitals the world has ever seen. Nebuchadnezzar carried many of the people of Judah into exile in this city. When Babylon fell to Cyrus, the Persian conqueror, in 539 BC,

some remained, while others returned to their native countries.

The Persians had a number of great emperors – Cambises, Darius, Xerxes – and their strategies conquered a vast region extending from Asia Minor and Egypt as far east as India. These conquests and the ensuing advance of the Persian empire were finally arrested at Marathon, in 490 BC, by the Greeks, who after a setback at Thermopylae and the sacking of Athens in 480 BC forced the Persians to return to Asia.

An efficient and stable administration enabled the Persians to perfect a system of fast communication by horse. They spoke an Aryan language and practised a version of Zoroastrianism. Some two centuries later, Alexander the Great finally conquered the Persian or Achaeminid Empire in 334–323 BC. Having conquered the whole of the civilized world from Macedonia to India, he died in Babylon in 323 BC. Greek culture was influential in other Middle Eastern countries through the Seleucids in Syria and the Ptolemies in Egypt, and through the later Byzantine and Roman Empires until the dawn of Islam.

The Persian Empire was revived by

the Parthians between 250 BC and 226 CE, and later by the Sassanids from 226 BC to 650 CE. There was at this time a close relationship between the Arabian Gulf and Mesopotamia, and in the latter fertile area was the site of Ctesiphon, the Persian capital when the Sassanids were conquered by Muslim Arab armies in the *jihad* or holy wars of 637–650 CE.

The Hebrews too made an important contribution to the religious and literary traditions of the ancient Middle East. They seem to have developed first as semi-nomadic tribes, brought together under a common traditional patriarch, a system characteristic of some Beduin tribes today. The Old Testament was probably finished while the Hebrews were in captivity in Babylonia. They were much influenced by the Canaanites of Palestine, part of whose land they conquered and inhabited. The time of Moses and the Exodus from Egypt is thought to have been early in the thirteenth century BC. The Hebrews were never an important people politically and the great empires of Egypt, Mesopotamia, Greece and Rome ruled them successively, although occasionally the Hebrews gained inde-

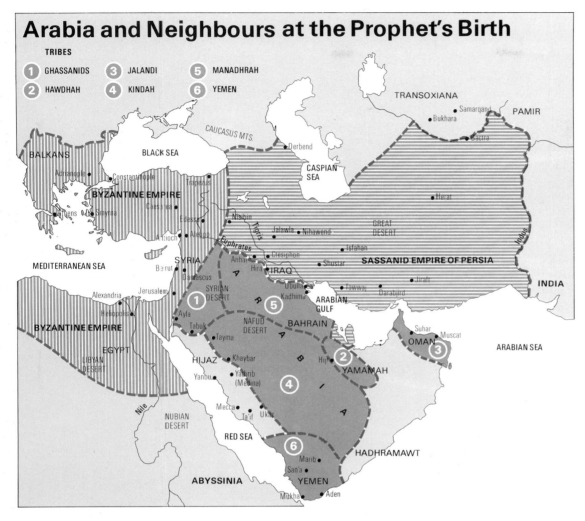

Arabia and Neighbours at the Prophet's Birth

TRIBES

1. GHASSANIDS 3. JALANDI 5. MANADHRAH
2. HAWDHAH 4. KINDAH 6. YEMEN

ern and southern kingdoms. During this time the 365 day calendar was devised. This was followed by the dynastic era in which the two kingdoms were consolidated and Egyptian power expanded into Syria and Palestine. The Old Kingdom saw the building of the pyramids, followed by further conquests in Nubia during the Middle Kingdom, although there was some disintegration between these periods. Then came the Empire, during which the Hebrew Exodus from Egypt took place. Under Ikhraton, father-in-law of Tutankhamun, sun-god monotheism was practised temporarily. Sovereignty over Egypt changed hands from a Libyan to a Nubian Dynasty, but was returned to the Egyptians during the Lower Empire. Persia was the last power to rule Egypt before the Arab conquests of the seventh century CE.

Although the Arabian Peninsula now has valleys and alluvial plains as fertile as those which originally encouraged settlements in the Fertile Crescent and in Egypt, its oases have also been populated for many thousands of years. During the Ice Ages which rendered so much of Europe uninhabitable, the Arabian region had enjoyed a temperate climate and evidence remains of numerous watercourses. The earliest Arabs were divided by custom into the nomads of the north and the city dwellers of the south, although some integration had occurred by the time of Muhammad. (To this day the vast deserts of the Peninsula are peopled by the Beduins, whose early raids into civilized territory led to cultural exchange across the area). The Hebrews, Aramaeans, Assyrians and other Semitic peoples migrated in large numbers to underdeveloped territories, and it is likely that they set up the Hyksos dynasty of Egypt in the eighteenth century BC.

Not long after the time of the Nile and Mesopotamia civilizations the southern part of Arabia became a populated commercial centre specializing in the production of frankincense and myrrh, both of which were in great demand from the Romans. The region also traded in the silks and spices and jewellery which were brought from the Indies and East Africa to the Eastern Mediterranean. Northern civilizations were supplied with precious metals, of which a quantity of gold and copper was mined in Arabia itself. Goods were transported by camel from one trading centre to another along a network of caravan routes

pendent control of their "promised land" for brief periods between their arrival there under Joshua in the thirteenth century and their final futile rebellions which were cruelly put down by their Roman overlords in 66–70 CE and 132–135 CE.

The Phoenicians, the northern Canaanites who originated in what is now the Lebanon and the coast of Syria, became the greatest Semitic seafarers and traders during a period of growth which started in the twelfth century BC. Through their far-flung voyages they disseminated their cultural influence. Their alphabet, and the resulting great improvement in communication, was a major development which took place in the Semitic territory between Sinai and Syria, the homeland of the Phoenicians. Several other forms of alphabetic script were devised; pictographs of Egyptian type gave rise to alphabets which are still used in the Middle East, and are the basis of the European alphabet and those of India and Mongolia. The Minoans of Crete had led the civilized world in seafaring but were replaced by the more adventurous Phoenicians, who traded in tin from Western Europe, silver from

Spain, and Tyrian purple dye from the Mediterranean and tropical seas. Carthage was their great colonial possession, situated in north Africa, not far from present-day Tunis. Other homeland cities included Tyre, Sidon and Jubayl. Carthage almost defeated Rome in the three Punic (Phoenician) Wars of the third and second centuries BC, but was finally destroyed by the Romans in 146 BC.

Parallel with the existence of the Hebrew Kingdom was that of Syria, whose capital was Damascus. The Syrians, known earlier as Aramaeans, fluctuated between alliance and war with the Hebrew people. Their close links with the Phoenicians included a similar alphabet and language, which survived as the language of the people of Palestine until it was replaced by Arabic a millennium later. They were equally successful in spreading their commerce abroad.

Of all the very early civilizations the one which left the most splendid cultural legacy was Egypt. The predynastic period had its beginnings in the days of the rise of Mesopotamia, when its provinces, known as *nomes*, were united into north-

Acceptance of the Prophet's message transformed the Eastern world from the Atlantic shores to the Indus and, later, beyond. The threads of earlier cultures were drawn together and under the inspiration of Islam a new and confident civilisation flowered.

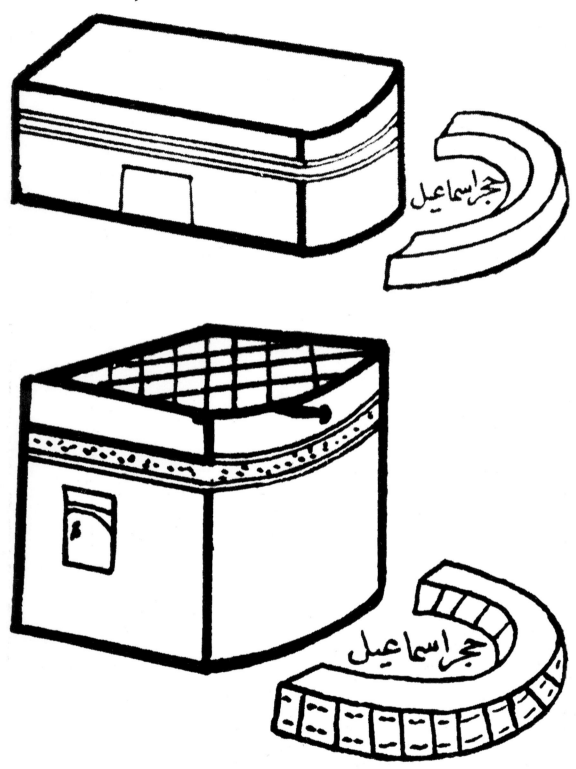

The reconstruction of Abraham's Ka'bah (top) and the Ka'bah of the Holy Prophet Muhammad (above), as calculated from ancient chronicles, demonstrate the consistency of design throughout the immense period – nearly five thousand years – of its existence as the holiest of shrines.

fanning out from Arabia to Egypt and Babylonia. Some of these routes are still used by pilgrims to Mecca and Medina, although the camel is no longer the most popular method of transport. Agriculture was difficult, but a sophisticated system of irrigation included the building of dams to retain flood water for the dry season. One such dam was at Marib, built of limestone and so well designed that it stood intact almost up to the birth of Muhammad.

The Kingdoms of Southern Arabia were subject to frequent change and internecine warfare. Ma'in and Saba, the probable domain of the Queen of Sheba, were two of the earliest which rose to power. Others included Awsan, covering approximately the area now known as Aden, Qataban to its north-east and Hadhramawt to the east of Qataban. The powerful tribe of Himyar in the south-west gave its name to contemporary civilisation there. Oman had been a centre of trade and ship-building for many centuries, and Dhofar the source of frankincense, a major commodity of international commerce.

Some time after the first settlements, the northern portion of the country was taken over by the Nabataeans. The Nabataean capital was al Petra, but their southernmost stronghold at Madain Salih, in north-western Saudi Arabia, was of great importance in controlling the trade routes. The influence at Madain Salih evident in the fine façades of the tombs, with their pilasters and pediments, is wholly Hellenistic. The Nabataeans, too, controlled the trade route to the Greek and, later, Roman worlds from the northern Gulf through al-Sawf. Their remarkable technology involved the construction of dams, rock cisterns and irrigation systems, some of which are usable today. With the rise of Rome, the Peninsula's commercial wealth came under military threat, but an invasion launched by Aelius Gallus in 24 BC ended in failure. Having overcome one hurdle, however, south-western spice trade routes based on such cities as Dedan, Yathrib (modern Medina) and Najran, fell at another. Trade began to decline when the Greeks and

"Blessed" Mecca and "Radiant" Medina were the sites of the first converts.

Romans discovered the Arab methods of sailing to India on the monsoon winds, and the people of the once-prosperous south migrated northwards. Once-prosperous towns along the trade routes that withered include that of Qaryat al-Fawr, recently excavated by the University of Riyadh, on the way from the south-west to the east, skirting the Rub al-Khali.

In the fourth and sixth centuries CE, south-western Arabia fell under Abyssinian rule, and it was during the year 571, when Mecca successfully rebuffed an attack by the Abyssinian Abraha, that the Prophet Muhammad was born in the Holy City.

The birth of Muhammad was a momentous event in history. The followers of Islam today number some five hundred million. Muhammad was the son of Abdullah and Aminah, of the tribe of Quraysh; he became an orphan when still young and spent part of his boyhood among the Beduins of the desert. At twenty-five years of age he married Khadijah, also of the Quraysh tribe, and entered a life of meditation. Soon after, in 610 CE, he experienced his first revelation and began his role as a prophet spreading the message of the one, all-powerful God and the day of judgement to come.

The early converts were few and slow to follow his teachings, but the turning point came in 622 CE when two hundred followers eluded the vigilance of the Quraysh and slipped into Medina. Seventeen years later the *hijrah* migration was described by the Caliph as an essential part of the Muslim experience. The Prophet assumed the role of warrior, judge and civil administrator, winning several victories against the Qurayshis and their supporters, among them the Medinese Jews. From being a religion within a state Islam became the State.

Although an unschooled man he was responsible for the Qur'an, regarded by Muslims as their spiritual and behavioural guide. Within his life span Muhammad established a religion that replaced Christianity in most of Asia and Africa, and laid the foundations of an Empire that was soon to embrace a large part of the then civilized world.

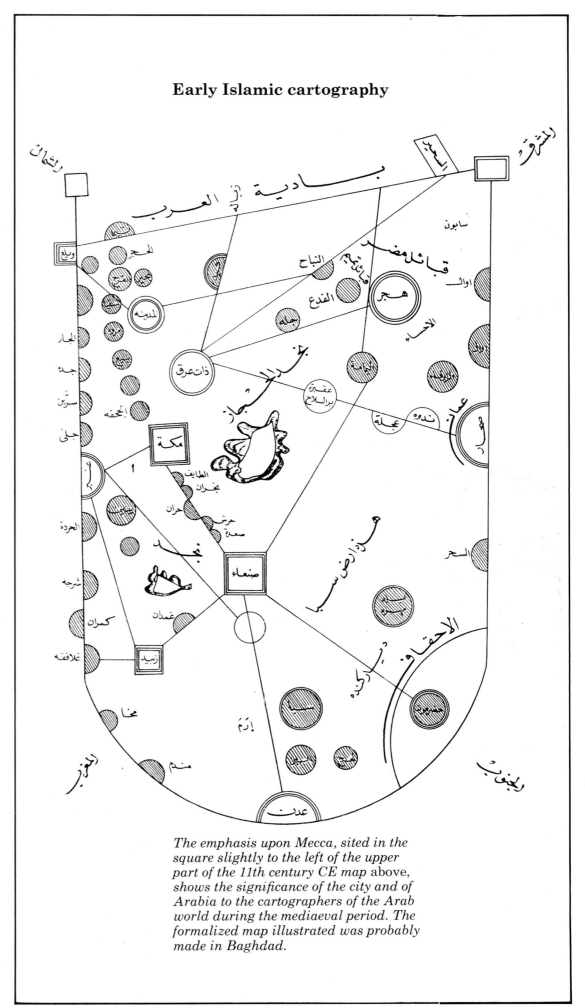

Early Islamic cartography

The emphasis upon Mecca, sited in the square slightly to the left of the upper part of the 11th century CE map above, shows the significance of the city and of Arabia to the cartographers of the Arab world during the mediaeval period. The formalized map illustrated was probably made in Baghdad.

The Rise of Saudi Arabia to the Mid-20th Century

THE modern state of Saudi Arabia began to develop in the Najd region of central Arabia some two hundred years ago. From the start of the Islamic era to the middle of the eighteenth century CE Arabian history is made up of the separate stories of a number of individual regions. Despite contacts between these regions and the unifying force of Islamic civilization, the political and religious development of Arabia was by no means uniform. More information is available about the important coastal areas – the Hijaz, Yemen and south Arabia, Oman and Hasa on the Gulf – than about central Arabia, the heartland of the future Saudi state.

Until the European expansion into the Indian Ocean after the fifteenth century, the Hijaz – the region containing the two main sanctuaries of Islam, those of Mecca and Medina – was the area of most significance to the outside world. For reasons of prestige, as well as for the financial benefit which accrued from control of the annual pilgrimage, powerful Muslim rulers frequently sought to establish their ascendancy over it. In the tenth century CE a descendant of the Prophet declared himself Sharif of Mecca, and the Sharifate thus founded survived, sometimes independently, sometimes under outside control, until ibn Saud conquered the Hijaz in 1925. Most frequently it was the ruler of Egypt who controlled the Sharifate, and after 1517, when Egypt became part of the Ottoman Empire, the governor of Egypt was recognized as having authority over the Hijaz on behalf of the Ottoman sultan.

Yemen too, because of its position at the mouth of the Red Sea, was of interest to the rulers of Egypt, who on occasions exercised political control over the area. From the early ninth century CE a number of independent dynasties established themselves in the Yemen, and at the end of the century two competing schools of thought in Shi-ite Islam, Isma'ilism and Zaydism, won support among some sections of the population. The Makramid dynasty of Najran, which arose in the eighteenth century and with whom the Saudi rulers came into conflict, espoused a form of Isma'ilism, but ultimately it was Zaydism which prevailed in most of Yemen. In 1636 CE, following an Ottoman withdrawal, the Zaydi Imam occupied San'a and united the greater part of Yemen under his authority. Despite the breakaway of the southern part of his territories, including the port of Aden, at the beginning of the eighteenth century CE, the Zaydi Imamate in the Yemen survived into the twentieth century.

Oman has a similar history, being ruled for much of the period by a non-Sunni Imam, and subject to tension between the tribes of the interior and the towns of the coastal region. The Imams

Venerated Places

Almost equal in sanctity to the two Saudi Arabian cities of "Mecca the Blessed" and "Medina the Radiant" is Jerusalem, and its Qubbat as-Sakhra, Mosque of 'Omar *pictured here* and al-Aqsa Mosque. Sites in Damascus and in Baghdad, both seats of the Caliphate, are also revered. It was in Damascus and Jerusalem that the Omayyid built their mosques. Apart from its very ancient Arab association, Damascus was associated with the relic of John the Baptist, and Jerusalem with Solomon, Jesus and Muhammad's ascensional vision.

followed the Ibadhi Kharijite form of Islam. They established their power in the ninth century and, ruling from the interior, managed to maintain it with interruptions down to the sixteenth century. In 1507 CE the Portuguese captured Muscat, the main port, but in the middle of the next century the Omanis recovered it. In the succeeding period the division between the coastal region, centred on Muscat, and inner Oman intensified. The Saudis were sometimes able to establish their authority in inner Oman by way of Buraymi.

The region of Hasa on the Gulf came at times under the authority of powerful rulers in Iraq, and at other times had independent rulers. From the late ninth to the late eleventh century Hasa was the centre of an Isma'ili state which, at its height, became involved in Iraq and Syria and for a while even removed the Black Stone from the Ka'bah. In 1591 CE the Ottomans brought Hasa under their rule, but in 1669 a local family, the Banu Khalid, drove them out, and between 1694 and 1709 actually took control over the emirate of Diriyah away from the Saudi family. By the end of the eighteenth century, however, the tables were turned and the Saudi rulers of Diriyah were able to defeat the Banu Khalid and install their own nominee in Hasa as a preliminary to taking over the region completely.

Information about the pre-Saudi history of Najd and inner Arabia is fragmentary. For the outside world Najd was important because of the pilgrim route which crossed it from the Gulf to the Hijaz, but the area remained largely independent. The population was mainly nomadic, but here and there conditions did allow the growth of sizeable settlements. One such area was that of Wadi Hanifah near Riyadh, where, by the fifteenth century CE, a number of independent emirates or principalities had established themselves. Here the Saudi state had its origins.

The Saudi family traces its descent from Mani ibn Rabia al-Muraydi, who came, about the middle of the fifteenth century CE, from Hasa to settle in Wadi Hanifah. By the beginning of the seventeenth century his descendants had established themselves as rulers of a small emirate centred on Diriyah to the north of Riyadh. Shortly before 1720, Saud ibn Muhammad, the eponymous founder of the family, became ruler.

He was succeeded, on his death in 1725, by his son Muhammad. It was under Muhammad that the Wahhabi form of Islam was espoused, and the expansion of the emirate began.

Wahhabism takes its name from Muhammad ibn Abd al-Wahhab, who was born in 1703 CE into a family of religious scholars at Ayayna, the centre of another emirate in Wadi Hanifah, to the north of Diriyah. He was brought up to follow the Hanbali Law School, the most rigorous of the four law schools of Sunni Islam, and from an early age was noted for his strictness. In the course of his education he became influenced by the ideas of ibn Taymiyya, a theologian and jurist who died in 1328 CE and who had argued for a purification of Islam from what he considered to be accretions to the primitive faith. His ideas had some influence, especially among followers of the Hanbali Law School, and ibn Abd al-Wahhab came to believe that the essential monotheism of Islam had been compromised by excessive veneration of the Prophet Muhammad and other "saints". This veneration was most commonly expressed in pilgrimages and visits to minor sanctuaries and to the tombs of holy men; so ibn Abd al-Wahhab preached against these. He also insisted on the stricter implementation of penalties – such as death for adultery – fixed in the Qur'an, and he forbade certain innovations, notably the smoking of tobacco.

In 1745, after setbacks elsewhere, ibn Abd al-Wahhab settled in Diriyah, where he was favourably received by Muhammad ibn Saud. This event marks the beginning of a seventy-year period of expansion for the Diriyah emirate, the first of three distinct phases in the history of the Saudi state. Modern Saudi Arabia is the product of the third of these phases. Wahhabism seems to have provided the Saudi power with an ideological basis for expansion which the competing emirates lacked. It appealed equally to the tribes and to the settled population – the latter provided the main support for the dynasty in the first two phrases, and the tribes were crucial in the third.

By the end of the eighteenth century CE the emirate of Diriyah had extended its authority over the Najd, finally gaining control of Riyadh in 1773. This extension of political power was accompanied by the spread of Wahhabism and the implementation of its teachings.

Tombs of holy men raised above the ground more than about thirty centimetres and other minor sanctuaries were destroyed. By 1792 when ibn Abd al-Wahhab died, his ideas had already proved more directly influential than those of ibn Taymiyya ever were.

The rapid expansion of the Saudi emirate inevitably provoked fear and hostility in neighbouring non-Wahhabi states. The Sharif of Mecca undertook a series of expeditions against the Saudi state which now bordered his in the Hijaz, but these expeditions were unsuccessful, and in 1803 CE, shortly before the death of Abdul Aziz, who had succeeded his father Muhammad in 1765, a Wahhabi army brought Mecca under Saudi control. Two years later Medina was taken. In the north the Ottoman governors of Iraq supported the anti-Wahhabi tribes on the border between Iraq and Arabia, but they too were unable to hold back the Wahhabi forces. In 1802 Wahhabi raids into Iraq reached a climax when the tomb at Karbala of Husayn ibn Ali, the Prophet's grandson, whom most Muslims regard as a martyr, was sacked, together with its neighbouring town. However, the Wahhabis were not strong enough to take and hold the towns of Iraq.

The sack of Karbala provoked the hostility of most Muslims, Sunni and Shi-ite, and the occupation of the Hijaz brought the Saudi state into direct conflict with the Ottoman sultan, who regarded himself as the guardian of the Holy places for the whole Muslim world. At first the sultan was unable to act, but in 1811 CE the Albanian, Muhammad Ali, having secured control of Egypt, organized, at the sultan's command, an expedition against the Wahhabis. In 1812 forces from Egypt, led by Muhammad Ali's son Tusan, took Medina and in the following year Mecca. Abdul Aziz had been assassinated in 1803, probably by a Shi-ite Muslim seeking vengeance for the sack of Karbala, and was succeeded by his son Saud. Saud himself died in 1814, and his successor, his son Abdullah, had to conclude a truce with Tusan, ceding control of the holy towns to Muhammad Ali. In 1816, however, fighting began again, an army from Egypt invaded Najd, and in 1818 CE Diriyah was taken. Abdullah was sent in captivity to Istanbul, where he was executed. This was the end of the first distinct phase in the history of the Saudi state.

The second stage ran from 1824 CE, when Turki, the son of the executed Abdullah, seized Riyadh from Muhammad Ali's forces, until the last two decades of the nineteenth century, when the Saudi state was taken over by the Rashidi rulers of Ha'il in Jabal Shammar. Riyadh now became the capital of the Saudi state, and from there Turki extended his authority over

own rule over the Saudi state. Between 1838 and 1843 CE Faisal's rule in Riyadh was interrupted when Muhammad Ali again sent a force to invade Najd and set up another member of the Saudi family as ruler under the supervision of Muhammad Ali's agent in Riyadh. Faisal himself was taken prisoner to Cairo, but escaped and re-established his rule with the help of Abdullah ibn Rashid.

time an independent sheikhdom.

It was Abdul Aziz ibn Abd ar-Rahman, usually called simply ibn Saud, who initiated the third phase in the history of the Saudi state, lasting from the beginning of the twentieth century CE until the present day. In 1902 he was able to take advantage of the weakness of the Rashidi power, following the death of Muhammad ibn Rashid in 1897, in order

Western Travellers in Arabia

The dangers of desert travel and Arab caution towards non-Muslim intruders deterred Westerners until quite recently. In 1761 Carsten Niebuhr, a German in the service of Denmark, travelled in portions of Western Arabia. In 1814, the Swiss J. L. Burckhardt became one of the first Christians to enter Mecca, convincing his challengers by his outstanding knowledge of the Qur'an and its language. The British explorer Richard Burton, setting out in 1851 disguised as an Afghan, followed suit, and later (1876–78) travelled to Midian. At much the same time another Englishman, Charles Doughty, was travelling in north-western and west-central Arabia (1875–78). First to enter the "cradle of the Arab race", as Lady Anne Blunt called the Najd, was the Finnish professor Wallin, reaching Ha'il in 1848. The Levantine Italian Guarmani, also in disguise, started from Jerusalem in 1863, with a commission to buy horses, and reached Tayma, Burayda, Ha'il and Jawf. Then the Jesuit missionary Palgrave, disguised as a Syrian merchant, reached Ha'il and Riyadh in 1864. First of the undisguised travellers in the Najd, the Blunts reached Ha'il in 1879. Of all the subsequent outstanding travellers in

Richard Burton (1821–90) assumed Afghan guise and travelled as a pilgrim.

St. John Philby (1885–1960) explored and mapped more widely than any other.

Arabia – Alois Musil, T. E. Lawrence, Bertram Thomas, Wilfred Thesiger among others – none covered half as much territory as St. John Philby.

Charles Doughty (1843–96) wrote his Travels in Arabia Deserta *after travels in the Hijaz.*

Gertrude Bell (1868–1926), a fine Arabist and tribal expert, reached Ha'il in 1912.

Bertram Thomas (1892–1950) crossed the Rub al-Khali in 1931, from Salala to Qatar.

Wilfred Thesiger (b.1910) made several journeys in the Rub al-Khali in the 1950s.

the whole of Najd, inner Oman, and Hasa, which had been occupied for a time by Muhammad Ali's forces. Abd ar-Rahman ibn Hasan, a grandson of ibn Abd al-Wahhab, was appointed by Turki to be *qadi* of Riyadh, and he, together with his son, Abd al-Latif, was largely responsible for the continued development of Wahhabism in the nineteenth century.

In 1834 CE Turki was assassinated in a dispute between members of the Saudi family, but his son Faisal managed to wrest power from the rebels who had seized Riyadh. In the following year Faisal appointed Abdullah ibn Ali ibn Rashid to be his governor in Ha'il. Rashid's descendants were eventually to extend their power and establish their

Faisal's death in 1865 CE was followed by a struggle for power between two of his sons, Abdullah and Saud; a conflict which enabled the Ottomans to win back Hasa and the ruler of Ha'il, Muhammad ibn Rashid, to extend his power over the Saudi state, while ostensibly seeking to uphold the rights of Abdullah. By the time of Abdullah's death in 1889 CE, the Saudi state was no more than a province of the territory ruled by the Rashidis from Ha'il. Two years later Abdullah's son and successor, Abd ar-Rahman, was expelled from Riyadh by Muhammad ibn Rashid who appointed a puppet governor there. Abd ar-Rahman and his family, including his young son Abdul Aziz, who had been born about 1880, fled to Kuwait, which was at this

to recapture Riyadh with the help of what was really no more than a raiding party from Kuwait. The following ten years were spent in inconclusive fighting against the Rashidis, who received support from the Ottomans, and it was not until 1912 CE that ibn Saud took a step which was to prove decisive – the inauguration of the *Ikhwan* movement. During his exile in Kuwait and the fighting with the Rashidis, ibn Saud had come to see the military potential of the nomadic tribes if their customary resistance to state control could be overcome. Realizing that he must settle the tribesmen and give them a motive for uniting, he organized them into a religious brotherhood (*Ikhwan* means "brethren"), the aim of which was the militant

The House of Saud

1   From whom the Jifuwi branch of the House of Saud derive their name

2   From whom the Abdullah al-Turki branch of the House of Saud derive their name

3   Known as "al Kabir", a name retained by his descendants

FAHD   The Seven Sons of King Abdul Aziz by the late Hassa bint Sudairi, who are known as the Al Fahd

△   Member of the Council of Ministers

☐   Government Service (including the armed forces)

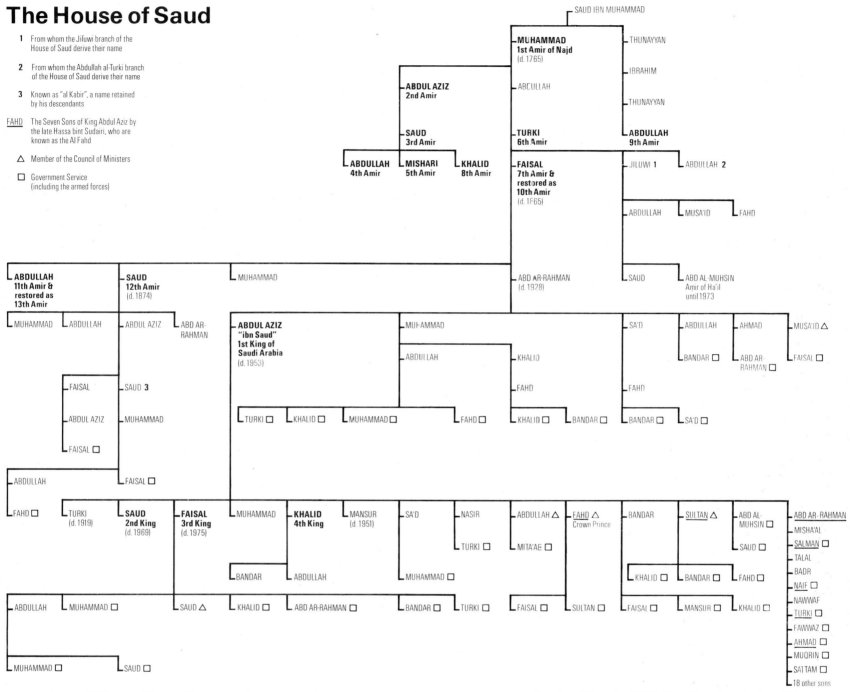

expansion of Wahhabism. The members of the movement were to settle in military encampments called *hijrahs*, just as at the time of the Arab Conquests the tribesmen had abandoned their nomadic way of life in Arabia for the garrison towns of the conquered territories. The first *hijrah* was founded at Artawiyya in 1912. Nobody knows the exact number of *hijrahs* which were established, but it may have been as high as two hundred. The number of warriors in each of them varied between ten and ten thousand.

With the help of the *Ikhwan*, ibn Saud took Ha'il in 1921 CE and the whole of the Hijaz, including Mecca, in 1924–25. Any further expansion in Arabia or its border areas would entail a clash with Great Britain, which was involved as

protector or mandatory power in all of the territories now bordering the Saudi state. Indeed clashes had already occurred. To the *Ikhwan*, such political considerations appeared a betrayal of the doctrine of holy war against all infidels (i.e. non-Wahhabis) with which they had been inculcated. Relations between ibn Saud and the *Ikhwan* deteriorated rapidly in the late 1920s as the *Ikhwan* began to act more independently. In 1929 they massacred a party of Najdi Wahhabi merchants, and the revulsion which this act aroused among the settled population of the Najd, as well as among several of the tribes, strengthened ibn Saud's hand sufficiently for him to take action against the *Ikhwan*. At the battle of Sabalah in

March 1929 ibn Saud put the *Ikhwan* to flight, and their power collapsed. Early in 1930 a number of their leaders surrendered to the British authorities in Kuwait, whence they were extradited by ibn Saud. He spared their lives but imprisoned them in Riyadh. This marked the end of the power of the *Ikhwan* as a force independent of ibn Saud. Some of their *hijrahs* continued to exist, but were now under government control. Eventually the *Ikhwan* were incorporated in the National Guard.

After 1930 ibn Saud began the transformation of the state which is still continuing. The battle of Sabalah marked the end of the era in which the history of Saudi Arabia can be discussed only in traditional terms.

From Abdul Aziz to the Present Day

TODAY'S Saudi Arabia under King Khalid – energetic, swiftly developing, yet profoundly respectful of tradition – is the direct heir of the Saudi Arabia created by Abdul Aziz ibn Saud. King Khalid is the fourth King in the present dynasty of Saudi rulers, succeeding his brothers Faisal and Saud. It is easy to overlook the fact that he is only one generation away from the founder of this stable, forward looking state.

King Khalid's father, Abdul Aziz ibn Saud, is remembered by all who knew him for characteristics which distinguished him among the Arabs of his generation. Physically, he was outstandingly tall; self-disciplined to be hardy, he relished battle and was indifferent to injury. Spiritually, his faith dominated his life; he was deeply devout, and steadfast in upholding the puritanism preached to his forbears by the eighteenth century Islamic reformer, ibn Abdul al-Wahhab. Mentally, he was a master of politics; his appraisal of men and their capacities was shrewd, and his grasp of world affairs astounding in one who during his long life paid only three brief visits outside his native Arabia, and never left the Arab world. Lastly, his basic instincts – integrity, a sense of honour, of justice, of humour – added up to a nature that brought him success despite early vicissitudes in his chequered life.

He was born in or about 1880 CE into a family – the Saudis of southern Najd – that had formerly been great but was then living in penury and exile after defeat by its northern rival, the Rashids of Ha'il. He spent his childhood in Kuwait, dreaming of restoring his family's fortunes. At twenty-one, he took advantage of some leisurely skirmishing between Kuwaitis and Rashidis to slip inland with forty picked companions and, in a night of surprises and sharp sword thrusts, to recapture his home town, Riyadh. This exploit brought him his first acclaim, and to this day Riyadh, in all its other buildings fashionably modern, preserves at its heart the old mud fort that is his people's memento of his daring. In 1902 his father, glad to reward determination allied to piety, named him Emir of Najd

and Imam of its puritanical brand of Islam.

Thereafter, he simultaneously spread religious reform and Saudi power, sometimes in battle, sometimes in the name of Wahhabism (a movement which appealed for a return to the true teaching of Islam), sometimes through persuasiveness or through respect for his military success. By 1926 he had captured the Holy Cities of Mecca and Medina and the whole Red Sea coastal province of the Hijaz. He declared himself King of Hijaz and Najd, and in 1932 renamed his kingdom Saudi Arabia.

As always happens, conquest brought complications. He owed to his belligerent *Ikhwan* the conquests that enabled him to dominate Arabia, yet was obliged to suppress them, because he could not condone their wish to carry Holy War abroad. Again, although Wahhabism had become a matter of course in the austere climate of Najd, it was less acceptable in the more sophisticated and easy-going Hijaz. In overseas Islam, too, the thought of Wahhabi fanatics in charge of Mecca and Medina caused deep disquiet. These misgivings he was within two or three years able to dispel, partly by ensuring the safety of the pilgrimage, partly by his handling of the *Ikhwan*, partly by the tact and moderation that he showed to anxious visitors. Equally tactfully, he slowly introduced his own people to innovations that they saw as heresies, but which he knew must come if his country was to grow great – concessions sold to infidels, the telephone, pilgrimage by motor transport, wireless telegraphy. But it was in his dealings with great powers that he best showed the acumen, and the awareness of Arab limitations, which made him an outstanding diplomat. For instance, though he hated the two Hashimite brothers whom the British had installed as rulers in neighbouring Iraq and Transjordan, he punished tribal or religious forays into their territory. Again in 1934 when armies led by his sons were on the verge of conquering Yemen, to their chagrin he ordered them to withdraw, because he realized that their approach to the confines of Aden

The great Abdul Aziz ibn Saud (right) *was swift to perceive the potential of his country's oil wealth and to encourage prospecting by foreigners like the early American oilman* (above), *robed for the desert.*

and the coast of Eritrea was antagonizing both Britain and Italy. He was always circumspect with the British, surrounded as he was by their sea power, their mandates and their dependencies. Yet he was friendly; even during the darkest days of the Second World War, he warned them of local pitfalls and backed them to win in the end. Only on the subject of Palestine did he censure them, then and later. As he listened,

The first decisive act in the restoration of the Saudi dynasty was the capture of Riyadh by Abdul Aziz in a raid of astonishing daring, on January 15th, 1902 CE, with a handful of men.

conscious of Arab impotence, to broadcasts about the British handling of Palestine's dismemberment, tears, it is said, poured down his cheeks.

At home, the greatest boon that he gave his people was internal security. Until his reign, all towns were walled, all gates barred at nightfall, all desert journeys undertaken at risk from raiders or feuding tribes. At the sight of strangers, friend could be told from foe only by some conventional gesture such as waving a headcloth or throwing up sand; if no such sign were given, the safest course was to gallop out of sight. Ibn Saud put an end to these hazards. His ways of doing so were to appoint trusted Najdis as regional governors, usually members of his vast family or of related stock – as-Sudayris, al-Jiluwis or ath-Thunayyahs; these outposts he furnished with the mobile wireless trucks that enabled him to keep a watch – miraculous to the tribes – on desert behaviour; he also travelled widely and frequently among them, often cementing loyalties as he went by arranging a marriage between some sheikhly family and his own. By the time of his death, town walls were a thing of the past; he had induced the *Ikhwan* survivors to settle in agricultural colonies, and a

Abdul Aziz re-established the Saudi dynasty in the Najdi heartland in January 1902 by his remarkable assault on the Musmak Fortress of Riyadh (top left), a memorial of which survives in the spear-tip lodged in the woodwork of the door (left): the weapon was thrown, that fateful dawn, by one of Abdul Aziz' companions, ibn Jiluwi. Riyadh was restored as the Saudi capital, in place of the defeated enemy's capital at nearby Diriyah (above), today a largely ruined city.

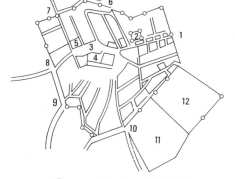

Riyadh in 1918

**adapted from a sketch
by H. St. John Philby**

1	THUMAYRI GATE	7	ZUHAYRI GATE
2	MUSMAK FORTRESS	8	BADIYYAH GATE
3	MAIN SUQ	9	MURAYQIB GATE
4	QASR OF KING ABDUL AZIZ	10	DAKHANAH GATE
5	GREAT MOSQUE	11/12	NEW QUARTER
6	SUWAYLIM GATE		

traveller could stop and pray at the lawful hour or camp at nightfall without fear of molestation, as he can today.

When ibn Saud won his kingdom, it was pitifully poor. It produced only the bare necessities of life; its so-called roads were tracks; it had no ports; its sole source of foreign exchange was pilgrimage dues. Religious learning apart, education was scanty; he had to resort to foreign Arabs as his advisers. All but one of his immediate entourage were literally advisers, for though he listened to information, he took all decisions, however trivial, himself. The exception was the one Najdi among them – his Minister of Finance, Abdullah Sulayman. Ibn Saud, though the equal of anyone in political skill, negotiation or paternalistic power of decision, hated adminis-

tration and was not good at it. As the business of his kingdom swelled and paperwork piled up, he was fortunate in having at his elbow for over twenty years one Najdi possessed of executive ability. When the outbreak of the world economic crisis of the early 1930s seriously reduced the numbers making the pilgrimage, the repercussions magnified beyond management his kingdom's endemic poverty. At this moment of crisis, a stroke of fortune relieved his plight.

In 1932, oil was discovered in Bahrain, an island visible from the Saudi mainland. Mining geologists suspected that oil deposits might underlie the mainland also. An American oil company, offering to pay gold for prospection rights, enabled the desperate King and Finance

Minister to round a tight corner. So began the exploration and discovery that, once the Second World War was over, turned Saudi Arabia's oil production into the most promising and wealthiest venture in an oil-rich peninsula.

Ibn Saud was abstemious throughout his life. His tastes were simple. Prayer and reading the scriptures took up many hours of each day; late in life he composed his own anthology of religious wisdom, sayings and proverbs. He rejoiced in family life; children and grandchildren were his delight; a cluster of them surrounds him in every informal photograph. Since at his death he left behind him forty-seven living sons (the youngest under seven) and unnumbered daughters, children were always in plentiful supply. He could be irascible, but not for long. Among his greatest pleasures were desert life and pursuits, camping for part of every year, hunting, hawking, tests of horsemanship, camel racing. Whether in tent or palace, his mornings were spent giving audience in a *majlis* open to all his subjects, hearing grievances, righting wrongs, dispensing reward and punishment. Duty done, he liked to spend his afternoons in the

of fact. It is said that when he captured Ha'il in 1921, a traitorous defender let him into the town by one of its five gates; he honoured the captains of the other four and punished the traitor. He handed out judgement with assurance and well-remembered imagination – summary execution for a villain, coupled with compassion for the victims of his crime, the shaving off of the beard and moustache of a young man who had simply been pert. Until crippled by arthritis, he liked to join in fun or horseplay; part of his personal success with his subjects was the spontaneity with which he rubbed shoulders with a crowd or joined in a war-dance. He loved an apt quip. Once, chatting tête-à-tête with a British envoy, he mentioned the contrariness of his English friend, St. John Philby. The envoy countered with the story of the British mum watching the Guards march by: "Everyone's out of step but my Johnnie." The king laughed till his sides ached, and then roared for his entourage to come and hear the joke. (Philby, often described as his "British adviser", was never this, but rather his walking encyclopaedia and verbal sparring-partner – a refreshing change from the sycophants round his throne;

he always mistrusted Philby's capricious judgement.)

By 1950 – a year in which oil production topped twenty-five million tons – a hard life was taking its toll of his great frame. An old eye trouble worsened; old wounds generated arthritis; unwillingly, he took to a wheel chair; inch by inch he lost his grip as he fought a long last illness. He grew unequal to controlling the waste of oil revenue by princes rendered profligate by this sudden inflow of money. Shortly before his death in 1953, Philby overheard him whisper the old adage that a man's possessions and his children are his worst enemies. Perhaps he would have done well to observe the Arabian custom of leaving the choice of a successor to his heirs; as it was, fatherly indulgence caused him to name a Crown Prince, and for once his judgement faltered. Not until a decade after his death did a worthy son – the late King Faisal – succeed to the Kingdom that his father had won for Islam and the Saudi family. Statesmen blessed with ibn Saud's moral stature, high principles and common sense are rarities; by any standards, he must be reckoned among the greatest in the first half of our century.

peace of the desert, on some restive horse when in his prime, travelling by car in old age. A tremendous talker, his evenings were spent in discourse; topics on which he liked to dwell were theological niceties, such as the distinction between pure and impure belief; desert genealogies, which he had at his fingertips; the details of old campaigns; success with women; magic; the properties of scents, medicines or aphrodisiacs.

Legend and anecdote sometimes tell more of a man's character than a recital

Up to the First World War, Turkey claimed a sovereignty over Arabia that was never more than nominal, and not even that so far as King Abdul Aziz was concerned. The war affected Arabia principally in the Hashemite area of the Hijaz, where T. E. Lawrence came to fame – not least in his role in the destruction of the Turkish-controlled Hijaz railway, of which some relics (left) survive in the desert to this day. Hashemite rule did not long survive the Great War. By December 1925 Medina and Jiddah were Abdul Aziz', and in January 1926 the principal citizens of Mecca offered their allegiance to Abdul Aziz.

"From log cabin to White House" was a phrase once coined by an American author to epitomize the life of Abraham Lincoln. From desert obscurity to world status is no less a shift of fortune, and perhaps the more remarkable of the two in that it sums up the career not of one man – the late King Faisal of Saudi Arabia – but of a whole nation.

Changes of this magnitude within the span of a lifetime are seldom wholly due to the worth or character of a single individual. Outside agents such as a freak of timing, or the unwisdom of others – or a simple stroke of luck – often play their part. Yet King Faisal ibn Abdul Aziz ibn Saud made a great personal contribution to his own rise to fame and power. When historians come to assess him, they will refer first to the spiritual reserves underlying the inner calm which enabled him to bide his time when things were not going his way, and secondly to the cautious reasoning and balanced judgement that made him a first-class negotiator. Add to these assets a presence marked by a fine bearing, inborn dignity and grace of manner, and you have the outlines of a portrait that is filled in by the story of his life.

He was the fourth son of a father who had won back from a rival – the Emir of Ha'il – the family patrimony of Najd in central Arabia, after almost a generation of exile in Kuwait. At Faisal's birth, Riyadh, the capital which ibn Saud had recovered less than four years before, was hemmed in by the enemies of its puritanism and its claim to spiritual superiority. The Rashids of Ha'il lay to its north, the Turks in the coastal province of Hasa to its east, and their myrmidon the Sharif of Mecca on the Red Sea coast to its west. Riyadh was in those days a dour place, dependent for life on dates and herding; its gates clanged shut at dusk and at the hours of prayer; at night, no glimmer of light revealed its existence except when, in Ramadan, a huge arc lamp was hoisted above the palace flagpole to signal the breaking of the fast. Faisal was educated by the customary *qadi*, and knew only family pleasures – hunting, horse and camel racing, hawking, picnics in the gardens of the neighbouring *wadi*. Desert excursions were unsafe, except for in well-armed bands, owing to the prevalence of raiders, tribe against tribe.

But before Faisal was out of his 'teens, this state of isolation had begun to

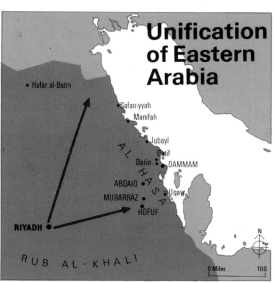

Unification of Eastern Arabia

By 1920, the fortresses of eastern Arabia (illustrated this page) *had all fallen to Abdul Aziz. But the Turkish hold on the area had been broken on a moonless night in April 1913 when Abdul Aziz, with 600 men, scaled the walls of Hofuf and surprised the defenders.*

change. His father the Emir ibn Saud had chased the Turks out of Hasa province (1913), had established treaty relations with the British in the Gulf (1915), and had conquered Ha'il (1921). He had made large tracts of the desert safe for travellers and when, in 1919, his new friends the British offered a member of his family a trip to England as a reward for services in the First World War, he chose Faisal for the treat. Maybe he picked a boy of only fourteen because his eldest son, Turki, had died in the influenza epidemic of 1918 (as had his favourite wife and some 25,000 of his people); anyway, he reckoned Faisal to be the child most likely to profit from a new experience. Faisal justified the choice. With the dignity that was to mark him throughout his career, he exchanged swords with King George V and, in the freezing cold of a post-war December, gravely accepted the visits that were thought suitable to his years – to the Zoo, to the Greenwich telescope and to *Chu Chin Chow*.

By 1925–1926, when his father overpowered the Sharifian family and conquered the Holy Cities of Mecca and Medina, he was thought old enough to command an army. He brought up the reinforcements for which his father sent in order to capture the sea port of Jiddah. Later, still only twenty-nine, he was to prove his military capacity more conclusively by commanding the most successful of the armies used by his father on the last of his campaigns – that of 1934 – by means of which he settled his frontier with the Yemen. Faisal's army, which sped down the coastal plain of the Red Sea, was the spearhead of this operation.

For all his success in the field, it was in the council chamber that Faisal's talents showed up best. Mecca and Jiddah once

The decisive incorporation of the southwest (top pictures: *Abha's fortress*) *into the young kingdom was assigned by Abdul Aziz to his young son Faisal* (later King) pictured opposite, *while he himself subdued the last strongholds in Hijaz* (above) *and to the north, including Ha'il and Shenayah* (far right).

conquered, ibn Saud proclaimed himself king of the Hijaz and Najd; but he could not be everywhere at once and he appointed Faisal his Viceroy in the Hijaz, with his seat in Mecca. Here the responsibilities were great, for the whole of the Islamic world outside Arabia was exercised, if not aghast, that its Holy Cities should have passed into the hands of unlettered desert religious reformers who might in their zeal destroy the essential features of the pilgrimage and tamper with the seats of Islamic learning at Mecca and Medina. For several years after 1926 anxious delegations poured in from more sophisticated lands –

Egypt, India, Indonesia, Iran, Iraq. Whenever possible, ibn Saud received and reassured these delegations himself. When he was there, his sons, if they appeared at all, took the customary place behind his chair. But at times he was forced to be absent because of the demands of Najd, where his warriors were champing to carry their Holy War into Iraq and needed curbing. In his absence, visitors to Mecca were received by Faisal.

Faisal was likewise his father's deputy in many dealings with non-Islamic states. In 1926, he was sent to Europe to broaden his mind in Britain and France, and five years later he embarked on a wide-ranging tour that included Soviet Russia. (Saudi-Soviet relations at the time were good, for Soviet Russia, with its own Muslims in mind, had been one of the first foreign states to recognize the new King and his Kingdom.) Ibn Saud throughout his life continued personally to handle dealings with foreigners if they

Murabba Palace

Abdul Aziz' Palace of Murabba in Riyadh is today preserved as a memorial to his achievement – with its traditional decoration and weaponry, it is characteristic of the period.

It was here at Qasr al Murabba that the ailing King spent the last years of his life, yet maintaining his strict routines of life.

A selection of flintlock rifles, used by King Abdul Aziz' soldiers in the early days of the unification of the Kingdom, are preserved at the Palace (*above*).

Emir Faisal represented Saudi Arabia, a Founder Member, at the U.N.

came to Arabia – for instance, to negotiate frontiers or seek concessions, but abroad he left everything to Faisal, whom he appointed as his Foreign Minister.

The Second World War changed the status and outlook of most Arab lands. They joined forces in a League; they gained admission to the United Nations; they gave new forms of expression to their nationalism. Some began to earn income from the oil that had been discovered before the war; most planned to use this new wealth for development and welfare. Looking back, it is odd to remember that, at this stage, the states which made all the running in the Arab League were Egypt, Iraq and Syria; Saudi Arabia's contribution to the League's budget was seven per cent of

King Faisal ibn Abdul Aziz combined inspirational leadership with sound management, and respect for the past with sagacious innovation.

the total as against Egypt's forty-two per cent. Only from 1950, when it made its "fifty-fifty" arrangement with the Arabian-American Oil Company (Aramco), did Saudi Arabia throw off its image of barren desert, backward inhabitants and poverty.

Faisal, who during the war had further broadened his experience of the world by visiting the United States with his half-brother Khalid (now King Khalid), became a figure of note in world conclaves. At the San Francisco Conference which inaugurated the United Nations, at meetings of the Arab League, in the United Nations Assembly, his dignified figure and graceful robes (he never wore Western dress) singled him out for attention. His father, smitten from 1950 with the sad illness of which he died in 1953, became wholly dependent on the two eldest of his thirty-five surviving sons – Saud, the Crown Prince, who had inherited touches of ibn Saud's humour and gaiety, and Faisal, who was more like him in his piety and austerity, and in his grasp of human foibles.

When the old King died and Saud succeeded him, the younger, graver brother became Prime Minister as well as Foreign Minister. At the time, Saudi Arabia lacked the institutions and the administrative framework that were becoming necessary if it was to handle its mounting revenue and play its potential role in Arab affairs. Faisal watched with misgiving the extent to which King Saud, using a king's personal powers to the full, slipped with his whole court circle into habits of extravagance which ate up the new revenue. Incredibly, by 1958 princely extravagance was such that the national exchequer was in debt. At this moment of crisis, Faisal was induced by the country's wisemen – the *ulamas*, literally 'scholars', meaning men of religious learning – to step in and take over. With the assistance of a devout and cautious Pakistani financier, he set up the Saudi Arabian Monetary Agency (SAMA), which devalued the currency and within two years had put money matters to rights.

But two years of economy and restraint were not popular with the court, and by tradition kings have the last word. When King Saud sought to recover prestige and popularity by promising his sycophants "reforms", Faisal, who was sure that reforms would not be brought about, handed in his resignation. During the years between 1960 and 1963,

he needed all the inner reserves at his command; seldom seen in public except at Friday prayers, on pilgrimage, or living as a country gentleman among his orchards in the hills below Ta'if, he was obliged to watch a brother far gone in health and megalomania letting a prosperous kingdom go to ruin. The last straw was defection and flight abroad by members of the armed forces. Once again, the *ulama* used their influence to bring Faisal back. From 1963, he picked up the reins of power, and in 1964 his brother was deposed and he became king.

The role was not easy. To the right of him, the *ulama* and the more pious members of his family were pressing for a return to the austerity of his father's day; to his left, and in the forces, young men who had been abroad urged "modernization" and less rigorous adherence to the strict rules of religious extremists. Princelings resented his curbs on their extravagance. Faisal, as was his wont, steered towards compromise. He permitted television but not the cinema; he promoted secular and technical education for boys, but kept girls' education under the jurisdiction of the Sheikh al-Islam – the chief religious authority. His middle way was not everywhere popular, and in 1969 and 1970 he was obliged to stamp out revolt in the armed forces and among the would-be modernizers. Whatever his personal inclinations (and he cannot have enjoyed the glare of lighting for the television cameras that he permitted even during audiences) he never forgot that it was the *ulama* who had helped him to restore the kingdom to its proper course.

Foreign policy, too, presented its problems. Nasser's Egypt, the most powerful of his neighbours, had to his consternation taken up arms in support of the republicans against the royalists in Yemen; Aden, which the British were about to leave, was a hotbed of left-wing parties fanned by Egyptian propaganda; Syria and a newly-republican Iraq were flirting with his bugbear, Soviet Russia. He sought to create for himself a new base by visiting Islamic countries and establishing an Islamic summit that would include Iran and Pakistan. But this plan foundered because the Islamic states had differing political priorities. It won him little beyond the respect he already commanded as Defender of the Faith and guardian of its Holy Places.

The Palestine War of 1967 abruptly changed his role in foreign affairs. Egypt, till then a rival, was humiliated and truncated. So was Jordan. Jerusalem, the third holiest city of Islam, fell into Israel's hands. Faisal set about providing financial support for the states on Israel's borders. Nasser's death in 1970, and the passing of Egypt's presidency to a less dominant figure, Anwar Sadat, opened Faisal's way to the leading role in Arab affairs which, with his usual dignity, he now assumed. Though in his late sixties and often far from well, he made long journeys to Arab summits in order to have his say.

To him Zionism and Communism were twin evils, and he warmly approved when, in the summer of 1972, Sadat dismissed his Soviet advisers. Now nothing stood in the way of the full-blooded alliance that was capable of dominating the Arab scene – the marriage of Saudi wealth with Egyptian manpower and technical superiority. In July 1973 King Faisal gave the world an idea of what was in his mind when for the first time he publicly mentioned his country's power to cut back oil deliveries if President Nixon did not modify his support for Israel. The Arab oil embargo that accompanied the general oil price-rise during the October War of 1973 was applied only with his customary caution, but a repetition could be all-important since Saudi Arabia owns forty per cent of the world's known oil reserves.

At the time of Faisal's death, his country was one of the richest in the world in liquid funds. Riyadh, seventy years earlier a village, was a city throbbing with activity, besieged by salesmen and technical experts out for contracts to fulfil the developments he had in mind, pierced by dual carriageways, humming with traffic, twinkling at night with the lights that outline mile on mile of ribbon development, yet with *suqs* that fall quiet, empty of their menfolk, at the hour of prayer.

Saudi Arabia's government is highly centralized. Though competent and well trained Saudis are now available to run it, King Faisal personally took most of the important decisions. On the Prophet's birthday, 1975, one of his scores of nephews, the son of a much younger half-brother, slipped into his audience chamber and fired three shots at the King over the shoulder of the Kuwaiti Oil Minister whom the King was receiving. Perhaps we shall never

King Khalid today exercises the unifying role of an always-accessible popular monarch.

can immediately replace. We also know that the Arab world as a whole – a body which needs all its strength at a time of trouble – was deprived at a blow of a head who commanded worldwide respect and attention whenever he chose to speak his mind.

The stability of the Kingdom stood the test of this capricious act. King Khalid, as the younger brother next in line, moved naturally into the role of leader of the nation. The wide experience and talents of the immediate family – exemplified by Prince Fahd, the Crown Prince, as First Deputy Prime Minister, and Prince Abdullah Abdul Aziz, Second Deputy Prime Minister and Head of the National Guard in Riyadh – ensured the smooth continuance of the mechanics of government and administration. Within six months of assuming power, King Khalid presided over the launching of the country's monumental second five year plan.

Yet like his brother and father, the present King honours the essentially Arabian character of his roots. Born in 1913, in his father's capital of Riyadh, he received his education in the Kingdom before he took part in several military expeditions with his father. He also had various other positions of responsibility for governmental administration, which included his being sent, as further proof of his father's trust, to represent the Kingdom on many foreign missions. In 1934 he was appointed assistant to his half brother, Faisal; and when Faisal came to power in 1965, Khalid was named Crown Prince.

On the thirteenth of March 1395 AH (25th March 1975 CE) HM King Khalid bin Abdul Aziz became King of Saudi Arabia. He was swift to fill the massive responsibilities of his office. Contact with his people was maintained by weekly audiences. A series of visits was undertaken to neighbouring Islamic leaders (*see* Foreign Affairs). Saudi Arabia's initiation in world financial affairs and the Arab world was fully sustained, and the King's personal touch widely recognized.

know whether the assassin struck out of vengeance for the death of a puritanical brother who had, some years back, tried to tamper with a television mast, and been shot by guards in the course of a scuffle at its base; or whether he acted out of radical notions picked up while he was sampling three American universities without much success; or whether a mixed-up kid was prompted by both these ill-assorted motives. What we know for sure is that his bullets deprived his countrymen of a leader with a store of wisdom and experience that no-one

The Islamic World

GREAT BRITAIN

U.S.S.R.

GERMANY

ATLANTIC OCEAN

FRANCE

RUMANIA

YUGOSLAVIA

ITALY

BULGARIA

BLACK SEA

CASPIAN SEA

ARAL SEA

KAZAKHSTAN

SOVIET CENTRAL ASIA

SINKIA

PORTUGAL

SPAIN

ALBANIA

GREECE

TURKEY

SYRIA

IRAN

AFGHANISTAN

MOROCCO

TUNISIA

MEDITERRANEAN SEA

LEBANON

IRAQ

JOR

ARABIAN GULF

PAKISTAN

NEP,

ALGERIA

LIBYA

EGYPT

UAE

GULF OF OMAN

INDIA

RED SEA

OMAN

ARABIAN SEA

MAURITANIA

MALI

NIGER

CHAD

SUDAN

YEMEN

SOUTH YEMEN

SENEGAL

GAMBIA

GUINEA-BISSAU

GUINEA

VOLTAIC REP

DAHOMEY

TOGO

NIGERIA

CENTRAL AFRICAN REPUBLIC

ETHIOPIA

SOMALIA

SRI LANKA

SIERRA LEONE

IVORY COAST

GHANA

LIBERIA

CAMEROON

GABON

CONGO

ZAIRE

UGANDA

KENYA

TANZANIA

ANGOLA

ZAMBIA

MOZAMBIQUE

MADAGASCAR

92

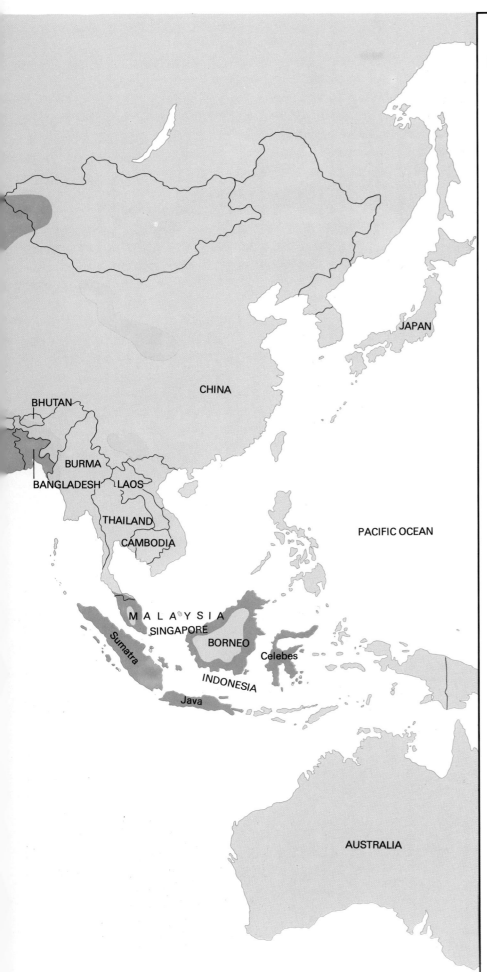

5
Islam

To Saudi Arabia, the holy cities of Mecca and Medina are a sacred trust, exercised on behalf of all of Islam. To the fountainhead of their faith every year flock pilgrims in their hundreds of thousands, to offer their "submission", as is the meaning of Islam, to God's will as revealed through the Prophet Muhammad.

From its foundation in the Arabian heartland, Islam today circles the globe and is the accredited faith of some 500 million people. It is constantly making new converts among those without belief.

Saudi Arabia as the Heartland of Islam

THE religious pre-eminence of Saudi Arabia in the Muslim world is vouchsafed by the fact that it contains the two cities of Mecca and Medina, where Islam was born and where it matured under the Prophet Muhammad himself, and where the Qur'an was revealed. Mecca also has the Ka'bah, Islam's central shrine, while the tomb of the Prophet and his mosque are in Medina. The Saudi regime earned the gratitude of all Muslims by ensuring the safety of pilgrims under the strong hand of King Abdul Aziz ibn Saud, who enforced the strict Shari'ah rules of law and order. The late King Faisal brought a new political dimension by pursuing a policy of Islamic solidarity, as distinct from pure territorial nationalism.

Islam is a world-wide faith. There exists today a world Muslim community about seven hundred million strong (some Muslim agencies put the number at around eight hundred million) which, despite sectarian differences, feels bound together in one faith: every Muslim must recite the profession of faith, "There is no God but Allah, and Muhammad is his Prophet", with awareness of its meaning and full consent from the heart. The first proselytizers were, of course, the Arabs themselves, and rightly so. The Qur'an repeatedly states that it is "a Reminder *for the whole world*", that differences of tribes and peoples, of tongues and skin-colour, are signs of God's power and mercy, but that real rank in God's sight depends on piety and virtue, and that the Prophet himself was "sent only as a mercy *to all mankind*". This universal character of the Islamic teaching was also strongly underlined in the Prophet's Farewell Pilgrimage sermon, which declares the religious ideal to be indifferent to racial and other natural differences.

The fact remains that Islam's origins lie in an Arab milieu and that it has a clear Arab base. Muslim thinkers have considered this point and given explanations to rationalize it. Thus, ibn Khaldun holds that the Prophet had to be born in Arabia, whose people were not primitive, yet were close to the natural state of man and therefore possessed of natural manly virtues and minds unencumbered by preconceived notions. Indeed he had to be born among the Meccan tribe of Quraysh, who, once converted to Islam, had the necessary power and prestige to protect and propagate it. It is, of course, historically true that when Mecca joined Islam, the rest of Arabia followed. Shah Walig Allah of Delhi adds that it was part of the divine plan to replace the older Middle Eastern civilizations with a new civilization which would have a moral freshness and virility that could be supplied only by the Arabs, once they had been nurtured by Islam.

Be that as it may, there was undoubtedly a religious ferment in Mecca and Medina prior to the appearance of the Prophet. While the Jews of Medina longed for a Prophet to make them victorious over the Arabs there (*Qur'an* II, 83), Arab intellectuals in Mecca, having accepted neither Judaism nor Christianity, desired a new Arab Prophet so that "they may be better guided" than the Jewish and Christian communities (*Qur'an* XXXV, 42; VI, 157; XXXVII, 168). When the Meccans opposed the Prophet, the Qur'an repeatedly reminded them that he had been raised up "from among themselves" and that they knew him well because he had lived among them for so long. Even more emphatically, the Qur'an time and again states that it is revealed in a "clear Arabic tongue" (*Qur'an* XVI, 103; XXVI, 195; also XII, 2; XIII, 37; XX, 113), for "if We had made it a non-Arab Qur'an, they (the opponents) would have said, 'Why are its verses not clearly set out?'" (*Qur'an* XLI, 44). This last statement refers to the belief of the Arabs that the Arabic language is the most expressive and eloquent.

That the Prophet, since he was an Arab himself, should communicate to his people in Arabic, and that they should be the first addressees of Islam, was, of course, natural. But the statements of

Focus of the annual pilgrimage of hundreds of thousands of devout Muslims is the Ka'bah of Holy Mecca which pilgrims circle seven times – the first three times preferably hastening round three of the sides.

The Way to Mecca

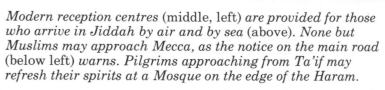

Modern reception centres (middle, left) are provided for those who arrive in Jiddah by air and by sea (above). None but Muslims may approach Mecca, as the notice on the main road (below left) warns. Pilgrims approaching from Ta'if may refresh their spirits at a Mosque on the edge of the Haram.

the Qur'an about its own nature go much further, since it regards itself as miraculous and challenges its opponents – those Arabs who were proud of their literary perfection – to produce anything like it (*Qur'an* X, 38; XI, 13; XXVIII, 49). In these verses, the Qur'an is emphasizing that its source is Divine, and cannot be the composition of a human mind, even that of the Prophet himself; and it is, indeed, clear that the speech of the Prophet, outside of Revelation, is of a different quality from that of the Qur'an. Muslim theologians early deduced the doctrine that the Qur'an is "inimitable" and hence untranslatable. Many Western scholars also think that it is not really translatable – which is why Arthur J. Arberry called his English rendering *The Qur'an Interpreted*, rather than *The Qur'an Translated*. For centuries, the religious scholars of Islam did not allow the Qur'an to be translated. This law has been quite recently relaxed in the interest of the wider dissemination of Qur'anic teaching; but they still insist that no translation be published without the Arabic text.

The second major source of Islamic doctrine and practice – particularly in the field of Law, which stands at the

centre of the entire Islamic system – is the Sunnah (Example or Model) of the Prophet – that is his precepts and conduct, both in private and public activity. The Sunnah interprets and elaborates the teaching of the Qur'an, and is embodied in certain authoritative works. These do not only include what the Prophet actually said or did. At a very early stage, the Muslim jurists decided that the entire body of Arab practices and customs to which the Prophet had not explicitly objected and *hence had tacitly approved of, is part of the Prophetic Sunnah*. This concept of the "tacit (*sukuti*) Sunnah" thus sanctified the entire gamut of Arab life – essentially Meccan and Medinan after its reform by the Qur'an and the Prophet. In its outward expansion and during its long development it was certainly modified, elaborated and changed (on the basis of the principle of *ijtihad*, or fresh thinking), but it always served as the normative base of reference. In the outermost regions of Islam, such as Indonesia, much of pre-Islamic custom (called *Adat*) still prevails, but the religious leaders there have been exerting steady pressure to change the situation.

Besides being the birthplace of Islam,

A fully-serviced tented city accommodates the pilgrims on their arrival for their approximately week-long ritual of contrition and worship.

Mecca is the object of the annual pilgrimage (*hajj* – q.v.) undertaken by Muslims to the Ka'bah Sanctuary (the Haram), also called the "House of God (*bayt Allah*)". A pre-Islamic Arab site, it was officially adopted by Islam in the year 1 AH (623 CE), after reforms purging it of idolatrous practices and implications. It is, for all Muslims, the most holy place, where the Divine comes into special touch with the earth. Muslim mystics (Sufis) in particular developed a mystique of the Ka'bah, regarding it as the earthly manifestation of a metaphysical Divine reality. Throughout the centuries, almost every Muslim, no matter how distant his abode, has aspired to visit Mecca, thus rendering it the metropolis of Islam, and the *hajj* the greatest living religious epic on earth. Scholars and saints – side by side with common folk – have usually visited Mecca, often more than once in their lifetime, to meet scholars and spiritual leaders from other parts of the Muslim world. Many stayed on in Mecca for

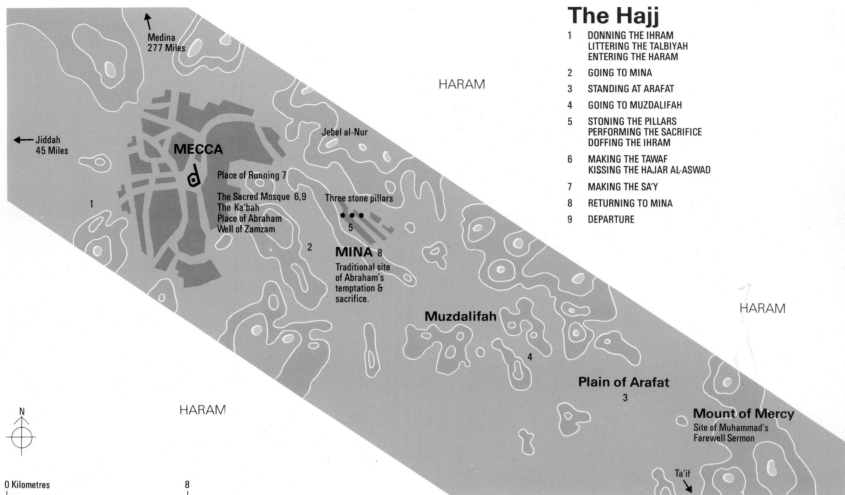

The Hajj

1 DONNING THE IHRAM
   LITTERING THE TALBIYAH
   ENTERING THE HARAM

2 GOING TO MINA

3 STANDING AT ARAFAT

4 GOING TO MUZDALIFAH

5 STONING THE PILLARS
   PERFORMING THE SACRIFICE
   DOFFING THE IHRAM

6 MAKING THE TAWAF
   KISSING THE HAJAR AL-ASWAD

7 MAKING THE SA'Y

8 RETURNING TO MINA

9 DEPARTURE

(Map labels) Medina 277 Miles · HARAM · Jebel al-Nur · Jiddah 45 Miles · MECCA · Place of Running 7 · The Sacred Mosque 6,9 · The Ka'bah · Place of Abraham · Well of Zamzam · Three stone pillars · MINA 8 Traditional site of Abraham's temptation & sacrifice. · Muzdalifah · HARAM · Plain of Arafat · Mount of Mercy Site of Muhammad's Farewell Sermon · Ta'if · HARAM · N · 0 Kilometres 8

study, reflection and spiritual enlightenment, some earning the honorific name "Allah's neighbour (*jar Allah*)". Ibn Arabi (d. 1240 CE) of Spain, perhaps the greatest name in Muslim mysticism, entitled his *magnum opus*, which he wrote at Mecca, *Meccan Illumination* (*Futuhat Makkiyah*).

Since 1925 CE, the quantity of pilgrims has increased immensely. Whereas at the *hajj* in the summer of 1925 the number of pilgrims was estimated at one hundred thousand, at the *hajj* celebrated in December 1974 there were well over a million and a half. This tremendous increase is partly due to the fact that more Muslims can now afford to go on the pilgrimage, but the main reason lies in the development of Saudi Arabia. The Saudi regime has acquitted itself admirably as protector of the Holy Cities. King ibn Saud's primary task was to put an end to the lawlessness which deterred Muslims from performing the *hajj* for fear of robbery and murder. Inheritor to the puritanism of his ancestors he strictly enforced the penal law of the Shari'ah, which ordains severe punishments for theft and murder. At the same time there have been steady improvements in air travel, roads, water, electricity and the availability of better and more hygienic accommodation.

The prestige of Saudi Arabia in the international Muslim community has grown gradually but tangibly. Although the new Saudi regime has never made theocratic or caliphal claims, its policies represent a broad-based Islam and a robust realism which have won for it the respect both of peoples and of governments. Turkey, which had been alienated since World War I and had virtually banned Turks from performing the pilgrimage, removed these restrictions in 1965, and at the pilgrimage in December 1974 the Turkish contingent was the largest from outside Arabia. Due primarily to the religious basis of the state, the Saudi monarchy is the only one in the world to eschew the use of such symbols of worldly power as the crown and the throne; an egalitarian practice much respected by all Muslims, whether Arab or non-Arab.

King Faisal, in particular, brought a new dimension to the Saudi rule by his active policy of pan-Islamic solidarity – a policy sustained by King Khalid (e.g. over bringing peace to Lebanon). The acute crisis created by Israel's occupation of Arab lands and particularly by her takeover of Jerusalem presented him with a special challenge. After the incident in 1969, when the Aqsa Mosque in Jerusalem – the third most holy place for all Muslims, after the Ka'bah in Mecca and the Prophet's Mosque in Medina – King Faisal played a central role in organizing the Islamic summit meetings held in Morocco in 1969 and in Pakistan in 1974. A permanent Islamic Secretariat has been established, with headquarters in Jiddah, and financed by Saudi Arabia, to bring about closer co-operation among Muslim governments. At semi-official level, the Saudi government had already set up an important organization called The World Muslim Congress (*Rabitat al-Alam al-Islami*), with which many other Muslim organizations all over the world have become affiliated or associated. In April 1974, 158 Muslim national and international organizations, big and small, held a meeting in Mecca under its auspices. Whereas the Congress discusses primarily religious problems and socio-political issues arising from them, the Secretariat addresses itself to matters of politics and intra-Muslim development.

The Hajj

"And complete the Hajj *and the* Umrah *in the service of God. But if you are prevented (from completing it) send an offering for sacrifice such as you may find. And do not shave your heads until the offering reaches the place of sacrifice. And if any of you is ill or has an ailment in his scalp (necessitating shaving) he must in compensation either fast or feed the poor or offer sacrifice."*

HOLY QUR'AN, II

Medical facilities (top) and nourishment (centre) are available to pilgrims as they adopt the simple Ihram *garb of two pieces of white towelling.*

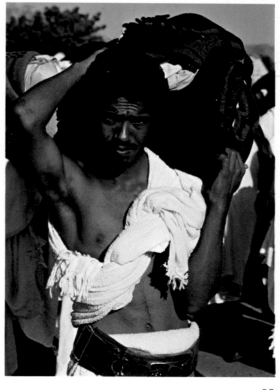

AFTER belief in the one God (Allah), the performance of regular, ritual prayers, fasting during the month of Ramadan and the giving of fixed alms (*Zakah*), the *hajj* is the fifth pillar of Islam, a fundamental duty which a Muslim, male and female alike, must perform at least once in his lifetime if he or she has the material means to do so.

Long before the Prophet Muhammad began to preach Islam and summon the Arabs and all mankind back to the worship of the One True God, indeed since time immemorial, the barren valley of Mecca had been a place of pilgrimage venerated by the Arabs, both settled and nomadic. It had been associated with the Patriarch Abraham, the Friend of God, who was the first to establish there a house to the glory of God. In the Holy Qur'an (II, 122–123) we read: "And lo! Abraham and Ishmael raised the foundations of the House saying: 'Oh Lord! accept this from us. Thou art, indeed, the All-Hearing, the All-Knowing. Our Lord! and make us submissive to Thee and of our progeny a nation submissive to Thee and show us our rites and turn to us in Mercy. Indeed, Thou art the All-Forgiving, All-Merciful. Our Lord! send amongst them a Messenger of their own who will recite to them Thy signs.' "

Again we read (III, 91–92): "Indeed, the first House (of worship) established for men was at Bakka (Mecca), full of blessing and guidance for all men. In it are clear signs, the Station of Abraham. Whoever enters it shall be safe. Pilgrimage thereto is a duty men owe to God, all those who can afford the journey. But if any reject this, God is in no need of any of His creatures."

And so the ancient pilgrimage to Mecca became incorporated in Islam and the guiding lines of its performance were laid down by the Holy Qur'an (II, 193 ff.): "And complete the Hajj and the Umrah in the service of God. But if you are prevented (from completing it) send an offering for sacrifice such as you may find. And do not shave your heads until the offering reaches the place of sacrifice. And if any of you is ill or has an ailment in his scalp (necessitating shaving) he must in compensation either fast or feed the poor or offer sacrifice. And when you are in safety again, if anyone wishes to continue the Umrah on to the Hajj he must make an offering such as he can afford. But if he cannot afford it he should fast three days during the Hajj and seven days on his return, making ten days in all. This is for those whose household is not settled in the Sacred Mosque. And fear God and know that God is strict in punishment. The Hajj is in well known months (Shawwal, Dhu 'l-Qa'dah and Dhu 'l Hijjah). If anyone undertakes that duty in them let there be no obscenity, nor wickedness, nor quarrelling in the Hajj. And whatever good you do God knows it. And take provision for the journey. But the best of provisions is fear of God. So fear him, all you who are wise."

The pilgrimage is made to Mecca, the most sacred city of Islam, where the Prophet Muhammad was born, where his mission was first revealed to him and where he began preaching Islam. In the centre of Mecca stands the Sacred Mosque (Al-Masjid al-Haram), a large open courtyard enclosed by cloisters, rebuilt and enlarged many times.

"When you press on from Arafat, then remember God at the Holy Waymark, and remember Him as He has guided you, though formerly you were gone astray. Then press on from where the people press on, and pray for God's forgiveness; God is All-forgiving, All-compassionate. And when you have performed your holy rites remember God, as you remember your fathers or yet more devoutly. Now some men there are who say, 'Our Lord, give to us in this world'; such men shall have no part in the world to come."

HOLY QUR'AN, II

him to the time of Adam. The Ka'bah has been rebuilt many times in the course of the centuries, once in the lifetime of the Prophet, before his mission, when he was chosen by chance to place the Black Stone in its position. In the north-east wall of the Ka'bah close to the corner in which the Black Stone is set and some seven feet above the ground is the door to the Ka'bah which is opened at special times. There is nothing inside the building, which was cleansed of its idols when the Prophet returned in triumph to Mecca early in 630 CE. The Ka'bah is covered with a black pall decorated with verses from the Qur'an. This is the *Kiswah* (garment) which from the Middle Ages was made in Cairo and brought ceremoniously to Mecca every year by the Egyptian pilgrims. It is now made

Pilgrims gather on the Mount of Mercy, the site of Muhammad's farewell sermon, to watch in prayerfulness as the sun descends over the Plain of Arafat.

Roughly in the centre of the Sacred Mosque stands the Ka'bah, the House of God, towards which all Muslims turn their faces in their daily prayers, no matter where they may be. The Ka'bah, as its name denotes, is a cube-shaped building of stone, the front (north-east) and back (south-west) sides being forty feet long, the other sides being thirty-five feet and the height fifty feet.

In the east corner, about four feet above ground level, is set the Black Stone in a silver frame. This stone (eight inches in diameter) is believed to be the only remnant of the first mosque built by Abraham and to go back even before

by local craftsmen.

The two remaining shrines inside the Sacred Mosque are the Station of Abraham (facing the door) where the Patriarch bowed down in prayer and the Well of Zamzam, north-east of the Ka'bah, which sprang up when Hagar was desperately seeking water for the infant Ishmael. Just outside the Sacred Mosque is the Mas'a (running place) between the rocky hillocks of as-Safa and al-Marwah, a distance of 440 yards. The Mas'a, which was until recently an ordinary street with shops, is now covered over and paved with marble flags. It was between these two hills that Hagar ran distractedly seeking water.

Pilgrimage to Mecca is of two kinds. There is the *umrah*, the Lesser Pilgrimage or Visit, which can be performed at

any time of the year and is confined to worship at the places mentioned above. Then there is the *hajj* proper, which combines the rites of the *umrah* with others outside Mecca and takes place only once a year in the first part of the month of *Dhu 'l-Hijjah*, the last month of the Islamic lunar calendar.

Again, the *hajj* and the *umrah* can be performed together (*Qiran*) or separately (*Tamattu*). The latter is chosen by pilgrims who arrive in Mecca some days before the ninth of the month, which day is the culmination of the pilgrimage. *Tamattu* entails either sacrifice at Mina or fasting during the pilgrimage and on return home.

Nowadays, with frequent and easy means of transport, the number of pilgrims to Mecca during the pilgrimage

"The Pilgrimage is in months well-known; whoso undertakes the duty of Pilgrimage in them shall not go in to his womenfolk nor indulge in ungodliness and disputing in the Pilgrimage. Whatever good you do, God knows it. And take provision; but the best provision is godfearing." HOLY QUR'AN, II

"Indeed, the first House (of worship) established for men was at Bakka (Mecca), full of blessing and guidance for all men. In it are clear signs, the Station of Abraham. Whoever enters it shall be safe. Pilgrimage thereto is a duty men owe to God, all those who can afford the journey. But if any reject this, God is in no need of any of His creatures."

HOLY QUR'AN, III

Children count for no less than adults in the eyes of Allah, and throughout Islam, children at an early age are able to recite large portions of the Holy Qur'an.

month is very large, sometimes exceeding a million. Organizing such a vast number of people, seeing to their health and other needs, is a formidable task which the Saudi Government performs with great efficiency.

Most foreign pilgrims arrive either by sea or by air through Jiddah, the port of Mecca, and there the Government has a special *hajj* Administration. From Jid-

dah they go by bus to Mecca (some fifty miles away), each group of pilgrims being assigned according to their rites (Hanafi, Shafi'i, Maliki, and so on) to a *mutawwif* in Mecca. A *mutawwif* is a special guide and mentor whose duty it is to see that the pilgrims under his wing perform the rites of the pilgrimage correctly, have no difficulties while in the Holy Land and return to their homelands happy and satisfied, having gained the blessing of the pilgrimage properly performed. Each *mutawwif* has under him a number of assistants whose duty it is to accompany groups of pilgrims. Of course, a pilgrim who knows the language and is familiar with Mecca can dispense with a *mutawwif*, relying on one of the many guides to the *hajj* printed in Arabic or other languages.

Before entering the sacred territory surrounding Mecca – indeed, sometimes from the start of his journey – the pilgrim puts himself in a state of sanctity by ablution, prayer and donning the pilgrim's dress (*Ihram*), which for a man consists of two unsewn towels, one worn wrapped around the lower part of the body, the other thrown over the upper part, and unsewn sandals. There is no special dress for a woman except that her face must remain unveiled, no matter what her local customs may be. The reason for these regulations is to emphasize the equality of all pilgrims, high and low, before God.

On and off during his journey and until he enters Mecca the pilgrim chants a short formula of acceptance of the pilgrimage duties (the *Talbiyah*). This is: "Here I am in answer to Thy call, O God, here I am! Here I am! Thou hast no associate! Here I am! All Praise and Favour and Kingship are Thine! Thou hast no associate!"

The rites of the *umrah* are *Tawaf* (circumambulation of the Ka'bah), *Sa'y* (running between as-Safa and al-Marwah) and shaving of the head or clipping of the hair. On arrival in Mecca the pilgrim performs *Wudu* (ablution before prayer) and goes straight away to the Sacred Mosque which he enters preferably by the Bab as-Salam (Gate of Peace). Around the Ka'bah is a paved area (the *Mataf*) on which the pilgrim performs his *Tawaf*, beginning at the Black Stone and going around the Ka'bah seven times in an anti-clockwise direction. The pilgrim makes the first three rounds of the Ka'bah at a fast pace and the remainder at walking pace, all the while glorifying God and supplicating His favour and mercy in set phrases generally repeated after his guide. As the pilgrim passes the Black Stone he either kisses it, or touches it or simply makes a motion of his hand towards it. As the throng making *Tawaf* is generally very large, the last is by far the most common. A policeman is posted on either side of the Black Stone to keep the pilgrims on the move. It is a remarkable fact that the *Mataf* is never free from pilgrims, night or day, except at the times of congregational prayer. Muslims in no wise worship the Black Stone. They kiss or touch it because it is known that the Prophet Muhammad did so and thereby they establish a physical link between themselves and the Prophet. And he did so because it was a link be-

tween himself and Abraham. *Tawaf* is the first and last religious act of the pilgrim to Mecca.

After performing his *Tawaf* the pilgrim then proceeds to the Station of Abraham and there performs two cycles of individual prayer. Before going out from the Sacred Mosque to the Mas'a he may drink some water from the Well of Zamzam. This water is slightly brackish but is drunk in large quantities by the pilgrims, who often fill their water bottles with it to take home.

The second rite of the *umrah* is *Sa'y* (running) between as-Safa and al-Marwah. For this the pilgrim leaves the Mosque by the Bab as-Safa (Safa Gate) and mounts the rocky hillock of that name. After a short prayer he proceeds at walking pace towards the second

"Thus We appointed you a midmost nation that you might be witnesses to the people, and that the Messenger might be a witness to you. Turn thy face toward the Holy Mosque; and wherever you are, turn your faces towards it."

HOLY QUR'AN, II

An historic picture of Mecca, dating from the 1950s, shows the prevailing architecture backed by the so-called Black Hills. A minaret of the Great Mosque is seen in the foreground.

"God has appointed the Kaaba, the Holy House, as an establishment for men."

HOLY QUR'AN, V

Islamic dignitaries from home and abroad are permitted to enter the Ka'bah (far left and below), *which contains a spare and unadorned chamber, with no intervention of human artifice needed to add to its unique sanctity. Most pilgrims wish to kiss the Black Stone* (bottom left) *and to worship at the shrines of the Station of Abraham* (left) *and the Well of Zamzam.*

" 'Take to yourselves Abraham's station for a place of prayer.' " HOLY QUR'AN, II

off on his journey home.

But since it is vouchsafed to the vast majority of Muslims to make the pilgrimage to Mecca only once in their lifetimes, most pilgrims combine their pilgrimage with a visit to Medina, sometimes before, but generally after the pilgrimage. There they visit the Prophet's tomb and those of the early Caliphs in the Sacred Mosque. They usually spend several days in this second city of Islam – the city to which the Prophet Muhammad fled from persecution in his native city, where he established the Islamic State and where he lies buried with so many of his noble companions.

The pilgrimage to Mecca used to be an arduous and often perilous adventure, but today it is done in comparative comfort and perfect safety. Nevertheless, owing to the vast numbers of pilgrims, it is still a challenging enterprise, especially when the pilgrimage season falls in the summer months. Yet, when the *hajji* is safe at home with his family and when the month of the *hajj* comes round again he feels that there is nowhere he would rather be than with countless thousands from all corners of the earth thronging the Sacred Mosque and the streets of Mecca or standing in prayer on the Plain of Arafat.

Medina the Radiant

Second only to Mecca in sanctity is the city of Medina, whose night-time profile is dominated by the Great Mosque with its green dome and exquisite interior. It was to Medina that the Prophet fled (in 622 CE) when his teachings were registered by his fellow citizens in Mecca. Medina, whose ancient name was Yathrib, lay on a principal north-south caravan route. Its essentially Arabian character largely survives today.

Islam in Today's World

"SURELY in the creation of the heavens and earth and in the alternation of night and day there are signs for men possessed of minds who remember God, standing and sitting and on their sides, and reflect upon the creation of the heavens and the earth: 'Our Lord, Thou has not created this for vanity. Glory be to Thee! Guard us against the chastisement of the Fire.' "
Qur'an III, 187

Islam and Knowledge

"Hast thou not seen how that God sends down out of heaven water, and therewith We bring forth fruits of diverse hues? And in the mountains are streaks white and red, of diverse hues, and pitchy black; men too, and beasts and cattle – diverse are their hues. Even so only those of His servants fear God who have knowledge."
Qur'an XXXV, 26

"Say: 'Are they equal – those who know and those who know not?' Only men possessed of minds remember."
Qur'an XXXIX, 12

". . . God will raise up in rank those of you who believe and have been given knowledge."
Qur'an LVIII, 12

These verses are but a small sample of the many in the Holy Book of Islam, the Qur'an, where knowledge and men of knowledge are given such a high place. From them we can see that Islam looks at knowledge – including science – not just as a friend of faith and of God-fearing men, but, more important, as the right way to piety; hence the special position of the 'men of knowledge'. Islam not only encourages people "to seek knowledge from the cradle to the grave" (as the Prophet Muhammad has instructed his followers), but considers fact-finding and scientific discovery as a form of worship, provided no evil is intended. In fact, the

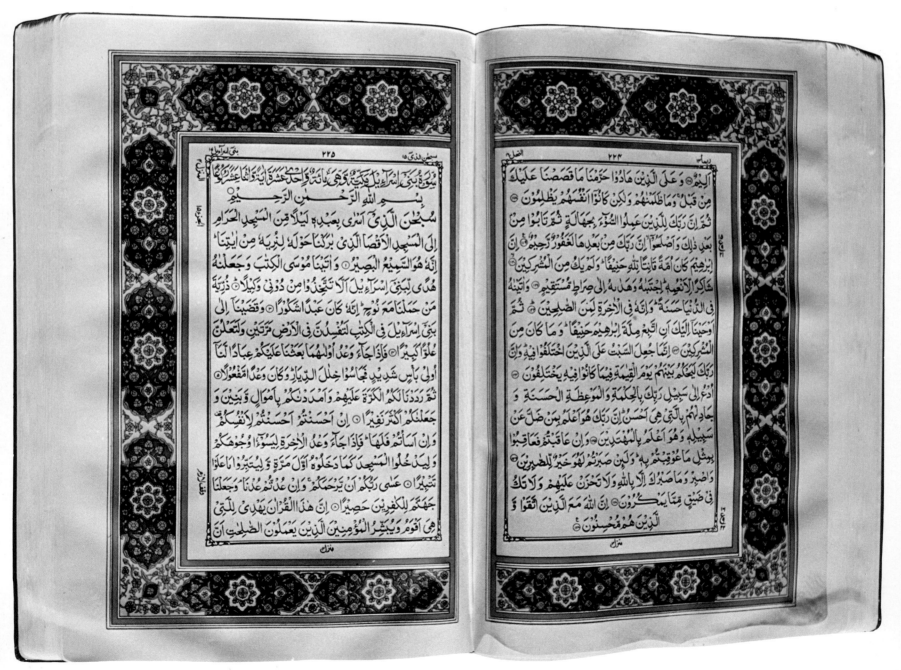

Prophet Muhammad is reported to have said, "To seek knowledge is obligatory on every Muslim, male and female." He also said, "Whoever takes a road in search of knowledge God will ease for him a way to Paradise." The first verses revealed by Almighty God to the Prophet Muhammad were directly related to the question of knowledge and the search for it. The revelation of the Holy Qur'an began with the words "Recite: In the Name of thy Lord who created, created Man of a blood-clot. Recite: And thy Lord is the Most Generous, who taught by the Pen, taught Man, that he knew not" (XCVI, 1–5). Reading and the pen – the basic tools in the search for, and dissemination of, knowledge!

The road to knowledge which leads to Paradise has many landmarks, and the Qur'an has much to say about them.

On the liberation of the mind from the shackles of convention, tradition and every sort of prejudice that may affect one's judgement, we read in the Qur'an: "And when it is said to them, 'Follow what God has sent down,' they say, 'No; but we will follow such things as we found our fathers doing.' What? And if their fathers had no understanding of anything, and if they were not guided?"

The Qur'an, holiest of the Islamic scripts, is believed by Muslims to have originated from God himself, dictated to the Prophet Muhammad. Binding not only in the faith but as a way of life, it has become perhaps the world's most influential book. It is recited frequently by believers and is constantly under study by scholars, as in a library of Medina (above).

In another part we read: "And when it is said to them, 'Come now to what God has sent down, and the Messenger', they say, 'Enough for us is what we found our fathers doing.' What, even if their fathers had knowledge of naught and were not guided?" (V, 104). These and other verses express the Qur'an's strong condemnation of blind imitation and the mere acceptance of traditions inherited from others, even from one's own father. The Qur'an actually gives mention to "thinking", the "mind" and synonymous expressions in no less than three hundred places.

Contemplation and observation are of equal importance: the Qur'an has instructed Muslims to take advantage of the gifts of mind and time provided to them by their Bounteous Lord. They are encouraged to go through the land and observe the marvellous and intricate systems in the skies as well as on earth, animate and inanimate. "Surely in the creation of the heavens and earth and in the alternation of night and day there are *signs for men possessed of minds*" (III, 87). "What, do they not consider how the camel was created, how heaven was lifted up, how the mountains were hoisted, how the earth was out-stretched?" (LXXXVIII, 17–20). "*Hast thou not regarded* thy Lord, how He has stretched out the shadow? Had he willed, He would have made it still. Then We appointed the sun, to be a guide to it . . . It is He who appointed the night for you to be a garment and sleep for a rest, and day He appointed for a rising. And it is He who has loosed the winds, bearing good tidings before his Mercy; and We sent down from heaven pure water so that We might revive a dead land, and give to drink of it . . ." (XXV, 46–50). "What, have they not *beheld* heaven above them, how We have built it, and decked it out fair, and it has no cracks? And the earth – We stretched it forth, and cast on it firm mountains, and We caused to grow therein of every joyous kind for *an insight and a reminder* to every penitent servant" (L, 6–8). There are many more examples; out of more than six thousand verses in the Qur'an no less than seven hundred deal with natural phenomena.

One of the necessary steps in the search for facts is the process of comparing and contrasting the evidence. Scores of Qur'anic verses teach us to do just that. "Not equal are the two seas; this is sweet, grateful to taste, delicious to drink, and that is salt, bitter to the tongue" (XXXV, 13). "It is He who sent down out of heaven water, and thereby We have brought forth the shoot of every plant, and then We have brought forth the green leaf of it, bringing forth from it close-compounded grain, and out of the palm-tree, from the spathe of it, dates thick-clustered, ready to the hand, and gardens of vines, olives, pomegranates, like each to each, and each unlike to each. Look upon their fruits when they fructify and ripen! Surely, in all this are signs for a people who do believe" (VI, 98).

The Qur'an teaches man to be careful and enlightened in his judgements, and to base these judgements on a foundation of knowledge, rather than mere guess-work. It teaches: "And pursue not that thou hast no knowledge of; the hearing, the sight, the heart – all of those shall be questioned of" (XVII, 38).

Humility also is a key feature of Qur'anic teaching. In order that we may

The essential simplicity of the faith is upheld by Saudi Arabia – in its village mosques (right), *and in the adherence to the rules of regular prayer* (far right).

not think that we know everything (and become arrogant or ignorant), the Qur'an tells the Prophet: "They will question thee concerning the Spirit. Say: 'The Spirit is of the bidding of my Lord. *You have been given of knowledge nothing except a little*' " (XVII, 87). "He knows what lies before them and what is after them, and *they comprehend not anything of His knowledge save such as He wills*" (II, 257).

The Views of Islamic Scholarship

Though the reaction of the Muslim masses to the scientific and techno-logical achievements of the present age is a mixed one, ranging from the dazzled and bewitched to the sceptic or non-chalant, it seems that the scholars of Islam agree on the following points.

Science and technology are not the property of any one person or nation, and they are not the products of any specific religion or ideology. So there is nothing wrong in accepting and contri-buting to them. In fact, whatever is beneficial to man in science and tech-nology is recommended for a Muslim. For the Prophet of Islam said: "Wisdom is the believer's lost camel, wherever he finds it he has the greatest right to it." The Holy Book of Islam tells us that scientific investigation leads to the dis-covery of the marvellous works of our Creator; therefore, it should be appreci-ated and encouraged. This explains the great contributions made by Muslim scholars who bore the torch of know-ledge during the Middle Ages when science and scientific investigation were regarded with suspicion elsewhere, particularly in the West.

Science and technology are a means of discovery. Neither they nor man are creators or substitutes for the Creator, because science only unveils what is already present in the universe. Therefore, scientific achievements, however marvellous, should not lead us to atheism; the two things are unrelated.

The Qur'an tells us that whatever is in the skies and whatever is on earth were made serviceable to man by his Lord and Master, Almighty God. "Have you not seen how that God has subjected to you whatsoever is in the heavens and the earth, and He has lavished on you His blessings, outward and inward?" (XXXI, 19). We are also told that man was created to be "On the earth a viceroy

"From whatsoever place thou issuest, turn my face towards the Holy Mosque."

(of God)" (II, 28), and that man has been honoured by God and given preference above many of God's creation (XVII, 70). Accordingly, we must not be slaves to things material, and we should be above the pursuit of sheer animal satisfaction. Man should take his responsibility seriously, remembering his proper place in the universal scheme.

Since science and technology are amoral, they can be used both to the advantage of man and to his disadvantage and destruction. The only way we can guard against the evil misuse of the scientific achievements of this age is by reviving religious consciousness and by

adhering to the moral values of Islam, values which preach man's responsibility to God, on the Day of Judgement, for the security and peace of his fellow men.

Science and technology can help man only in matters material. Faith alone can help him achieve spiritual satisfaction and psychological well-being. As the Qur'an puts it, "It is in the remembrance of Allah that hearts may find serenity and peace."

Renderings of the Qur'an from *The Koran Interpreted* by Arthur J. Arberry, published by Oxford University Press.

THE truest culture of Arabia rests not in things but in words, in the language. This is not only because in the nomadic life a man can possess no more than he and his camel can carry, but because the Holy Book, the Qur'an, is the fount of his culture as it is of his faith, and the verbal richness of the Qur'an is without parallel.

As Islam became established throughout Arabia, the followers of the Prophet drew on the heritage of Arab tribal thought. Adherence to the Holy Law constituted the primary act of faith. The absence of a priesthood meant that no clear distinction arose between the religious and the secular. No part of a man's daily life, or his thought, or his culture, lay outside his religion.

The religious scholars who chronicled the early centuries of Islam incorporated in their works the sagas and genealogies of tribal life as well as the career of the Prophet and the Community of the Faithful. The traditions they recorded became precedents for the legal and social fabric of Islam. This body of writing emphasizes the significance of human lives and human acts. It contributed to the forming of a self-aware Islamic culture in the Land of the Prophet.

For its part, the Holy Qur'an itself, in its style, not only took into consideration the poetic traditions of the Beduin, but also challenged their literary talent. Before the appearance of the Holy Book, the Beduin had no written

code of law, and only the custom of the blood vendetta ensured the protection of a man's life. Leaders had to rely on their own merits for their authority: it was necessary for such men to demonstrate the qualities which entitled them to their position. The spare nomadic life of the Beduin offered little chance for the development of the material arts. Only those forms which could survive the harsh demands of their existence were cultivated.

The nomad jealously nurtured his language as his single unalienable good. By nature he was, and is, a rhetorician. The poet, the man of eloquence, was prized almost above all others in the community. His gifts and powers, believed to have been inspired by spirits, had already

Weaponry

Glass, wood and leather are the traditional materials for decorated shields. The leather is of camel hide, and the wood is often tamarisk.

Powder horns (above) *take their design with surprising literalness from the shape of ram's horns. The silversmith's craft in Arabia has for centuries been lavished on the hilts of swords* (left) *and daggers, and their sheaths.*

Although skilled smiths plied their trade in every permanent settlement, the development of intricate workmanship in precious metals was largely confined to major centres such as Mecca, Jiddah and the Gulf ports. Metal work was often imported from Oman and Yemen. On the other hand, distinctive designs evolved in central Arabia itself, and regional styles emerged in, for example, Qasim and Sudayr. Until the second quarter of this century, it was customary for every male to regard himself as properly dressed only when he was also armed – either with dagger or rifle or both – if for ceremonial rather than strictly defensive purposes.

evolved a complex art form. Poets sang of their lives, loves and land, but they also served as promulgators of the virtues and merits of their own tribes. The obligations of social values such as hospitality, generosity and courage were a matter of honour. Failure to uphold this unwritten code resulted in insult, and it was in this respect that poetic panegyrics possessed an enormous moral force for the Beduin, and had a regulatory effect within the community. The Prophet himself had to contend, through Muslim poets, with opponents who used the gift of poetry against him in Medina.

The first revelations to Muhammad were spoken in rhymed prose consisting of short phrases. These were taken down during his lifetime and were grouped into chapters which became collectively known as the Recitation, or Qur'an.

There is no trace of Arabic prose before Islam, and although examples in the same form may have existed before, they were never written down. It was only the special nature of Muhammad's messages which caused them to be recorded. The Holy Book's concern was not to produce a literary work, but to communicate the meaning which formed itself in it. To do this, the Qur'an initially employed a forceful, rhythmic and rhyming prose, for example:

"We have taught Muhammad no poetry, nor does it beseem him to be a poet. This is but a warning, an eloquent Qur'an to admonish the living and to pass judgement on the unbelievers."
Qur'an XXXVI, 69

Islam gathered in not only the poetic traditions but the practice of pilgrimage. Mecca's sanctity, reaffirmed and redefined by Muhammad, had attracted pilgrims from very ancient times. The last stopping place on the route from the south, lying somewhere between Ta'if and Mecca, was the fabled town of Ukaz. Here, during the four-month season of the "holy truce", travellers gathered to meet their fellows, to trade, to recuperate for the last leg of their journey, and to recite.

Poems were composed in honour of the powerful and were paid for in gold and silver. Swift fame was guaranteed to the

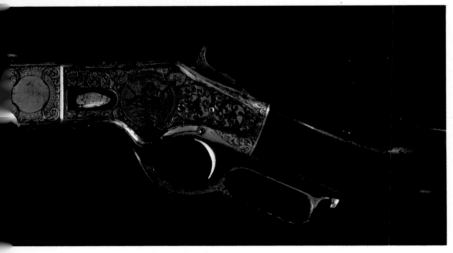

Chasing

Influences from Oman and Turkey have mingled with traditional Arabian techniques to produce a variety of designs for dagger-hilts and sheaths (shown here).

With the introduction of firearms in the late eighteenth century, metal-smiths turned their skills to the decoration of rifles.

successful poet. Here first developed the *Qasidah*, the ode in celebration of desert heroes – "appearing with Homeric suddenness", as Philip Hitti, the historian, has written, "and surpassing the Iliad and Odyssey in metrical complexity and elaboration."

Unquestionably, the poetic rhythms have been influenced by the gait of the camel. First to emerge was the rhythmic prose of the sages and travelling poets. From such prose grew the *Rajaz*, the four or six beat metre, rhymed prose for the father and a song for the mother, spoken or sung to the lilt of travel by camelback.

And so eloquence was, and has been ever since, allowed its place in Arabian culture. The flow of poetry and well-turned precepts has continued down the centuries, sagas of battles, journeys, loves and loyalties, moral tales and aphorisms as guides to the conduct of life, passed by word of mouth, from generation to generation, sometimes sung or chanted, sometimes accompanied by the stringed *rababa*.

The pure doctrine discouraged dancing and licence, and any extravagance of display or decoration. Yet no group in Saudi Arabia are without their traditions of communal rejoicing. And the sense of elegant design and craftsmanship is evident from the meanest artefact or utensil of daily life to the finest and most intricately wrought of garments or weapons.

The nomadic life of the desert has always existed in interdependence with the settled life of the oasis, or well-watered south-west, or the cities and ports. No Saudi Arabian settlement is without its craftsmen of ancient tradition – bronze-smiths, brass-smiths, gunsmiths and swordsmiths, potters and weavers and dyers, makers of incense burners and coffee mortars, makers – and players – of musical instruments. In the earlier past would have been found fletchers and bowmakers, and specialists in the manufacture of intricate bird traps. And in the ancient past – revealed today in the new Riyadh Museum established by the Director of Antiquities – elegant stone tools were worked by the Neolithic inhabitants of the Rub al-Khali and Eastern Province.

Home Utensils

Amid the onrush of 20th century technology, Saudi Arabia is taking decisive steps to preserve its ethnological history. Riyadh has a fine Museum of Archaeology, both for the public and for research. Six further local museums are planned by the Department of Antiquities – at Hofuf, el-Awda, Tayma, al-Jawf, Najran and Jizan.

Incense burners are used in tents and houses to pervade the atmosphere with fragrance.

Metal inlays of this perfume container show influences of Damascus or Turkey.

This elegant water jug is used for rinsing the right hand before eating.

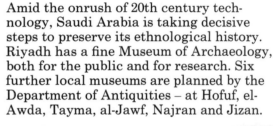

Pots and pitchers are widely made, both on wheels and by coiling the clay.

The singing voice is often accompanied by the one-stringed rababa.

In the preparation of coffee, beans and cardamom are pounded in mortars.

Highly decorated brass-bound chests are a distinctive product of the Gulf area. Such chests were in the past part of the dowry of a newly-wed bride.

The main centres, above all Mecca, would attract those with the finer skills: calligraphers and illuminators of holy manuscripts, ceramicists and workers in gold and silver thread, fine leather-workers, cabinet-makers and chest-makers (this was a speciality of the Gulf, with its sea-faring tradition), and those skilled in embossing and engraving, especially of guns.

Many of these crafts, in humbler form, were carried on within the tribe. Today they are indeed challenged by the importation of mass-produced goods from abroad. But the day of the craftsman in Saudi Arabia is not yet ended. For the market remains. Those things that are essentially "Arabian" are constantly sought by the discerning.

Fine jewellery in the form of thinly beaten and wrought pendants, necklaces and hair jewellery is widely favoured among the women.

Throughout the country, doors are often finely carved and studded, while in the Eastern Province, a tradition has persisted of decorating doors with elaborate designs in natural paints. The wood is often imported from India. Elaborately devised locks are locally made, to deter intruders.

The Government of Saudi Arabia

KEY TO ABBREVIATIONS

Min.	Minister
Dep. Min.	Deputy Minister
Asst. Dep. Min.	Assistant Deputy Minister
D.G.	Director General
Asst. D.G.	Assistant Director General
Gen.	General
Cttee.	Committee
Admin.	Administration
Org.	Organisation
Tech.	Technical
Govt.	Government
Agric.	Agriculture

✿ Newly formed Ministeries (1976)

Public Morality Cttee. Western Province — Public Morality Cttee. Najd & Eastern Provinces — Royal Protocol — Royal Advisers — His Majesty's Private Office

Central Planning Organisation — Office of the Comptroller Gen. — Military Section — Agency for Technical Cooperation — Bureau of the Presidency of the Council of Ministers

Vice President

Council of Ministers Regulations Cttee.

Public Works Dept. — Grievance Board — Supreme Council for Education — National Guard — Holy Mosque Religious Supervision

Court for Review of Corrupt Practices

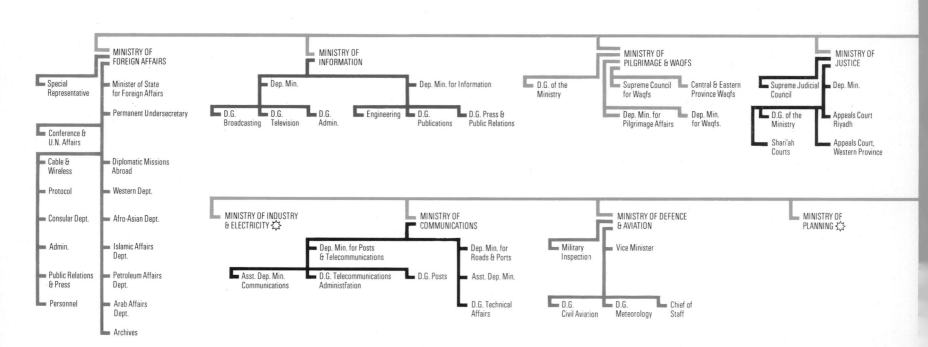

MINISTRY OF FOREIGN AFFAIRS
- Special Representative
- Minister of State for Foreign Affairs
- Permanent Undersecretary
- Conference & U.N. Affairs
- Diplomatic Missions Abroad
- Cable & Wireless
- Western Dept.
- Protocol
- Afro-Asian Dept.
- Consular Dept.
- Islamic Affairs Dept.
- Admin.
- Petroleum Affairs Dept.
- Public Relations & Press
- Arab Affairs Dept.
- Personnel
- Archives

MINISTRY OF INFORMATION
- Dep. Min.
- Dep. Min. for Information
- D.G. Broadcasting — D.G. Television — D.G. Admin.
- Engineering — D.G. Publications — D.G. Press & Public Relations

MINISTRY OF PILGRIMAGE & WAQFS
- D.G. of the Ministry
- Supreme Council for Waqfs — Central & Eastern Province Waqfs
- Dep. Min. for Pilgrimage Affairs — Dep. Min. for Waqfs.

MINISTRY OF JUSTICE
- Supreme Judicial Council
- Dep. Min.
- D.G. of the Ministry
- Appeals Court Riyadh
- Shari'ah Courts
- Appeals Court, Western Province

MINISTRY OF INDUSTRY & ELECTRICITY ✿
- Dep. Min. for Posts & Telecommunications
- Asst. Dep. Min. Communications — D.G. Telecommunications Administration

MINISTRY OF COMMUNICATIONS
- Dep. Min. for Roads & Ports
- D.G. Posts — Asst. Dep. Min.
- D.G. Technical Affairs

MINISTRY OF DEFENCE & AVIATION
- Military Inspection
- Vice Minister
- D.G. Civil Aviation — D.G. Meteorology — Chief of Staff

MINISTRY OF PLANNING ✿

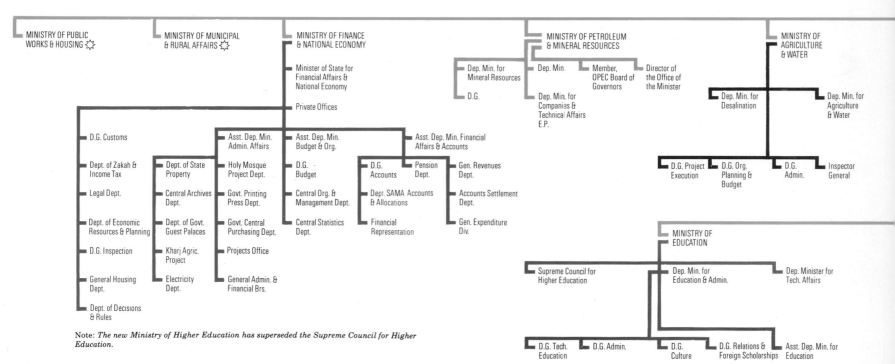

MINISTRY OF PUBLIC WORKS & HOUSING ✿
- D.G. Customs
- Dept. of Zakah & Income Tax
- Legal Dept.
- Dept. of Economic Resources & Planning
- D.G. Inspection
- General Housing Dept.
- Dept. of Decisions & Rules

MINISTRY OF MUNICIPAL & RURAL AFFAIRS ✿
- Dept. of State Property
- Central Archives Dept.
- Dept. of Govt. Guest Palaces
- Kharj Agric. Project
- Electricity Dept.

MINISTRY OF FINANCE & NATIONAL ECONOMY
- Minister of State for Financial Affairs & National Economy
- Private Offices
- Asst. Dep. Min. Admin. Affairs
- Asst. Dep. Min. Budget & Org.
- Asst. Dep. Min. Financial Affairs & Accounts
- Holy Mosque Project Dept.
- D.G. Budget
- D.G. Accounts — Pension Dept. — Gen. Revenues Dept.
- Govt. Printing Press Dept.
- Central Org. & Management Dept.
- Dept. SAMA Accounts & Allocations — Accounts Settlement Dept.
- Govt. Central Purchasing Dept.
- Central Statistics Dept.
- Financial Representation — Gen. Expenditure Div.
- Projects Office
- General Admin. & Financial Brs.

MINISTRY OF PETROLEUM & MINERAL RESOURCES
- Dep. Min. for Mineral Resources
- Dep. Min.
- Member, OPEC Board of Governors
- Director of the Office of the Minister
- D.G.
- Dep. Min. for Companies & Technical Affairs E.P.

MINISTRY OF AGRICULTURE & WATER
- Dep. Min. for Desalination
- Dep. Min. for Agriculture & Water
- D.G. Project Execution — D.G. Org. Planning & Budget — D.G. Admin. — Inspector General

MINISTRY OF EDUCATION
- Supreme Council for Higher Education
- Dep. Min. for Education & Admin.
- Dep. Minister for Tech. Affairs
- D.G. Tech. Education — D.G. Admin. — D.G. Culture — D.G. Relations & Foreign Scholarships — Asst. Dep. Min. for Education

Note: *The new Ministry of Higher Education has superseded the Supreme Council for Higher Education.*

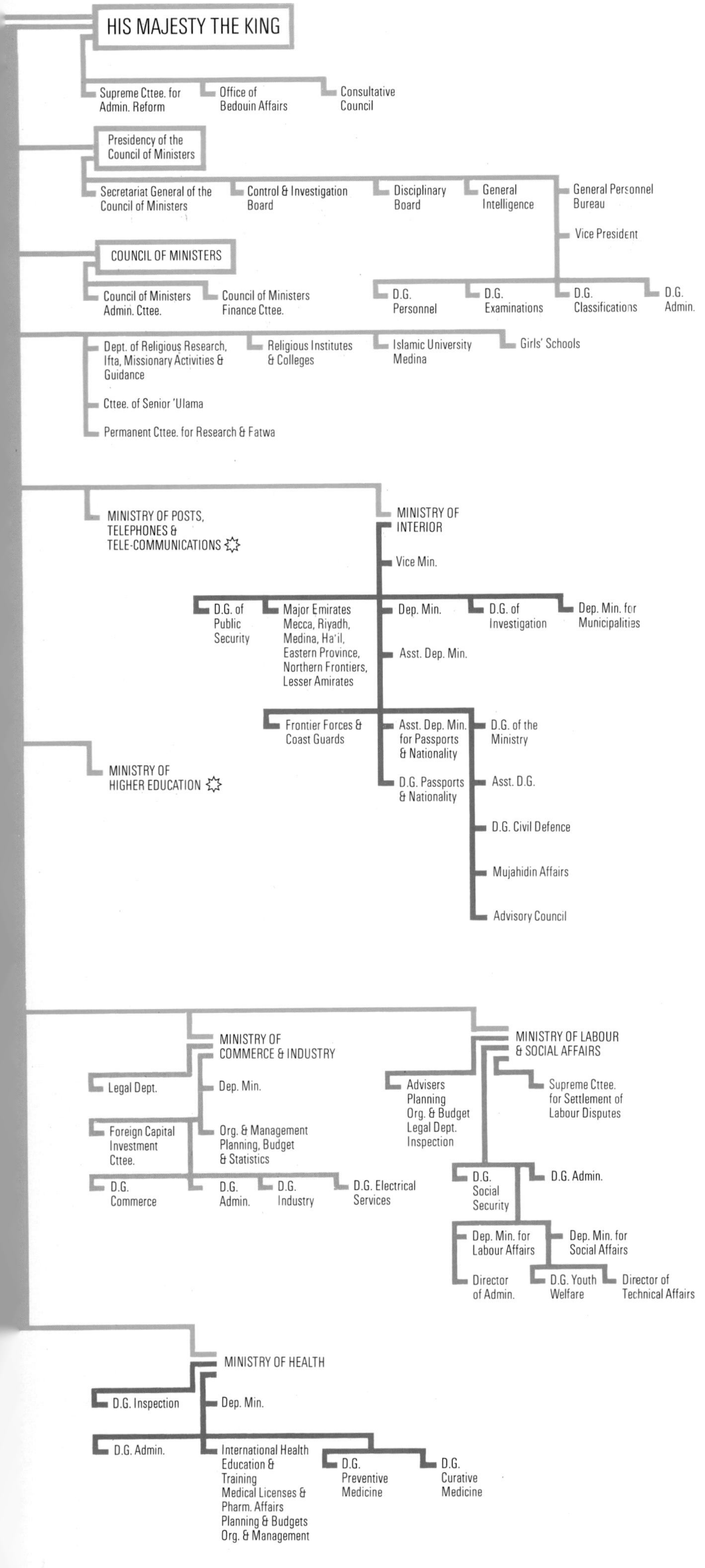

HIS MAJESTY THE KING

- Supreme Cttee. for Admin. Reform
- Office of Bedouin Affairs
- Consultative Council

Presidency of the Council of Ministers

- Secretariat General of the Council of Ministers
- Control & Investigation Board
- Disciplinary Board
- General Intelligence
- General Personnel Bureau
  - Vice President
  - D.G. Personnel
  - D.G. Examinations
  - D.G. Classifications
  - D.G. Admin.

COUNCIL OF MINISTERS

- Council of Ministers Admin. Cttee.
- Council of Ministers Finance Cttee.

- Dept. of Religious Research, Ifta, Missionary Activities & Guidance
  - Religious Institutes & Colleges
  - Islamic University Medina
  - Girls' Schools
- Cttee. of Senior 'Ulama
- Permanent Cttee. for Research & Fatwa

MINISTRY OF POSTS, TELEPHONES & TELE-COMMUNICATIONS ☼

- D.G. of Public Security
- Major Emirates Mecca, Riyadh, Medina, Ha'il, Eastern Province, Northern Frontiers, Lesser Amirates
- Frontier Forces & Coast Guards

MINISTRY OF HIGHER EDUCATION ☼

MINISTRY OF INTERIOR

- Vice Min.
- Dep. Min.
  - D.G. of Investigation
  - Dep. Min. for Municipalities
- Asst. Dep. Min.
- Asst. Dep. Min. for Passports & Nationality
  - D.G. of the Ministry
- D.G. Passports & Nationality
  - Asst. D.G.
- D.G. Civil Defence
- Mujahidin Affairs
- Advisory Council

MINISTRY OF COMMERCE & INDUSTRY

- Legal Dept.
- Dep. Min.
- Foreign Capital Investment Cttee.
- Org. & Management Planning, Budget & Statistics
- D.G. Commerce
- D.G. Admin.
- D.G. Industry
- D.G. Electrical Services

MINISTRY OF LABOUR & SOCIAL AFFAIRS

- Advisers Planning Org. & Budget Legal Dept. Inspection
- Supreme Cttee. for Settlement of Labour Disputes
- D.G. Social Security
- D.G. Admin.
- Dep. Min. for Labour Affairs
- Dep. Min. for Social Affairs
- Director of Admin.
- D.G. Youth Welfare
- Director of Technical Affairs

MINISTRY OF HEALTH

- D.G. Inspection
- Dep. Min.
- D.G. Admin.
- International Health Education & Training Medical Licenses & Pharm. Affairs Planning & Budgets Org. & Management
- D.G. Preventive Medicine
- D.G. Curative Medicine

7
Government

A monarchy built upon consultation and consent has proved flexible enough to sustain benevolent and enlightened rule in a period of unprecedented change. The Qur'anic foundation has held firm, supporting the complex structures required to govern a modern state.

The lines of authority and rule, evolved from the days of King Abdul Aziz, but formalized under the late King Faisal, give to Saudi Arabia a coherent and effective Government structure; the diagram opposite should be reviewed in the light of latest developments.

Monarchy

MORE than any other country in the modern world, Saudi Arabia is identified with her monarch. The King represents his people in a unique and individual way; he is their champion and they trust him. He speaks to them directly on all major matters which affect the welfare, honour and interests of the nation.

Kingship in the Arab lands has always been based on identity with the teaching of the Prophet and on prowess in war and peace. In addition, the people have expected their king to acquire wisdom, experience and the art of diplomacy.

Although the monarchy of Saudi Arabia is often described abroad as 'absolute', this is not accurate in the sense that Far Eastern monarchies were at one time absolute. No divinity has ever attached to Islamic kings. They are as their subjects are. Allah, alone, is God and under him all men are equal. One does not bow to an Arabian monarch.

The King's role is to lead his nation and keep in constant touch with the people. The legislative and executive power in Saudi Arabia is exercised by the Council of Ministers. When they draft a decree, they submit it to the King for signature. He may return it for further consideration, but the whole active operation of the government machine is carried out by the Council.

The King appoints the Prime Minister, who in turn chooses his colleagues, whose names are submitted to the King. There is thus a working relationship between the King and his Council. The Prime Minister has wide powers of supervision and control over the Ministries and departments, and he is responsible for directing the policy of the State. He also gets reports from the audit council and from the Grievance Bureau, a Saudi Arabian version of the Ombudsman.

The proof of the efficacy of any given form of government is the success it achieves. Saudi Arabia has greatly strengthened her power and prestige in the Arab world. Increasingly beneficial agreements have been made with the foreign oil companies, and the negotiations involved in achieving these agreements revealed the modernity and tenacity of the Saudi Government. The standard of living of Saudi Arabia's people has been improved at a rate which no-one could have foreseen, and at the same time friendly relations with other powers in the West and in the East have been preserved and promoted. It is undeniably a success story.

Saudi Arabia has no intention of introducing Western-type parliamentary democracy. In this unique country the Qur'an appears a firmer basis for law, order and progress than the ballot box. Moreover there must be a wide degree of real democracy in a nation where the individual dignity of all men is recognized. The Head of State is available to anybody with a petition to present or a complaint to make, and this right is constantly exercised; the King is referred to by his given name. Ordinary citizens can and do have direct access to him on fixed days of the week. The King personally initiates the appropriate action or enquiry.

The monarchy of Saudi Arabia is refined by the Islamic concept of government which considers that "every shepherd is responsible for his flock" (as the Prophet said), and "were a sheep to fall from the bank of the Euphrates [the governor] will be responsible on the Day of Judgement for having failed to make

Administration

a safe path for it." It reflects the tribal notion of administration exemplified by the proverb, "The master of the people is their servant".

The House of Saud – the Royal Family of Saudi Arabia

When the late King Abdul Aziz ibn Saud by royal decree in September 1932 changed the name of his realm from "Hijaz and Najd and its Dependencies" to "The Kingdom of Saudi Arabia", not only did the new style express the unity of a greater part of the Arabian Peninsula than at any time since the Prophet Muhammad but also forever identified the new country with the family of its founder – the House of Saud.

Today, His Majesty King Khalid bin Abdul Aziz bin Abd ar-Rahman Al Faisal Al Saud, seventh son of the late King Abdul Aziz and the third to succeed him, is ruler of the modern Islamic state of Saudi Arabia, in the government and administration of which other members of the Royal Family also play an active and leading role.

Major posts, however, are often filled by Saudi citizens who are not connected to the Royal Family.

SAUDI ARABIA is an Islamic monarchy which has been developing from monarchical to ministerial rule. The duties of the King-Imam are defined in the Shari'ah law (religious Islamic law as recorded in the Qur'an and interpreted in the Hadith, the Prophet's sayings) which recognizes the Imam not as an absolute hereditary monarch but as one who reigns in order to rule for the public good.

The modern history of Saudi Arabia begins with the recapture of Riyadh by King Abdul Aziz ibn Abd ar-Rahman Al Faisal Al Saud in 1901. Other conquests followed and the Kingdom's international position was confirmed by a series of treaties, the most important of which was the Treaty of Jiddah signed in 1927, when Britain recognized the complete independence of the Kingdom in return for a pledge by King Abdul Aziz to abstain from attacking the Gulf Sheikhdoms which were under British protection. In 1932 the name Saudi Arabia was adopted.

The Royal Decrees, proclaimed in 1953 and 1958, which provided for a Council of Ministers and laid down its functions, may be regarded as the beginning of the "constitutional regime",

the first formal step towards the system of popular consultation recognized by the Shari'ah law.

At the present time King Khalid heads the Government as Prime Minister, and the First Deputy Prime Minister is Crown Prince Fahd. The other members of the Council of Ministers – some of whom belong to the Royal Family – include the Ministers of Finance and National Economy, Justice, Defence and Aviation, Transport, Communications, Commerce, Industry and Electricity, Agriculture and Water, the Interior, Higher Education, Education, Information, Petroleum and Mineral Resources, Health, Labour and Social Affairs, Pilgrimage and Waqfs, Planning, Public Works and Housing, Municipal and Rural Affairs, and Foreign Affairs.

Ministers are responsible to the King. Almost all the apparatus of modern government – ministries, civil service, budgeting systems and so on – have been set up since 1955; in the early 1950s the Ministry of Finance was the only executive department of government. An independent judiciary and a modern judicial system were part of a reform programme begun in 1962, but the first

There is the aspect of formal grandeur, exemplified by the Guest Palace in Jiddah (far left), and the Council of Ministers' offices, the Riassa Palace, in Riyadh (left). Yet an essential characteristic of kingly rule is that the monarch himself is available in person to any one of his subjects. This is a weekly fact of life in Saudi Arabia. The aggrieved citizen knows he can himself bring his plea to the King.

Minister of Justice was not appointed until 1970.

Although there are no elections and no political parties, Saudi Arabia has its own form of Islamic democracy. All men are regarded as equal, and differences are minimized between the rich and the poor, the governors and the governed. Ministers and officials keep their doors open so that anyone with any business can call in, without prior appointment, and be offered refreshment in accordance with Arab customs. A morning visitor to a senior official may find himself waiting with a large number of other callers; and since most of the official's morning may be spent receiving visitors in this way, he often needs to return to his office in the evening to do uninterrupted work when the office is closed.

An element of decentralization was introduced in 1963 when the country was divided into four provinces: Western (Hijaz), Central (Najd), South Western (Asir) and Eastern Province (Hasa), each with an appointed governor, or Emir, who is charged with local administration, maintenance of order and implementation of Shari'ah judgements. Various ministries have field offices, and the Ministry of the Interior is responsible for appointing the Emirs, but Saudi Arabia has no effective local government as the term is understood in Western democracies. The municipalities are completely dependent on central Government for funds. The people expect the Government to provide whatever utilities and services are necessary, and the Government accepts an obligation to do so. The only form of local election is for council members, called al-Majlis al-Batadi, who have a purely advisory function, their advice being directed to the chief municipal executive. A new "district system" of local administration was approved in principle by Royal Decree in 1963.

Oil provides nearly all the Government's revenue. There is no income tax. This dependence on oil is too great, and many of the Government's plans are aimed at diversification: by increasing the area of land under cultivation, settling the nomads, and stimulating industrialization.

The Ministry of Education is the largest government department with about 50,000 administrators and teachers throughout the country, of whom 2,800 are employed centrally in the ministry headquarters in Riyadh. Great efforts are being made to educate the people. Saudi students do not have to pay fees, and are given generous allowances from the Government which amply cover their expenses. In 1967 the Kingdom's third university, King Abdul Aziz University, was founded in Jiddah (the others are Riyadh University, founded in 1957, and the Islamic University, Medina, founded in 1961). The University of Petroleum and Minerals, which might be described as a technological university, produced its first graduates in 1970. In 1975 King Faisal University was established in the Eastern Province. Riyadh's University of Imam Muhammad ibn Saud was preparing to include colleges of Arabic languages, Social Studies, and Shari'ah (Islamic law) and the High Institute of Judiciary.

The General Personnel Bureau is responsible for staffing policies throughout the public service. Considerable efforts are being made in the direction of administrative innovation and reform, and impressive training schemes are being introduced to improve the structure and processes of public administration. The Institute of Public Administration, which was established in Riyadh by Royal Decree in 1961 as a semi-independent public agency, provides training and further education for civil servants, undertakes research, and assists government departments in reorganization and reform. It is probably the biggest and best equipped institute of its kind in the Middle East.

The Government's general objectives are to provide for national security and economic and social stability, and to raise the living standards of the people, while maintaining the religious and moral values for which the Kingdom, as the original homeland of Islam, is so well known.

The most difficult administrative problem, for the foreseeable future, is the shortage of skilled manpower. Although increased efforts are being made to remedy this deficiency, it is unlikely that the Government will achieve its social and economic objectives without considerable help from non-Saudis, and such achievement may be at the expense of some of the religious and moral values which are an essential and distinctive element of Saudi society. It will be a matter of great interest to see how Saudi Arabia continues to develop towards objectives which anywhere else would be considered virtually irreconcilable.

Law

IN Saudi Arabia – uniquely in the modern world – Islamic law, in its Hanbali interpretation, still reigns virtually supreme. Article Six in the Fundamental Law of the Hijaz, 1926, unequivocally declares that "The law in the Kingdom of the Hijaz shall always conform to the Book of God, the Sunnah of the Prophet and the conduct of the Companions of the Prophet and of their Pious Followers." A year later King ibn Saud proposed that a code of Islamic law should be drawn up based not only on the doctrine of the Hanbali school but on that of whichever school seemed closest to the Qur'an and Sunnah (or practice of the Prophet) on the particular point concerned. The Hanbali *ulama* (scholars learned in the school of law named after the great jurist-theologian Ahmad ibn Hanbal, who died in 855 CE) persuaded him to abandon this project, and regulations issued in 1928 and 1930 made it obligatory on the *qadis*, or judges, to follow the recognized Hanbali texts. But in 1934 he affirmed his own policy, when he said: "We are seekers of the truth. We will accept what is sound in any school of thought or from any *alim* (learned Muslim scholar) . . . We obey neither ibn Abd al-Wahhab (the founder of the Wahhabi school of thought) nor any other person unless what they said was clearly endorsed by the Book of God and the Sunnah of the Prophet. God made us – me, my fathers and ancestors – preachers and teachers according to the Qur'an and the Sunnah. So, whenever we find strong proof in any of the four schools, we will refer to it and be bound by it. Should we fail to find the evidence there, then we would resort to the teachings of Imam Ahmad ibn Hanbal".

Until about the middle of the last century, Islamic law (the Shari'ah or "path to a watering place") was dominant throughout the whole Muslim world. It was regarded as being firmly based on divine revelation, the only way in which man could distinguish between virtue and vice.

How was the divine will to be ascertained? First, from the Qur'an or "Book of God", which is regarded by orthodox Muslims as having been written from eternity in Arabic in heaven and revealed to Muhammad, as occasion demanded,

Modern and efficient administration and ministerial buildings are scattered throughout Riyadh and Jiddah and the towns of the Eastern Province. Frequently architects and designers have succeeded in combining the requirements of large official structures with a markedly Arabian flavour in the façades. Such is true, for example, of the Ministries of Agriculture (above) and Petroleum (below), both in Riyadh, and Jiddah's Saudia headquarters (left).

by the archangel Gabriel. But there is comparatively little in the Qur'an which is of direct legal significance; so the second of the *usul al-fiqh* (or sources of the divine law as put together and systematized by the jurist-theologians of Islam) was the Sunnah or practice of Muhammad, equally inspired in content although not in form, and derived from a mass of Traditions (*ahadith*) as to what he had said, done or allowed to be done. Even this, however, was not enough. In very early days a judge or jurist would, where necessary, fall back on his own opinion (*ra'y*) of what was consonant with the spirit of the faith. But the view soon gained ground that this was far too fallible and subjective a source for a divine law: too fallible, so *ijma* or the consensus of the Muslim community (in practice, that of its jurists) came to be accepted as another reliable indication of the divine will; too subjective, so the "opinion" of an individual judge or jurist was replaced by *qiyas*, or the science of analogical deductions from one of the primary sources.

In early days, any qualified jurist was regarded as entitled to exercise *ijtihad*: that is, to go back to the authoritative sources of the law and deduce from them the solution to a particular problem. But soon the jurist-theologians began to draw together in schools, based in some cases primarily on a geographical area, and in others on their allegiance to some outstanding lawyer or theologian. With the crystallization of these schools, most Muslims came to regard the "door of *ijtihad*" as having been virtually closed, and all future lawyers as mere *muqallids* (men bound to accept as authoritative the views of the great scholars of the past). With the passage of time, moreover, the number of law schools in orthodox or Sunni Islam became limited to four: the Hanafis, Malakis, Shafi'is and Hanbalis. The Hanbali school relied on traditional rather than "speculative" material.

There were, however, a very limited number of Muslim jurists who not only proclaimed that the "door of *ijtihad*" had never been closed, but that they were themselves *mujtahids*, or men who had the right to exercise the faculty of *ijtihad*. Hence the suggestion made by King ibn Saud about following the doctrine of whichever school seemed closest to the Qur'an and Sunnah on any particular point. The opposition of the Hanbali *ulama* was not only to such

freedom of choice but to the very idea of any official compilation of the divine law. As a result, the law in Saudi Arabia is still derived principally from some six Hanbali texts, although some *qadis* exercise a certain amount of discretion.

The degree of legal orthodoxy which still prevails in Saudi Arabia contrasts with the course of development, since the middle of the last century, in the greater part of the Muslim world, where the Shari'ah has been progressively displaced by codes of commercial, criminal and even civil law which are largely of Western inspiration, and the Shari'ah, as such, has been chiefly confined to the law of personal status (marriage, divorce, succession, etc). Even in this sphere, moreover, the Islamic law has often been reduced to a codified form, during the last half century, by legislation based on a process of selection and reinterpretation. As a result, Saudi Arabia is virtually the only country today in which the criminal law of Islam is still in full force – characterized first by the treatment of homicide and wounding primarily as civil wrongs which involve blood-money or some other form of compensation; then by the imposition of certain very severe penalties for a few precisely defined crimes such as theft, brigandage, illicit sex relations and the consumption of alcohol (provided the offence can be proved by the oral testimony of the requisite number of unimpeachable, adult, male witnesses); and by discretionary punishments in all other cases. This is why one sometimes still hears of an adulterer being stoned to death, or a thief having his right hand amputated.

Throughout the Muslim world, however, a number of other courts, such as those of the local governor, the police and the inspector of markets, have always exercised jurisdiction alongside that of the *qadis*, together with a Court of Complaints presided over by the Caliph himself or some powerful official appointed by him, which acted, *inter alia*, as an unofficial court of appeal. And none of these other courts were, in practice, as strictly bound by the Shari'ah as were those of the *qadis*.

It was inherent in the theory of Islamic jurisprudence that there was exceedingly little scope for State legislation. According to a commonly accepted classification, all human actions were subsumed under one of five categories: what God had positively commanded, had recom-

mended, had left legally indifferent, had reprobated or had actually forbidden. So it was only in the middle category (things left legally indifferent) that there was, in theory, any scope for human legislation. For the rest, the Shari'ah was regarded as a divinely given blueprint by which all Muslims should try to abide.

In Saudi Arabia much of this concept still survives. Only comparatively minor concessions have been made to the exigencies of modern life – although it is true that, alongside the Shari'ah, there now stand an ever increasing number of administrative regulations promulgated by the Government. These certainly have the force of law; but they are normally termed either *nizam* (regulation) or *marsum* (royal decree) rather than *qanun* (which is the normal term for legislation throughout the Middle East). Such royal decrees have provided for a hierarchy of courts – Summary Courts, High Courts and a "Commission of Judicial Supervision". Summary Courts are of two types, one of which deals with Beduin affairs and the other with minor criminal and financial cases in urban areas. High Courts consist of three or four judges and try the more serious criminal and financial cases, together with matters of personal status or family law. In the more remote districts, local governors, sometimes assisted by a *qadi*, deal with crimes, civil litigation, tribal customs and mediation. The Office of the Chief *Qadi* and the Commission of Judicial Supervision have now been replaced by a Minister of Justice and a Supreme Judicial Council. The Supreme Judicial Council, which consists of twenty members chosen from the leading jurists and *ulama*, has the function, *inter alia*, of issuing *fatawa* or opinions on points of law and religion, and thus of adapting the law as traditionally accepted to the changing needs of contemporary life. But the ultimate responsibility for promulgating and implementing legislation remains with the Council of Ministers and with the King himself whose decrees have the force of law, who endorses the regulations formulated by the Council of Ministers and by whom sentences of execution or amputation must normally be confirmed.

From the first, King Abdul Aziz had himself acted both as chief executive and chief judge, to whom litigants might always appeal. But in 1954 a Board of Complaints (*Diwan al-Mazalim*) was set up, to which all complaints could be submitted for investigation and – with royal approval – final resolution. The Board also deals with administrative problems, questions of governmental corruption, disputes about taxation and matters which concern foreign nationals and their investments in Saudi Arabia.

One of the earliest and most important innovations was the establishment of a Council of Commerce in Jiddah in 1926 and the promulgation of a commercial code, or Regulations on Commerce, in 1931. In 1954 the Council was replaced by a Ministry of Commerce, and "Chambers of Commerce" were set up in Jiddah, Yanbu and Dammam to administer the Regulations (which are based on the Ottoman Commercial Code of 1850, but with all references to interest expunged). A number of concessions to modern life are being quietly introduced. Banks, for example, are now allowed to charge a "commission" (rather than "interest") on loans; and this is a matter of considerable importance, since people were apt previously to be charged a ruinous rate of interest in transactions which were completely illicit. Until recently, again, insurance contracts were allowed only in regard to maritime commerce; but this concession is now being extended to all forms of property, although not to life insurance.

There has been a spate of recent legislation. The General Personnel Regulation of 1957 was replaced in 1970 by the Disciplinary Code, which covers the behaviour, administrative negligence or defaults of civil servants, and the power of a Disciplinary Council – but with the proviso that any act which constitutes a crime or civil wrong still falls within the competence of the Shari'ah Courts. The Work and Workmen's Regulation of 1970 deals with labour disputes, injuries, dismissals, minimum wages and maximum hours of work; obliges all employers to enlist at least seventy-five per cent of their workmen from among Saudi nationals and to pay Saudis at least fifty-one per cent of the total sum expended on wages; and makes an employer responsible for any prohibited item, such as alcohol, brought to work by one of his employees. But administrative penalties which may be imposed under this law do not exclude the jurisdiction of the qadis in regard to the punishment of crimes or the computation of blood-money under the Shari'ah. Similarly, the Regulation on Motor Vehicles leaves

it to the police to investigate accidents and to determine questions of guilt, but reserves the allocation of blood-money to the qadis. The Regulation on Investing Foreign Capital, 1957, provides that at least fifty-one per cent of the controlling interest in an investment company must be owned by Saudi nationals, who must also make up three-quarters of the total number of employees and be paid no less than forty-five per cent of the total salaries paid by the company; the Regulation on Companies, 1965, established a special Committee for the Resolution of Disputes; and the Regulation to Control Commercial Fraud, 1961, lays down a variety of penalties.

Only in 1936 was the importation of slaves largely prohibited in Saudi Arabia, and not until 1962 was the status of slavery itself abolished. The theoretical implications of the abolition of slavery are of great significance, for Saudi Arabia has in this case demonstrated conclusively that it is both able, and at times willing, to abrogate by statute law what many would regard as a basic right under the Shari'ah – and to do so in deference to political pressure and the weight of contemporary world opinion.

Particular interest attaches to Royal Decree No 1135, by which the late King ibn Saud ratified the oil concession first granted to the Standard Oil Company of California and subsequently inherited by the Arabian American Oil Company (Aramco). This concession, while conforming to what has become a comparatively standard type of agreement in such cases, is *sui generis* in terms of the Shari'ah, which lays down in minute detail the conditions for a series of named contracts, rather than enumerating principles which would constitute a general "law of contract". Different parts of the concession would normally be classified under the Shari'ah as *ihya al-mawat* (cultivation of undeveloped land), *iqta* (grant or concession), *ijarah* (lease) and a form of *sharikah* (partnership); but it includes specific provisions which might strictly be held to invalidate each of these contracts or dispositions in their classical form. Yet this concession was certainly regarded as valid and binding by the King; and the Arbitration Agreement of 1955 expressly states that both the Government and the Company "respect all the obligations which they have undertaken" and "have never entertained the thought that they would not

be bound by the agreements they have made and now make with one another." There is, moreover, excellent authority in both the Qur'an, and in those traditions which are generally accepted by Muslims as authentic, for the proposition that Muslims are bound by their contractual stipulations – a principle wide enough to cover any contract which the exigencies of modern life may require. This principle is reinforced, in Hanbali teaching (which Saudi Arabia adopted), by the welfare (*maslaha*) of the individual and community.

In 1952, a Royal Decree promulgated new Regulations for the "Organization of Administrative Functions in the Shari'ah Court System". These provide for the *qadi*, as soon as a suit is brought before him, to fix a day for the plaintiff to be heard and to notify the defendant accordingly, and for the appropriate forms to be signed, writs of summons issued and files prepared. If two litigants appear and request an immediate hearing this request should be granted whenever circumstances permit; but in all other cases the *qadi* should study the case on the day before it is heard and the "special police post assigned to the court building, or nearby" ensure that the defendant is not only duly summoned but even, in some cases, brought to court by force (since all claims must be raised in the town in which the defendant is resident, provided this is within the Kingdom). Following the classical pattern, the *qadi* must ask the plaintiff to provide evidence for his claim and then ask the defendant to answer it, promptly if possible, or after a delay adequate to enable him to consult documents, accounts, etc, where this is necessary. Special provisions are included for those cases in which either party fails to appear; everyone, without restriction, is given the right to appoint a suitably qualified legal representative; and litigation must be conducted in public "except in circumstances in which the court considers it in the interests of morals for it to be in secret". Documents issued by registrars are to be refused by the court only when something in them is "contrary to the Shari'ah", and it is significant that documentary evidence appears to be freely admitted.

One of the major functions of the new Judicial Council is to resolve any conflict between the Qur'an and Sunnah on the one hand and the demands of modernization on the other.

Defending the Country

Saudi Arabia's vast size and scattered centres require relatively formidable defence forces. International reference sources list an army of some 36,000, an air force of 6,000, and a navy of 1,500. Its sophisticated weaponry included (1976) Lightnings, Mirages, Strikemasters (*right*), Hawk missile launchers, Jaguar patrol boats and hovercraft. Paramilitary forces are listed as including a 26,000 strong National Guard, of which an officer is pictured in ceremonial dress (*left*) and men in equestrian training (*overleaf*). *Below:* Air force cadets are put through basic training.

Army

36,000 men incorporating 4 infantry brigades, 1 armoured battalion, 2 reconnaissance battalions, 1 parachute battalion, 1 Royal Guard battalion, 3 artillery battalions, 3 AA battalions and 10 SAM batteries with *HAWK*.

30 AMX-30

25 M-47 medium tanks

60 M-41 light tanks

200 AML-60 & AML-90

Navy

1,500 men

4 *Jaguar* class fast patrol boats

8 SRN-6 hovercraft (coastguard)

20 patrol boats (coastguard)

Air Force

5,500 men

2 fighter ground attack squadrons with 21 BAC-167

2 fighter-bomber squadrons with:

14 F-5E

20 F-5B

2 interceptor squadrons with 35 F-52/F-53 *Lightning*

2 helicopter squadrons with 20 AB-206 & 10 AB-205

2 transport squadrons with:

9 C-130H

2 C-140B

World Affairs

AS the largest exporter of oil in the world Saudi Arabia's most valuable contribution to world financial stability lies in its restraining influence on increases in the price of oil. The Saudi Government differs from other OPEC members in fearing the effect on the world economy of an excessive oil price. It is acutely aware that a world recession could lead to a massive surplus of supply. The result, many Saudis believe, would be a scramble among the producer nations for markets and the imposition of harmful trade barriers; which would not at all fit in with the Saudi desire for orderly industrialization in co-operation with the West.

Saudi Arabia has remained unswervingly committed to the Arab cause in the continuing crisis over Israel, not hesitating to use its considerable economic authority to instil in the Western powers the need for an even-handed attitude. At the same time, the Kingdom has worked perseveringly for a concerted and realistic Arab policy – as witness its alignment with Egypt in 1975, during which a phased withdrawal of Israeli forces in Sinai was secured. Significantly it was Saudi Arabia that played host to the conference of Arab statesmen, sponsored by Saudi Arabia and Kuwait and under the chairmanship of Crown Prince Fahd, that led to the restoration of peace in Lebanon in 1976.

Backing by Saudi Arabia, in the form of loans, grants and guarantees for the less well endowed countries of the Islamic world, operates as a force for stability and more equitable worldwide growth. Many countries benefit from Saudi Arabia's international financial policies, including several sub-Saharan Muslim African states.

Saudi Arabia has become effectively the trustee of the Third World. In the field of aid, emphasis is placed on the needs first of the Islamic world, next of the Arab world, and then of the general community of Third World states. Development agencies and banks were being established in Riyadh during the 1960s and 1970s to provide help for developing nations, and other methods are being urgently considered. The UN Technical Assistance Board and Special Fund receives a generous flow of Saudi funds.

King Khalid demonstrated his personal commitment to his country's international role very swiftly after succeeding his revered brother in 1975. He paid visits to his major non-Arab Islamic neighbours: to Iran, for discussions with the Shah on strategic affairs and petroleum, and a few months later to Pakistan, for discussions with the influential Zulfikar Ali Bhutto, the Pakistan Prime Minister. At home, he conferred with King Hussein of Jordan. Reconciliation with Egypt, in which good personal relations with President Sadat have featured, has been significant in Saudi foreign policy.

Equipped with one of the finest conference centres in the world, Riyadh has become the natural capital for pan-Islamic or pan-Arab international conferences.

Above: *King Khalid (left) leads his country's delegation, including Crown Prince Fahd (right), in discussions on world and Arab affairs with Egypt's Head of State, Anwar Sadat.*

8
Industry and Development

Saudi Arabia came to riches through the long, hard school of poverty. There was to be no place for profligacy. Rather, the bounty of oil and mineral resource was to be made to provide, for generations to come, the infrastructure of modern statehood; and to fund a free economic system where human enterprise, working within a total plan, would ensure self-generating growth.

The boom of the world's most plentiful capital of mineral energy in the form of oil has turned Saudi Arabia from one of the poorest countries in the world to the richest of all, in terms of reserves, in scarcely more than a single generation. Some oil is obtained offshore (left).

Introduction

THE economic situation of Saudi Arabia in the last quarter of the twentieth century is unprecedented in the history of the world. This is a country whose sparse population had, historically, been subjected to a harsh, if ennobling, poverty, that came into riches beyond the range of dreams.

The Kingdom indeed proved to be blessed with the largest oil reserves of any country in the world; but it can certainly take personal credit for the skilful exploitation of these reserves and the sensible husbanding of the wealth that results. Saudi Arabia, by 1977, was standing second only to West Germany in monetary reserves: each year was bringing substantial increases in the funds available for spending.

Such a situation does not represent, as might be thought, an economic paradise. Indeed (as is described in the section on Development and Economy on page 150) it presents responsibilities and challenges which, in their way, are only a little less frustrating than poverty. The persistent danger is that of destroying the integrity of the

nation, which in its intricate patterns of family and society must always be a delicate and subtle complex, by the sudden and overwhelming nature of the change that the availability of virtually limitless funds can mean. The late King Faisal always attempted to separate oil from politics, thus allowing the petroleum industry to establish its own markets and reach its own decisions without his intervention for political motives. It was clearly a wise principle on which to base the conduct of government and one which has been carried forward under King Khalid; for to curtail artificially the flow of oil could so easily have resulted in distorting the world market for this vital product while at the same time building up at home pressures and difficulties of a different kind.

And so Saudi Arabia has accepted the fact of its wealth, with a courage and determination to make use of it to the maximum advantage of the nation both internally and abroad, and to use the surplus with traditional Islamic generosity among poorer nations.

It so happened that from the latter period of 1974, when oil first rose to its natural market price, the economies of many Western nations were entering the spiral of inflation because of a complex of reasons, most of them arising from home-generated political and electoral presures. Several major industrial countries were experiencing inflation rates in double figures: the major oil-producing states came in for ill-judged criticism. But the truth remained that the factor of increased petroleum costs worldwide was a negligible element in the inflationary spiral. Saudi Arabia has consistently appreciated the need for stable Western economy.

For the Kingdom openly accepts its dependence, for the coming period of history, on the skills and products that Western economies can offer. It has opened its arms to Western participation: first and foremost, of course, in its historic relationship through Aramco with the U.S., but also with Britain, France, West Germany, Japan and other major industrialized countries, in an immense range of new enterprises and

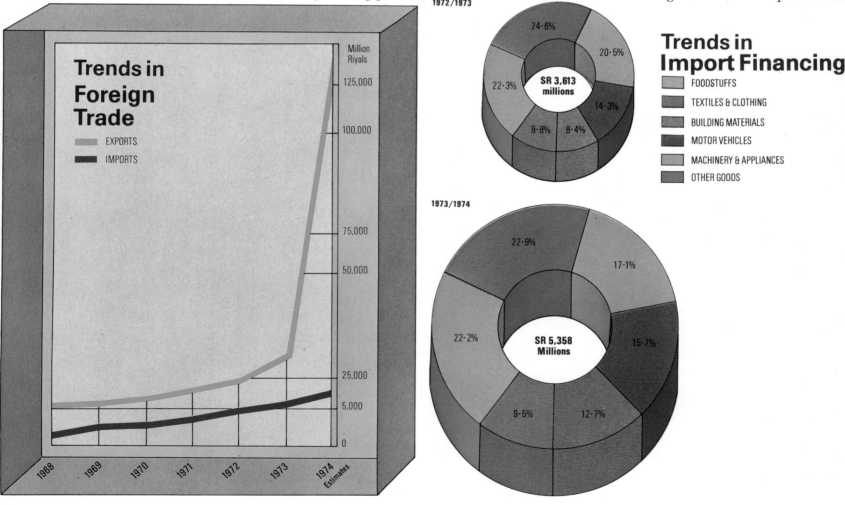

Trends in Foreign Trade

EXPORTS
IMPORTS

Million Riyals
125,000
100,000
75,000
50,000
25,000
5,000
0

1968 1969 1970 1971 1972 1973 1974 Estimates

Trends in Import Financing

FOODSTUFFS
TEXTILES & CLOTHING
BUILDING MATERIALS
MOTOR VEHICLES
MACHINERY & APPLIANCES
OTHER GOODS

1972/1973 — SR 3,613 millions: 24·6%, 20·5%, 22·3%, 14·3%, 9·8%, 8·4%

1973/1974 — SR 5,358 Millions: 22·9%, 17·1%, 22·2%, 15·7%, 9·5%, 12·7%

products, from defence and telecommunications to every kind of manufacturing plant, agricultural aid and irrigation technique, at the same time welcoming the skills and instruction that new techniques require.

Simultaneously, the Kingdom has sought to secure its future – a future which will stretch infinitely beyond the period of history in which petroleum and petroleum products are likely to be flowing and producing massive income – by encouraging investment abroad, both on its own account, as a government, and through the enterprise of its citizens.

The Saudi Arabian Monetary Agency (SAMA) has a team of advisers, which include international bankers, and a list of accredited money brokers with whom it is prepared to deal – a list of some fifty which includes all the leading European and American banks. A strong vein of conservatism runs through its national investment policy, and the precise areas where Saudi investment is concentrated are not in the main public. The major area of investment is generally considered to be the United States; American funds allow for a high level of liquidity in the opportunities available for the purchase of corporate stocks and bonds. A second centre is certainly London, which remains the banking and insurance capital of the world. It is in London that the Saudi International Bank (al Bank al Saudi al Alami) has been established, with SAMA holding a fifty per cent share and the rest held by such leading banks as Morgan Guaranty, National Westminster, and the Union Bank of Switzerland. This enterprise may well prove to be a prototype for the controlled use of government funds in international markets. Through such banks, with a high involvement of private enterprise, funds seem most likely to reach the right categories of production investment.

Private fortunes are inevitably being made in Saudi Arabia today, and these in turn lead to investment not only in Saudi Arabia itself, but abroad. Investment in property has its obvious attractions; but a wide range of non-speculative and imaginative investments have been reported, including film-making and sporting enterprises.

The third outlet for surplus is aid to needy countries. The order of priority that the Kingdom's generous policy of aid has followed has been established

for several years. The first tranche of aid is offered to needy countries of the Islamic world, then to the Arab countries with special needs, and then to the third world as a whole. This is a policy, incidentally, which reflects the order of priority that has prevailed in Saudi foreign policy.

The international banking world has reciprocated Saudi Arabia's external expansion with enthusiasm. There are two major Saudi-owned banks in operation, and with the encouragement of SAMA branches have been opened in all parts of the country by the Riyadh Bank and the National Commercial Bank. A third indigenous bank, the Bank al Jazirah, was making rapid headway by 1977. Other banks are increasingly seeking Saudi participation. For example, in 1976 the Algemene Bank Nederland set about reorganizing its operations in the country with an offer of sixty per cent of the new bank to Saudi investment. Such a structure may well set a pattern for the other major banks operating in the Kingdom, such as the First National City Bank N.A., the British Bank of the Middle East, the Arab Bank, Bank Melli Iran, Banque du Liban, United Bank (Pakistan) and the Banque de l'Indochine.

Meanwhile, the merchant banking field has been opened by a consortium consisting of the Chase Manhattan Bank, Schroder Wagg, Commerzbank and the Industrial Bank of Japan, together forming the Saudi Investment Banking Incorporation. Its aim will be, first, to provide medium term finance for industry.

Inevitably, the rapid increase in the supply of money has led to sharp and sometimes rapid inflation. Swift growth of the major cities has accelerated their attraction to the young in the scattered and isolated communities throughout the country. This phenomenon, common in the third world, has, in Saudi Arabia, led to immense pressure upon accommodation. Yet wages have increased sharply, and with the efficient running of the Organization for Social Insurance, enough of Saudi Arabia's wealth is reaching the mass of people to provide them with a vivid sense of an expanding availability of the material benefits of life and of expanding opportunities in a new yet very much Saudi Arabian Islamic context.

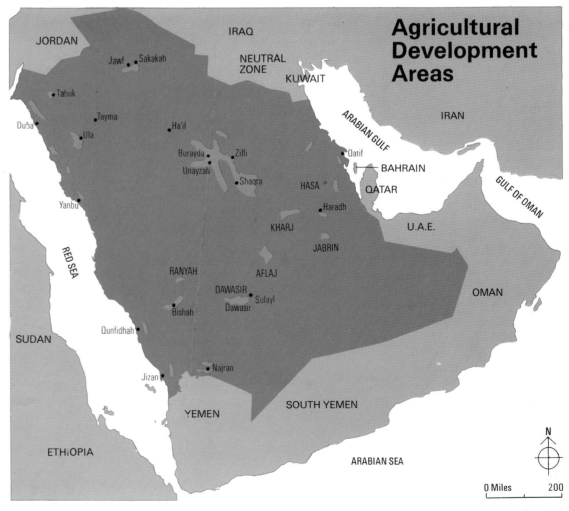

Agricultural Development Areas

Horticulture has been highly developed in experimental farms (right and above), *adding to the accumulated experience of skilled farming in the areas* (below and opposite) *naturally endowed with adequate rainfall.*

adoption of technology and agricultural mechanization, which necessitate large holdings. The official estimate of the area under agricultural ownership is about 1.9 million acres of which 900,000 acres are productive. Field crops such as wheat, barley, maize, millet and sorghum are harvested. The area planted with winter field crops is 239,059 acres compared with 701,797 acres of summer field crops.

Owing to the increasing national income and population, the growth rate in food consumption is high. About fifty-five per cent by value of total food consumed was domestically produced in 1391 AH (1971 CE); the remaining forty-five per cent was made up of net imports. Imports have grown much more rapidly than domestic production – by about

thirteen per cent over the 1382–1391 AH decade. Consequently the Kingdom's self sufficiency in food production has fallen significantly. An exception may be marine food, for which a growing demand offers the Kingdom a unique opportunity to increase food production with a minimum input of labour.

The labour force in agriculture is declining by 0.9 per cent annually; a decline reflected in abandoned farmland and partly depopulated villages, particularly in the South-Western region. Its main causes are low real incomes in agriculture and increasing opportunities for well-paid employment in other sectors.

The most binding constraint on Saudi agriculture is imposed by water (*See also* Geography and Climate). The general

availability of water in areas of cultivable soil is insufficient almost everywhere in the Kingdom: but studies conducted by the Ministry of Agriculture and Water have revealed that underground water resources are much greater than was believed ten years ago. Comparative studies of known water sources with recent national water consumption rates demonstrate that they should be sufficient for tens or even hundreds of years. Surface water is intermittent and primarily available in the south-western highlands and coastal areas, brackish water is abundant and sea-water is available for desalination in unlimited quantities.

It has been found that the eastern, northern and central areas of the Kingdom are compiled of sedimentary rocks

containing water-bearing formations which vary in quality and quantity. Such sedimentary deposits cover two-thirds of the country. Most of these deposits are represented by sandstone or limestone, which hold a considerable amount of ground water.

These aquifers contain water more than thirty thousand years old. Some formations are near the surface but some are very deep, so diving and pumping equipment are necessary to extract the water. Some of these formations are not rechargeable, so water resources, like oil resources, are diminishing. According to studies made by consultants, twenty-eight important sedimentary aquifers have been discovered. Artesian water, once tapped, reaches the surface under its own pressure, often at a high tem-

perature, from the heat of the earth's core.

As for surface water, Saudi Arabia is the largest country in the world without rivers. The annual rainfall does not exceed 100 mm, although the south-western parts of the country are affected by monsoons and the annual rainfall average in these areas might reach 500 mm. In general, rainfall is sporadic and variable. There can be periods of drought of up to seven years, great humidity, high evaporation, strong wind effects and rapid run-off floods.

The accumulation of salts in the soil is one of the permanent problems facing irrigated agriculture. All surface water contains some soluble salts in negligible amounts, but after several years of irrigation a harmful accumulation ap-

pears. Salts found in irrigation water remain in the soil, while water itself is lost by evaporation and drainage. Irrigation water is used in Saudi Arabia with a salt content ranging from one thousand to more than four thousand parts per million (ppm). Generally 3,150 ppm is considered the maximum for the safe watering of any plant; so salinity is a severe problem.

Irrigation agriculture has been and will continue to be by far the largest user of water. The demands made by agriculture on water supplies reflect crop needs and also determine minimum production and maximum cost levels. The depth of ground water in the Kingdom varies from a few feet to three thousand feet. Increased water usage for agricultural purposes will be per-

Healthy flocks of sheep for breeding purposes have been reared under scientific care at Haradh (above). Near Burayda (right) fat cattle on a private farm bear witness to skills in husbandry.

mitted only if it is clearly in the long-term public interest. A National Water Policy, with provisions for the enforcement of a National Water Code and National Water Standards, is being developed. Public awareness must be improved so that sound water management can be implemented and conservation practised throughout the Kingdom.

On the completion of studies carried out by the Ministry of Agriculture and

140

Water through consultant firms, comprehensive plans for decreasing the cost of agricultural production, raising production capacity in the agricultural sector and establishing an economic balance between domestic consumption and imports were approved. Finance priority will be given to projects which increase the national and individual income and also to programmes by which increased yields can be economically produced. Such projects include the irrigation and drainage scheme at Hasa, the Wadi Jizam dam, several other earth dams and a variety of agricultural experiments. Saudi Arabia has a good chance of achieving a high level of self-sufficiency. Depending on the quantities of water made available and the expertise of the cultivators, a great variety of crops is possible.

The three main objectives for agricultural development are to raise the *per capita* income and improve the welfare of rural people, minimize the

Kingdom's dependence on imported food and release surplus labour for employment in other sectors.

Fifteen research stations and demonstration farms have already been established and there are sixty-two extension units throughout the country. A Government subsidy on fertilizers has encouraged their use, and insecticides and pesticides are being distributed. An Agricultural Bank has been set up, and has continuously expanded interest-free credit to farmers. To encourage the adoption of modern technology and to increase farm production, the Government pays subsidies on selected imports and products.

The leaders of the country are committed to the processes of agricultural development. They recognize its connection with the maintenance of political stability.

A Saudi tractorman works land reclaimed from infertile loess.

Fruit, poultry and honey

Figs (*top left*), grapes (*middle left*) and pimentoes (*bottom left*) speak of diversity of fruit production. Contrary to popular belief, much of the soil of Saudi Arabia is cultivable. Only the sand desert will grow nothing. The great expanses of powdery loess "desert" would bloom if water could reach it. Where this has been possible, vivid patches of green enliven the dun of the landscape. Meanwhile, more specialist areas of food production are being exploited. Saudi Arabia is already a major exporter of fruit to neighbouring countries, and egg farms are run on scientific methods (*right, top and middle*), providing a protein diet for people who, in earlier generations, had depended largely on dates, rice and sorghum. Bee culture (*bottom right*) has recently been added to the country's indigenous industries.

Other successful crops of fruit include water-melon, squash and tomatoes. The development of cash crops has been greatly stimulated by the expansion not only of the water supply (usually from underground), but also of the road system. Many small trucking enterprises have sprung up, linking producers with their markets in other parts of the country.

Local production of such foods is swiftly changing dietary habits. Dates are seldom, today, a staple; although they remain an important supplementary food. At the same time, the reclamation of the desert and the marking out of new smallholdings act as a spur to settlement.

Communications

THE romantic view that travel and communications in Saudi Arabia depend on the camel, the caravan and the dhow, has long been belied by reality. For more than a generation Saudis have enjoyed most Western means of communication, from a complex modern road network to sophisticated telecommunications. The Ministry of Communications and the Ministry of Telecommunications and Postal Affairs have become two of the most active and important Ministries in the Kingdom. This importance is reflected in the "Physical infra-structure development" section of the 1395 AH (1975 CE) five year plan. International and inter-city transportation networks were to be developed in anticipation of increased passenger and goods traffic; so were the telecommunications and postal services. Old roads, airports, railways and ports were all due to be expanded and improved, and new ones were to be built. The realization of these ambitious plans during the subsequent five years necessitated complex planning, energetic recruiting of manpower, and very considerable budgetary allocations from the Government.

As the map on page 144 shows, there was already a substantial road network in the Kingdom. This was to be extended and in some areas replaced by all-weather tarmac roads linking the Kingdom with its neighbours, Jordan, Syria, Yemen and Kuwait. Rural roads were to be expanded to facilitate agricultural, mineral and industrial development. Studies and designs for 3,540 miles of primary roads, 4,000 miles of secondary and tertiary bitumen-surface roads, and 6,000 miles of new roads were being undertaken. "Back-up" services are as important as the actual construction processes, so laboratory testing of materials, road research, maintenance teams and improved safety measures had to be provided; SR 14,000 million was allocated for these purposes. (*See also* Construction.)

As the demand increased for imported capital and consumer goods to support the development of the economy, the major ports of Jiddah and Dammam expanded at a remarkable rate, as did the lesser ports of Yanbu and Jizan. More berths were to be constructed, and the amount of cargo handled per berth was to be increased. Specialized industrial facilities were to be set up at Jizan and Yanbu.

Minor Red Sea ports – Duba, Aflaj, Lith, Qunfidhah – and minor Arabian Gulf ports – Uqayr, Darin, al-Birk Zehma and al-Khubar – were being provided with improved facilities for small boats and fishing. Improved training programmes for the personnel of these ports were in hand.

Great distances and the difficult terrain of much of Saudi Arabia has made aviation a vital element in the transport network. At the time of writing there were forty-nine national and international airports served on a regular basis by Saudia, the national airline (*see* map): Kuala Lumpur, Taiwan and Tokyo were to be added by 1978. A fleet of five Tri-Stars, six Boeing 707s, two 720s and three 737s was operating by early 1977. Already, by 1974 CE (1394 AH) some 350,000 international and more than one million domestic passenger departures by scheduled flights were being recorded. Jiddah, Riyadh and Dhahran account for more than eighty per cent of air movements. The Civil Aviation Department has already vastly improved airport facilities, and this programme will be continued and expanded to provide for a rapidly growing volume of air traffic. Highly qualified personnel are being recruited to man the flight controls at all airports, for search and rescue, for freighting services, for information services, for the aeronautical training centre, and to represent the Kingdom in international aviation organizations.

The Saudi Arabian Government Railroad Organization (SGRO) owns, operates and manages the Kingdom's railways and the port of Dammam. The rail system has two main sections, one running between Riyadh and Dammam, the other between Dammam and Dammam port. The Arabian climate and landscape presents challenging maintenance problems, especially those caused by drifting sand and seasonal flooding. The Government was aiming to develop the railways so that they offered an increasingly economic, convenient and reliable mode of transport.

Wireless telegraph stations were established in Mecca, Ta'if, Jiddah and Riyadh long ago, in the reign of King

As Jiddah airport approached completion of its reconstruction, Dhahran's (above and opposite) *already stood as a triumph of architectural caprice.*

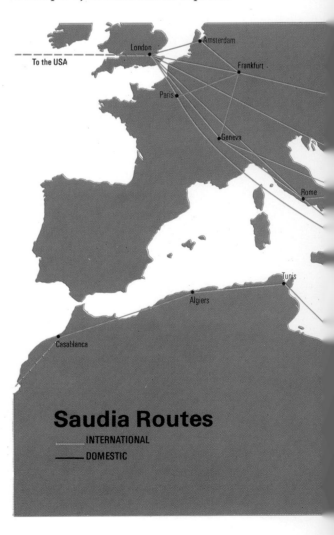

Saudia Routes

—— INTERNATIONAL

—— DOMESTIC

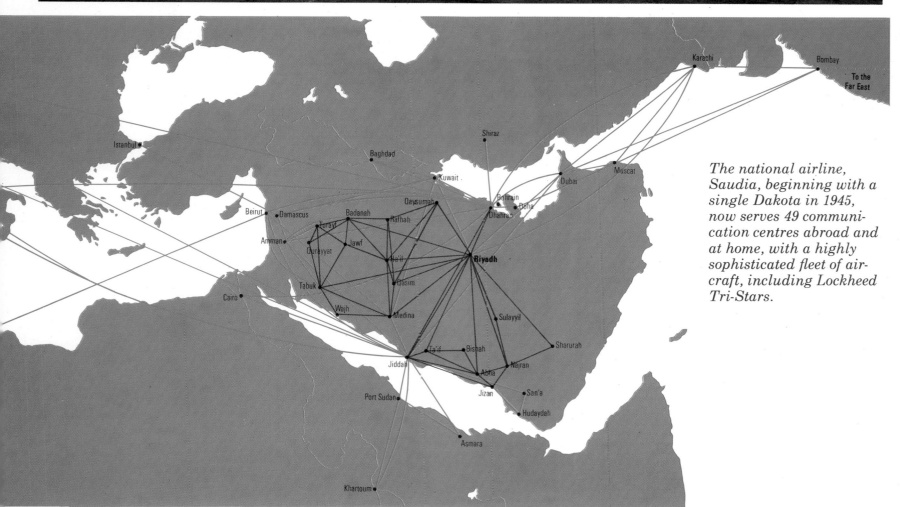

The national airline, Saudia, beginning with a single Dakota in 1945, now serves 49 communication centres abroad and at home, with a highly sophisticated fleet of aircraft, including Lockheed Tri-Stars.

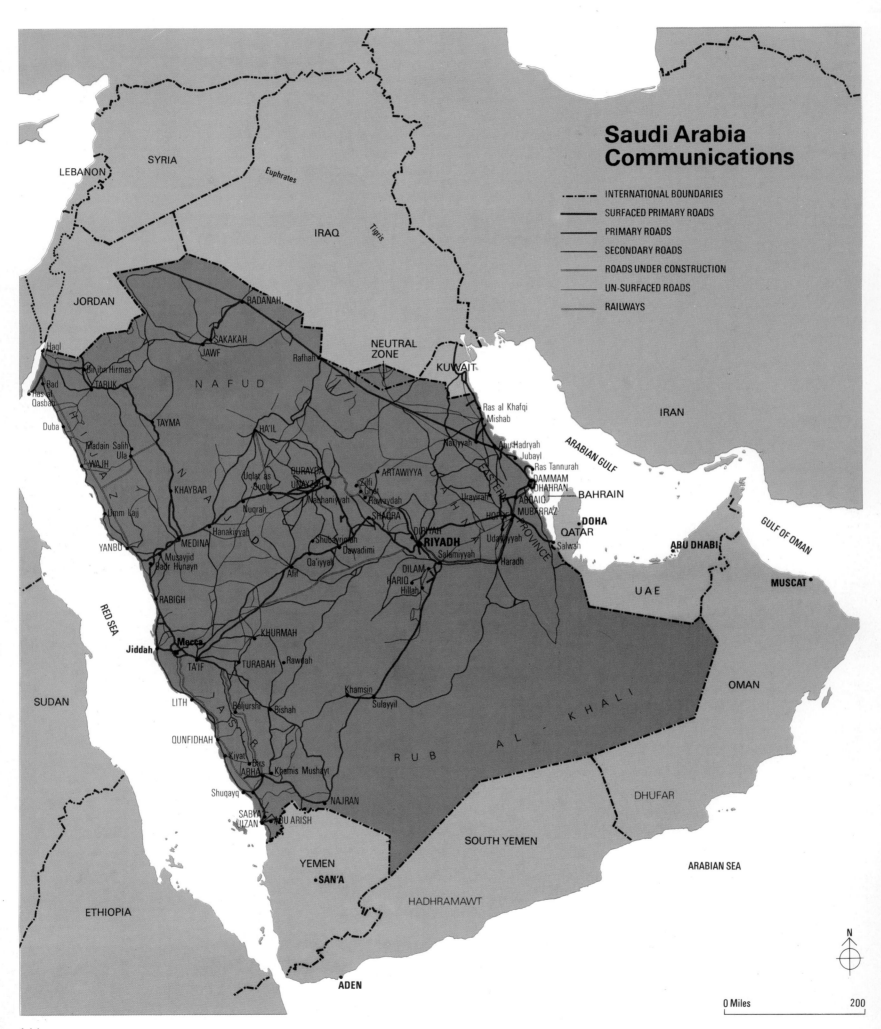

Saudi Arabia Communications

—·—·—	INTERNATIONAL BOUNDARIES
▬▬▬	SURFACED PRIMARY ROADS
━━━	PRIMARY ROADS
───	SECONDARY ROADS
━━━	ROADS UNDER CONSTRUCTION
───	UN-SURFACED ROADS
━━━	RAILWAYS

LEBANON

SYRIA

Euphrates

JORDAN

IRAQ

Tigris

NEUTRAL ZONE

KUWAIT

BADANAH

SAKAKAH

JAWF

Rafhah

Ras al Khafqi
Mishab

IRAN

ARABIAN GULF

Hagl

Bir ibn Hirmas

TABUK

NAFUD

Naftiyyah

Abu Hadryah
Jubayl
Ras Tannurah

Bad
Ras al
Qasbah

Duba

HIJAZ

TAYMA

HA'IL

DAMMAM
DHAHRAN

Madain Salih
Ula
WAJH

Uqlat as
Sugur

BURAYDA
UNAYZAH

ARTAWIYYA

Zilfi
Ghat

Ruwaydah

Urayrah

ABQAIQ
MUBARRAZ

BAHRAIN

DOHA

QATAR

Umm Lajj

KHAYBAR

Nathaniyyah

SHAQRA

HOFUF

Umm Lajj

Nuqrah

Hanakiyyah

Shubayriqah

DIRIYAH
RIYADH

Udawiyyah

Salwah

ABU DHABI

YANBU

MEDINA

Musayjid
Badr Hunayn

Afif

Qa'iyyah

Dawadimi

Salamiyyah

Haradh

GULF OF OMAN

DILAM
HARIQ
Hillah

EASTERN PROVINCE

MUSCAT

RABIGH

UAE

Jiddah

Mecca

KHURMAH

Khamsin

RUB   AL - KHALI

OMAN

TA'IF

TURABAH

Rawdah

RED SEA

Bishah

Sulayyil

LITH

Baljurshi

SUDAN

QUNFIDHAH

Kiyat

Bks

ABHA
Khamis Mushayt

NAJRAN

DHUFAR

Shuqayq

SABYA
JIZAN
ABU ARISH

YEMEN

SAN'A

SOUTH YEMEN

ARABIAN SEA

ETHIOPIA

HADHRAMAWT

ADEN

N

0 Miles   200

Abdul Aziz. Telephone systems followed and, in 1956, modern radio stations were set up. The Ministry of Communications (PTT) embarked upon large scale projects, both to develop the services, and to modernize the entire telecommunications system.

In 1974, the most modern means of long-distance communication was installed. Portable earth stations were established first at Riyadh, and later at Jiddah, working with the Indian Ocean satellite and using Rome as the gateway. Standard earth stations were then built in Riyadh and Ta'if. The portable ones will be moved to Abha and Burayda. Telephone, telegraph, telex and television systems also link Saudi Arabia nationally and internationally. New services and expansion projects were being undertaken in many places throughout the Kingdom, so that the installations would be less concentrated on the large centres of population.

Postal services have made considerable progress: a twenty-four hour service for inland mail was being widely established. But facilities were still antiquated and there was a shortage of trained manpower. Fixed sorting and delivery schedules improved the inland mail, but much remained to be done to make mail handling procedures more efficient; automation was necessary. New post office buildings and equipment were being set up, and mobile facilities tested. Recruiting methods, qualifications and pay scales were being studied, reviewed and improved. There are postal training courses in secondary schools. The National Computer Centre was being used to improve statistical and accounting methods. Specialized financial sections dealt with foreign post. The five year development plan aimed for "a prompt service of unquestionable reliability". The sophisticated changes which were planned would, when implemented, swiftly transform the whole of the Kingdom's communications system, so long overstrained.

A sophisticated road system has already given the well-populated areas of Saudi Arabia their vital ground communication links. Many roads, like the Jiddah–Ta'if highway, are monuments to modern road building. An efficient railway service links Riyadh and Haradh to the eastern port of Dammam.

Ports

Over seventy million tons of shipping docks annually at Saudi Arabia's major ports, of which the foremost is Jiddah (*below and right*). Jiddah has expanded enormously since the days of only a couple of generations ago when its principal traffic was shiploads of pilgrims bound for Mecca. Dammam (*bottom, far right*), and Jubayl on the Gulf have been built to cope with rapidly increasing traffic. Yanbu on the Red Sea coast was designated to become the country's second port, above all to relieve Jiddah. The immense inflow of goods led to acute congestion, especially at Jiddah, where ships were obliged to wait many weeks to unload. Urgent cargo had to be unloaded by helicopter. The main loading of shipped oil can take place by the pipeline off Ras Tannurah (*see also* page 182).

Port Handling Capacity & General Cargo Traffic

1 EXISTING CAPACITY **2** ADDITIONS UNDER WAY **3** PLANNED CAPACITY WITH MECHANISED HANDLING

Jiddah
IN MILLIONS OF TONS

9·6

37 BERTHS

6·2

7 BERTHS 3·3 2

12 BERTHS

TRAFFIC 1·4 1

1970 73 75 1980

Damman
IN MILLIONS OF TONS

8·2 4

7·4

32 BERTHS

7 BERTHS 2·6

TRAFFIC 1·4 1 9 BERTHS 3 1

1970 73 75 1980

Television

It was the late King Faisal who recognized television as a means of bringing to people in their homes a widening of knowledge and a more vivid sense of the unity and achievement of their own country. In a land where the public cinema was disallowed, the decision to create a national television network came as a surprise to some. A sophisticated service steadily developed, linked by Telstar to international networks for programmes and news from abroad, and bringing a familiarity with the affairs and leadership of the homeland among the people which would have been otherwise impossible.

With television established since 1964 as a widespread means of communication and education in the major cities and population centres, sophisticated studios produce a variety of indigenous programmes in Jiddah and Riyadh. Increasingly, local news events are covered by Outside Broadcasting units (left). *The advent of television has encouraged home-grown musical and dramatic talent* (below). *Original work by Saudis is now being written for television production.*

The Telstar link, originally operating from the Post Office site in Riyadh (above), *links Saudi Arabia with international television transmissions.*

Below: *Government employees in the media field are taught the multilingual techniques of their trade in a language laboratory.*

Development and the Economy

The resource of wealth is only one of the factors in an economy developing as fast as Saudi Arabia's. There is the factor of absorptive capacity – and, here, manpower and the country's infrastructure are paramount.

HAVING too much money may sound like an enviable problem, but, for Saudi Arabia, it is a real one with political and economic consequences. The country's immense oil revenues make it possible, in a way which is perhaps historically unique, for the Government to plan virtually any developments, including a total transformation of the economic and industrial base, without financial constraint. Theoretically everything can be done at one.

But, in practice, everything cannot be done at once. Pumping huge sums of money into a relatively undeveloped economy causes inflation, social upheaval and innumerable bottlenecks.

Opposite political pressures quickly arise, as they have in Saudi Arabia. On the one hand, there are impatient young Saudis who complain that the Government is moving too slowly. On the other hand, older and more cautious people are now asking for a slowdown, for a system of priorities, and for greater care in protecting a social structure which is inevitably being shaken by the speed of change.

Very rapid development continues to be the Government's declared aim, entailing – in principle – the expenditure of its entire revenue. The second development plan called for appropriations nine times larger than those of the first plan. The money, it was confidently predicted, would come from oil revenue, from foreign investment and from taxes on foreign economic activity in Saudi Arabia, while still leaving a considerable reserve balance, even allowing for a "significant inflation of costs".

How ambitious the plan was can be seen from the fact that Iran's expenditure target was barely half that of Saudi Arabia, despite the fact that Iran has a population five times as large and a much broader based administrative and economic infrastructure. It soon became evident that the Saudi Arabian Government could not disburse as much money on domestic expenditure as had been hoped; some of its projects would have to be postponed, or the time scale lengthened.

This is not necessarily a bad thing. Although there may be no contradiction between the traditional values of Islam and modern ideas of education, welfare and high consumption, the cultural shock produced by so much rapid spending and by the need to bring in some 500,000 people from outside the Kingdom could not fail to be very great.

There is, however, an international political aspect as well. Saudi Arabia, unlike some of the other oil-producing countries, has followed a policy designed to stabilize the price of oil and to help the economies of the Western industrialized nations. As Sheikh Ahmed Zaki Yamani, the Saudi Minister of Oil and Mineral Wealth, put it, "We know that if your economy falls, we fall with you."

This policy entails producing and selling oil – exploiting what is inevitably a wasting asset, however large – faster than would be justified by Saudi Arabia's own immediate financial needs. A plan for using the surplus revenue may be politically and psychologically necessary.

Much of the planned expenditure is devoted to building up the physical infrastructure which will be required for future development. Still more roads, for example, are urgently needed, both to carry food, fuel and labour across Saudi Arabia's great empty distances and to facilitate overland freight trucking from Europe. Such road-building is expensive; during the first plan, the cost per kilometre proved twice as high as had been anticipated.

New roads are also needed for the distribution of seaborne imports, a flow which must itself greatly increase. One of the highest priorities is to develop the country's seaports. Jiddah, Yanbu and Jizan on the Red Sea and Dammam on the Gulf have become notorious bottlenecks. Many weeks of waiting time for a cargo ship at any port in Saudi Arabia has become normal. Several hundred ships can often be seen lying at anchor, which means the risk of cargoes deteriorating in the heat and humidity, and extra costs which are passed on to the consumer.

The two principal ports, Dammam on the east coast, and Jiddah on the west, are both handling well above their planned capacity but they have not been able to keep pace with the increased volume of shipping. The development plan provides for the construction of additional berths and storage facilities. Meanwhile some floating quays are being brought to Jiddah.

Physical limitations have not been the sole obstacle. The port administration has also been inadequate, and there has been a lack of competent manpower – of drivers to use forklift trucks and cranes, of tally clerks able to read English, of skilled personnel to operate the radio network.

Even when barges have been cleared, the merchandise has sometimes had to be left waiting on the quays because there is a chronic shortage of warehousing and the importers were not ready to move their goods inland.

Urgent efforts are being made to deal with this congestion. New port authorities have been established, and a priority system for unloading various categories of goods has been instituted. Passengers and livestock have top priority, then goods which are in short supply or needed quickly for government contracts. American and British advisory teams have been brought in to streamline the organization of the ports.

The construction of several entirely new ports is being discussed. But improving the flow of goods through the ports themselves will be useless if the only result is to create new bottlenecks elsewhere which is what was still tending to happen by the later 1970s. Road access to the ports is not sufficient to carry the extra flow and, when the goods escape from that bottleneck, there is nowhere for them to be stored.

Importers have been looking for alternative routes. Airfreighting has increased, which has led to a pile-up of cargo at the airports. Smaller loads can come by truck from Europe, a seventeen-day journey, but delays have often built up at the frontier.

The whole situation vividly illustrates

Saudi Arabia's economic problem. So many things need to be developed simultaneously.

The shortage of water is another limiting factor. Irrigation has consumed, in recent years, about seventy-five per cent of the available water supply. The growing demands of industry and the cities cannot be met from local sources.

Even in the Eastern Province, where water has not hitherto been a problem, shortages could soon be felt, because this is also the region in which most of the country's oil and gas is situated, which means that industrial demand is growing very fast. By 1980 oil-well injection alone will account for a quarter of the predicted demand. The Jubayl industrial site will need as much water as Mecca.

The second development plan tackles this problem from both sides. On the one hand, it restricts to specially approved projects any further agricultural use of water, and it will steer new industrial enterprises to locations near the sea; and, on the other hand, it involves a massive programme of sea-water desalination. This desalination programme is intended to provide seventy-four per cent of the total water resources allocation – an additional output of some 314,000 cubic metres a day.

Industrial development requires large and continuous amounts of energy. During the foreseeable future, oil and natural gas will provide most of this energy, and Saudi Arabia is, of course, uniquely well endowed. The reserves should last for many decades. But alternative sources of energy are being actively explored. Consideration is being given, for example, to joint venture research and development work in solar energy and protein production from hydrocarbons.

The most acute and frustrating shortage, however, is of men. At managerial and professional level the need was expected to double between 1975 and 1980. Every trainable Saudi Arabian could be absorbed and there would still be a serious deficiency. The education and training programmes, which are already very large, will be hugely expanded. But there is a limit to what can be done. Money alone cannot provide teachers and train officers as rapidly as it can supply equipment. The teachers have to be taught. Some 54,000 more professional people were seen as needed in 1975, and of these almost two-thirds would become teachers. In addition,

there would need to be another 170,000 trained civil servants.

At the same time, the demand for production and service workers, and for labourers both skilled and unskilled, is huge. The vocational and craft training centres which are being planned cannot

hope to provide more than a fraction of them. Already twenty per cent of the country's work force come from abroad; by 1980 the proportion was expected to be larger – perhaps thirty-five per cent – consisting of at least 800,000 people.

This influx of manpower will create

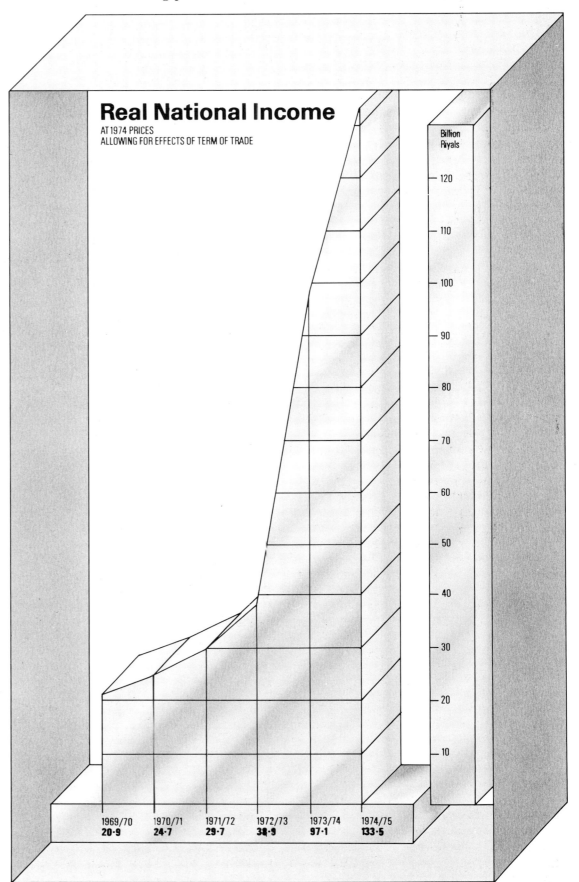

151

International Reserves of the Saudi Arabian Monetary Agency

IN MILLION RIYALS

INCLUDING PART OF GOVERNMENT'S SUBSCRIPTION TO IMF ☆
INCLUDING OIL FACILITY LENDING TO IMF ★

	☆ GOLD	FOREIGN EXCHANGE	★ INVESTMENTS	TOTAL
4 NOVEMBER 1964	350	2,279	48	2,677
30 APRIL 1965	350	2,536	101	2,987
24 OCTOBER 1965	349	2,839	118	3,306
20 APRIL 1966	349	2,971	237	3,557
14 OCTOBER 1966	349	2,987	294	3,630
10 APRIL 1967	349	3,463	414	4,226
30 OCTOBER 1967	349	3,487	598	4,434
29 MARCH 1968	349	3,222	755	4,326
22 SEPTEMBER 1968	574	2,799	848	4,221
18 MARCH 1969	574	2,900	687	4,161
11 SEPTEMBER 1969	574	2,342	696	3,612
7 MARCH 1970	574	2,242	691	3,507
1 SEPTEMBER 1970	574	2,343	789	3,706
25 FEBRUARY 1971	574	2,909	785	4,268
21 AUGUST 1971	574	4,404	825	5,803
15 FEBRUARY 1972	574	5,515	764	6,853
9 AUGUST 1972	574	8,193	802	9,569
3 FEBRUARY 1973	574	10,833	983	12,390
29 JULY 1973	574	14,086	1,624	16,284
23 JANUARY 1974	546	13,094	2,293	15,933
19 JULY 1974	546	28,689	10,347	39,582
12 JANUARY 1975	546	51,234	25,992	77,773

Money Supply

IN MILLION RIYALS

	CURRENCY OUTSIDE BANKS	PRIVATE DEMAND DEPOSITS	TOTAL
4 NOVEMBER 1964	892·9	516·9	1,409·8
30 APRIL 1965	963·7	517·8	1,481·5
24 OCTOBER 1965	977·8	537·7	1,515·5
20 APRIL 1966	1,061·8	569·9	1,631·7
14 OCTOBER 1966	1,103·6	618·5	1,722·1
10 APRIL 1967	1,219·5	666·6	1,886·1
3 OCTOBER 1967	1,241·4	701·1	1,942·5
29 MARCH 1968	1,370·2	759·3	2,129·5
22 SEPTEMBER 1968	1,373·8	739·6	2,213·4
18 MARCH 1969	1,466·2	803·8	2,270·0
11 SEPTEMBER 1969	1,452·5	808·3	2,260·8
7 MARCH 1970	1,566·9	838·6	2,405·5
1 SEPTEMBER 1970	1,528·3	812·1	2,340·4
25 FEBRUARY 1971	1,655·8	876·6	2,532·4
21 AUGUST 1971	1,641·6	967·8	2,609·4
15 FEBRUARY 1972	1,788·2	1,006·8	2,795·0
9 AUGUST 1972	1,951·2	1,309·4	3,260·6
3 FEBRUARY 1973	2,296·3	1,465·4	3,761·7
29 JULY 1973	2,487·8	2,259·3	4,747·1
23 JANUARY 1974	2,943·4	2,311·1	5,254·5
19 JULY 1974	3,374·5	3,195·2	6,569·7
12 JANUARY 1975	4,072·8	3,710·7	7,783·5

Currency in Circulation

IN MILLION RIYALS

	CURRENCY ISSUED	HELD BY S.A.M.A.	HELD BY COMMERCIAL BANKS	CURRENCY OUTSIDE BANKS
4 NOVEMBER 1964	1,038·0	97·8	47·3	892·9
30 APRIL 1965	1,135·2	88·3	83·2	963·7
24 OCTOBER 1965	1,126·8	99·1	49·9	977·8
20 APRIL 1966	1,284·4	125·8	96·8	1,061·8
14 OCTOBER 1966	1,283·3	119·1	60·6	1,103·6
10 APRIL 1967	1,441·9	137·0	85·4	1,219·5
3 OCTOBER 1967	1,441·8	138·7	61·7	1,241·4
29 MARCH 1968	1,621·9	150·5	101·2	1,370·2
22 SEPTEMBER 1968	1,622·0	177·6	70·6	1,373·8
18 MARCH 1969	1,825·8	248·1	111·5	1,466·2
11 SEPTEMBER 1969	1,713·3	200·0	60·8	1,452·5
7 MARCH 1970	1,893·2	216·7	109·6	1,566·9
1 SEPTEMBER 1970	1,852·8	238·2	59·2	1,528·3
25 FEBRUARY 1971	2,096·1	316·8	123·5	1,655·8
21 AUGUST 1971	1,925·8	221·5	62·7	1,641·6
15 FEBRUARY 1972	2,214·1	264·1	161·8	1,788·2
9 AUGUST 1972	2,254·5	234·5	68·8	1,951·2
3 FEBRUARY 1973	2,784·7	347·9	140·5	2,296·3
29 JULY 1973	2,857·0	251·9	117·3	2,487·8
23 JANUARY 1974	3,553·3	401·9	208·0	2,943·4
19 JULY 1974	3,926·0	395·1	156·4	3,374·5
12 JANUARY 1975	4,920·0	521·4	321·3	4,072·8

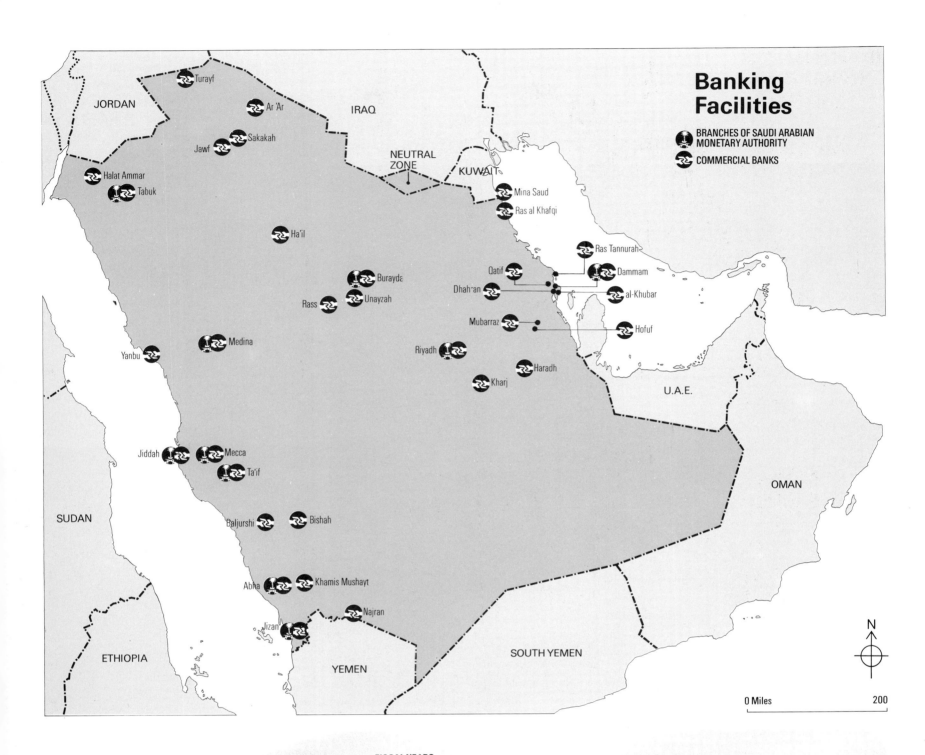

Banking Facilities

BRANCHES OF SAUDI ARABIAN MONETARY AUTHORITY

COMMERCIAL BANKS

JORDAN
IRAQ
NEUTRAL ZONE
KUWAIT
Turayf
Ar 'Ar
Sakakah
Jawf
Halat Ammar
Tabuk
Ha'il
Mina Saud
Ras al Khafqi
Ras Tannurah
Qatif
Dammam
Burayda
Dhah'an
al-Khubar
Rass
Unayzah
Mubarraz
Hofuf
Medina
Riyadh
Yanbu
Haradh
Kharj
U.A.E.
Jiddah
Mecca
Ta'if
OMAN
Baljurshi
Bishah
SUDAN
Abha
Khamis Mushayt
Najran
Jizan
ETHIOPIA
YEMEN
SOUTH YEMEN

N

0 Miles   200

Budget Government Expenditure

IN MILLION RIYALS

	FISCAL YEARS 1970/71	1971/72	1972/73	1973/74	1974/75	1975/76
COUNCIL OF MINISTERS	752·5	1,025·4	1,194·1	1,815·2	5,620·6	10,330·1
INFORMATION	75·9	118·2	165·4	249·7	321·8	802·6
FOREIGN AFFAIRS	59·2	79·1	107·9	153·0	221·5	327·2
DEFENCE & AVIATION	1,866·3	2 346·5	3,547·4	5,408·4	8,813·3	23,723·7
INTERIOR	827·5	1 379·6	1,867·2	3,227·6	6,601·5	19,278·9
LABOUR & SOCIAL AFFAIRS	187·6	309·8	347·0	525·8	1,406·6	3,891·9
HEALTH	177·1	279·3	420·9	582·8	1,163·0	3,197·4
EDUCATION	662·1	1,156·9	1,600·0	2,243·2	3,781·2	12,973·9
COMMUNICATIONS	632·6	1,482·6	1,435·1	2,282·5	4,558·2	11,564·6
FINANCE & NATIONAL ECONOMY	261·2	526·3	773·6	1,340·7	2,052·3	7,431·5
PETROLEUM & MINERAL RESOURCES	58·8	107·8	117·4	174·9	211·6	401·4
COMMERCE & INDUSTRY	24·3	49·8	70·1	90·7	164·3	841·8
AGRICULTURE & WATER RESOURCES	312·5	568·6	708·1	1,031·9	1,303·2	2,178·4
PILGRIMAGE & ENDOWMENTS	53·0	88·3	120·2	142·5	243·8	455·3
JUSTICE & RELIGIOUS AFFAIRS	102·3	93·3	108·1	132·1	204·5	353·8
FOREIGN AID	420·0	680·0	680·0	710·0	4,758·0	4,658·1
SUBSIDIES	109·1	140·5	155·3	147·0	1,317·6	6,924·4
PUBLIC INVESTMENT FUND	–	350·0	250·0	2,552·0	3,000·0	1,600·0
LESS EXPECTED SAVING	62·0	–	467·8			
TOTAL EXPENDITURE	**6,380·0**	**10,782·0**	**13,200·0**	**22,810·0**	**45,743·0**	**110,935·0**

There is more to hydrocarbons than oil. Natural gas is a fast-growing industry for industrial power; so, too, are petrochemicals, fertilisers produced from oil, and asphalt.

capital and skills in the industrial development of the country.

Hydrocarbon-based Industries

Over the five years from 1970 there were a number of major achievements. Examples are the forty-three per cent increase in production of the Ras Tannurah refinery between 1969 and 1974, the doubling of asphalt production and the great increase in fertilizer production. Over the following five years major developments will include the creation of new refineries, the construction of gas heating facilities and a programme for pipelines linking the various regions of the Kingdom.

In the longer term, Petromin will be concerned with various projects, including the expansion of existing refineries and the construction of new ones, leading in turn to the creation of gas heating plants able to produce 1,600 million cubic feet per day of gas for industrial use, and to the construction of several petrochemical plants, two fertilizer plants (ammonia and urea), a steel plant in Jubayl, sulphuric acid plants in both eastern and western regions and the necessary handling and storage facilities for these new products.

Non-hydrocarbon-based Industries

The most important non-hydrocarbon-based industry in recent times has been the cement industry, in which production increased one hundred per cent between 1969 and 1974. Its capacity will continue to increase rapidly in support of the major new construction programmes already under way. For example, plans for integrated grain storage, flour and feed milling complexes at Jiddah, Riyadh and Dammam were being realized in the latter 1970s. These complexes were to have a storage capacity equal to half a year's consumption of wheat. This expansion in cement production has been matched by the creation and development of other industries associated with the construction of new buildings – glass, furniture, textiles and fabrics, paints and plastics. In addition, new licences were issued by the Ministry of Commerce and Industry for companies involved in food processing, paper products, printing and publishing, leather and rubber, clothing, household goods and metal working.

Another important programme concerned the supply of irrigation equip-

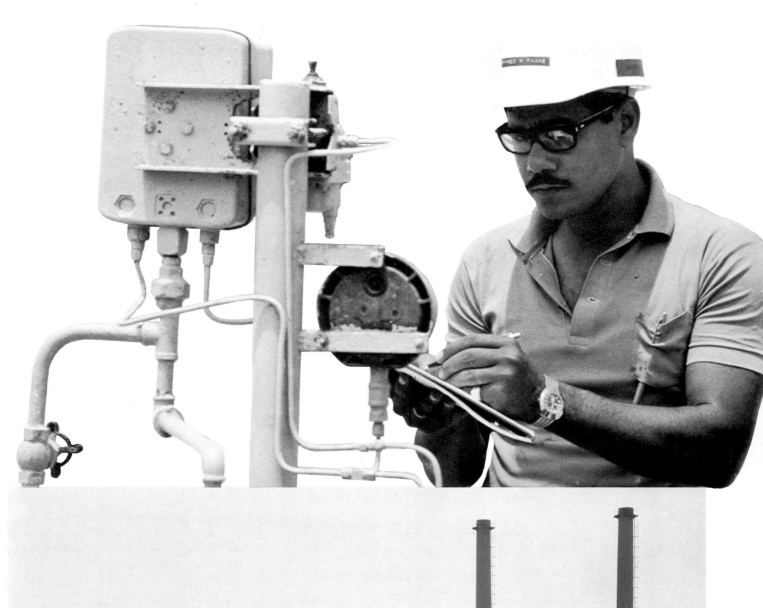

Industries firmly based on indigenous resources include natural gas at Haradh (left), *and water desalination* (above right and right).

159

*By the mid-1970s, Saudi Arabia was
producing no more than 50,000 tons of
its own iron and steel. But plans
existed to have increased this quantity
tenfold by the end of the decade.*

The economy flourishes under a system of free enterprise, by which both big ventures and small are given financial encouragement to build themselves up.

nical training "at the grass roots".

Financial support is as important as technical support, and the Saudi Industrial Development Fund was formed to provide venture capital and loans to private enterprise. The Fund is instrumental in liaising with the world financial community. The Saudi Arabian Monetary Agency (SAMA) encourages the expansion of equity and working capital for manufacturing enterprises provided by commercial banks and public and private investment funds.

The private investor is encouraged to take a stake in Saudi industry by the provisions of the Council of Ministers resolution of 1394 (1974 CE), enabling individuals to own shares in joint-stock companies. By 1396 (1976 CE) the Government had worked out ways of creating a capital market within the Kingdom to facilitate equity financing by private investors.

The siting of new factories is an integral part of government planning, and is implemented so as to open up new industrial areas in the Kingdom. Under the direction of the Ministry of Industry and Electricity, technical service workshops are being integrated into industrial estates at Jiddah, Riyadh and Dammam. New estates are envisaged in Mecca, Hofuf, Qasim and other secondary cities. Planning studies for a major industrial estate complex for hydrocarbon-based industries at Jubayl are under way.

To reinforce the financial and legal frameworks essential to industry, commercial codes are being improved so as to simplify the adjudication of business disputes and the clarification of legal matters. A major review of the laws which affect tendering is regarded as necessary to ensure that the operational problems of manufacturers – inflationary trends in costs, unforeseeable pro-

duction shutdowns and changes in tender specifications after bid approval – are recognized. Commercial law was being adapted to cover such transactions as mortgage, credit, licensing, royalty and insurance agreements. Many aspects of industrial business operation were not encompassed by the existing legal system.

With the speed of industrial expansion and diversification which the Kingdom has been experiencing, manpower mobilization and training presents a considerable challenge. Throughout the period of the plan, the Government was co-operating with manpower development agencies in supplying information concerning present and projected industrial manpower requirements, and in planning for recruitment and training. These agencies were implementing vocational training programmes and in-plant training, as well as enabling management and professional personnel to acquire specialized qualifications.

Planning for manufacturing industry is not restricted to a five year period. Longer term considerations are constantly being explored and provisions are made to deal with any unforeseen constraints on short-term programmes. One example will be the classification of development programmes into order of priority, in case critical shortages arise in the resources needed to carry out all these programmes simultaneously.

Saudi Arabia has not neglected small scale ventures in its drive to modernize industry. From its dependence on oil, it has diversified over a wide range, from large scale pipeline manufacture to the design and making of handicrafts in the rural communities. There are opportunities for workers at all levels of ability to help in building the economic strength of the Kingdom.

(*See also* Construction.)

KEEP CLEAR

Construction

The massive building programme has inspired the international community of architects and designers to stretch their skills and imaginations. All government projects are put out to international tender. British, American, Japanese, German, Lebanese, French, Italian and Egyptian architects have all been successfully at work. More recently, indigenous Saudi Arabian architects have played a part. New wealth spreading among the population has inspired originality in home building.

Given Saudi Arabia's low rainfall, ferro-concrete (left) has become the most-used construction medium. Though concrete absorbs rather than reflects heat, internal air-conditioning is de rigueur. Concrete has a plasticity which allows for imaginative design. Below: *the brilliantly lit Audit Department makes a striking focus of attention in Riyadh at night.* Right, *the Queen's Building in Jiddah, framed by the tall uprights of an hotel roof.*

The top of the water tower in Riyadh (top picture) *affords a splendid panorama of the city and its environs. An original roof design distinguishes an east coast villa* (above), *while a new hotel* (left) *encloses an elegant stairway. It is the cleanliness of the atmosphere and the strong light that have stimulated architects and designers into attempting forceful new ideas – both in detail, and on the grand scale – in new townships and universities.*

Probability of Oil Occurrence

■ FAVOURABLE
■ POSSIBLE

The first tanker was loaded on 1 May 1939.

In 1944 the Company's name was changed to Arabian American Oil Company (Aramco), by which it is known today. Mobil (formerly Socony-Vacuum Oil Company) and Exxon (formerly Standard Oil Company of New Jersey) obtained shares in 1946, and ownership of Aramco was divided on the basis of thirty per cent each for Socal, Texaco and Exxon, with ten per cent for Mobil.

The discovery and development of Saudi Arabia's oil fields began slowly, affected by transportation difficulties and material shortages resulting from the Second World War. Activity resumed in a limited way in the autumn of 1943 when plans were announced for a 50,000 barrels a day refinery at Ras Tannurah. With the ending of hostilities, Aramco's crude oil production jumped from an average 20,000 barrels a day before 1944 to 500,000 barrels daily by the end of 1949. By 1974, Aramco was producing 8,209,706 barrels of oil per day; its refinery at Ras Tannurah was turning out 482,411 barrels a day of products for marketing in Saudi Arabia and abroad.

Aramco accounted for ninety-seven per cent of Saudi Arabia's production,

but it was not the only oil company operating in the Kingdom. The Getty Oil Company was assigned a concession in Saudi Arabia's undivided share of the Neutral Zone in 1949 and, in co-operation with Aminoil (the American company carrying Kuwait's fifty per cent interest in the Neutral Zone), discovered oil in what is called the Wafrah field in 1953. The Japanese-owned Arabian Oil Company was assigned a concession by both Saudi Arabia and Kuwait to explore the offshore area of the Neutral Zone in 1958, and discovered oil in the Khafji field in 1960. In 1974, the Saudi share of daily production from the Neutral Zone amounted to 270,000 barrels a day.

At the end of 1974, Saudi Arabia's estimated crude oil reserves amounted to 181.2 billion barrels, representing about twenty-five per cent of total world crude oil reserves. Saudi Arabia is the third largest producer of crude oil in the world, topped only by the Soviet Union and the United States. Of the forty-six million barrels produced each day in the non-communist world, about eighteen per cent comes out of Saudi Arabia, and since ninety-eight per cent of Saudi Arabia's production is exported, Saudi Arabia is the world's biggest oil exporter.

The following illustrations give an indication of the magnitude and importance of Saudi Arabia as a world energy supplier. In 1974 Saudi Arabia's rate of liquid hydrocarbon production was equal to about one-tenth of all primary energy consumed in the non-communist world (including coal, oil, lignite, peat, gas, hydro-electric energy, geothermal energy, and nuclear energy). It could generate all the electricity produced in the whole of South America and Western Europe combined.

The trans-Arabian pipe line, known as Tapline, built by Aramco in the late 1940s, starts at Qaysumah, in northeastern Saudi Arabia, and runs for 542 miles to Lebanon's port of Sidon on the Mediterranean coast, through temperatures varying from a freezing 10° Fahrenheit to 120°

Such extreme temperature changes cause the steel to expand and contract, and can build up formidable pressures; but the stresses are absorbed, or "restrained", by careful design. A weak electric current is passed through the pipe to prevent corrosion. "Surge pressure control" is another safety device developed by Tapline engineers. If one of the unmanned pumping units suddenly

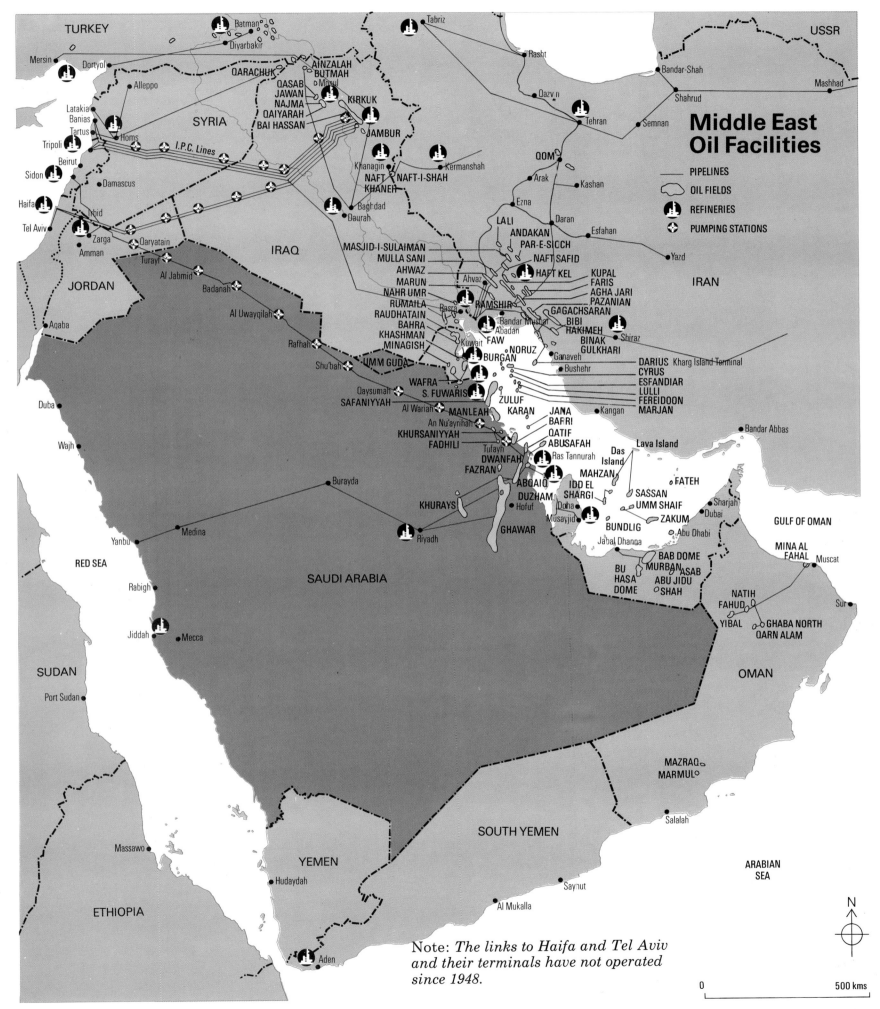

Middle East Oil Facilities

PIPELINES

OIL FIELDS

REFINERIES

PUMPING STATIONS

TURKEY

USSR

Mersin

Dortyol

Batman

Diyarbakir

Tabriz

Rasht

Bandar-Shah

Mashhad

Alleppo

QARACHUK

AINZALAH
BUTMAH

Mosul

Qazvın

Shahrud

Latakia
Banias

Tripoli

Tartus

Homs

SYRIA

I.P.C. Lines

QASAB
JAWAN
NAJMA
QAIYARAH
BAI HASSAN

KIRKUK

JAMBUR

Khanagin

Kermanshah

Tehran

Semnan

Beirut

Damascus

NAFT
KHANEH

NAFT-I-SHAH

Arak

Kashan

QOM

Sidon

Haifa

Irbid

Baghdad
Daurah

Ezna

Daran

Esfahan

Yazd

Tel Aviv

Zarga

Amman

Qaryatain

IRAQ

LALI
ANDAKAN
PAR-E-SICCH

IRAN

JORDAN

Turayf

Al Jabmid

Badanah

MASJID-I-SULAIMAN
MULLA SANI
AHWAZ
MARUN
NAHR UMR
RUMAILA
RAUDHATAIN
BAHRA
KHASHMAN
MINAGISH

Ahvaz

NAFT SAFID

HAFT KEL

KUPAL
FARIS
AGHA JARI
PAZANIAN

Aqaba

Al Uwayqilah

Basra

RAMSHIR

GAGACHSARAN

BIBI
HAKIMEH

BINAK
GULKHARI

Shiraz

Rafhah

Shu'bah

UMM GUDA

Kuwait

Bandar Mushal
Abadan

FAW

NORUZ

Ganaveh

Bushehr

DARIUS
CYRUS
ESFANDIAR
LULLI
FEREIDOON
MARJAN

Kharg Island Terminal

Duba

Qaysumah

Al Wariah

WAFRA
S. FUWARIS

ZULUF

KARAN

Bandar Abbas

SAFANIYYAH

An Nu'ayriyah

MANLEAH

JANA
BAFRI
QATIF
ABUSAFAH

Lava Island

Wajh

KHURSANIYYAH
FADHILI

Tufayh

Ras Tannurah

Das
Island

MAHZAN

FATEH

Medina

Yanbu

Burayda

KHURAYS

DWANFAH
FAZRAN

ABQAIQ
DUZHAM

IDD EL
SHARGI

SASSAN
UMM SHAIF
ZAKUM

Sharjah

Dubai

GULF OF OMAN

Hofuf

Doha

Musayjid

Jabal Dhanna

BUNDLIG

Abu Dhabi

MINA AL
FAHAL

Riyadh

GHAWAR

BAB DOME

BU
HASA
DOME

MURBAN
ASAB
ABU JIDU
SHAH

Muscat

RED SEA

Rabigh

SAUDI ARABIA

NATIH
FAHUD

YIBAL

GHABA NORTH
QARN ALAM

Sur

Jiddah

Mecca

OMAN

SUDAN

Port Sudan

Massawo

ETHIOPIA

YEMEN

Hudaydah

SOUTH YEMEN

Salalah

MAZRAQ
MARMUL

ARABIAN
SEA

Al Mukalla

Saynut

Aden

*Note: The links to Haifa and Tel Aviv
and their terminals have not operated
since 1948.*

N

0   500 kms

Exploration

Continued exploration for oil and gas proceeds not because any greater production is required, but to establish as precisely as possible the extent of the country's reserves. Proved oil reserves already make Saudi Arabia a substantially richer country than any other. The presence of oil is calculated in the first instance by trough-like geological "structures", but to strike an oil seam usually involves an extensive phase of trial and error. By the mid-1970s, thirty fields had been discovered in Saudi Arabia: eight offshore, nineteen onshore, and three extending over both land and water. Of these, fifteen were producing oil. The Ghawar field was the world's largest field onshore, and Safaniyyah the largest offshore. There were also seven commercial fields in the Neutral Zone which Saudi Arabia shares with Kuwait.

While heavy drilling materials must be dragged across the surface of the desert by specially designed vehicles (left and above), *camps are supplied by air-drop from helicopters* (above, right). *Rock depths can be calculated either by drilling, or seismically by blast* (right). *A gusher may produce black oil, or* (far right), *gas.*

Refining

The heart of the oil refinery at Ras Tannurah (*left*), is the bubble car or fractionating column of the crude distillation unit. Into the bottom of the car is fed the heated crude oil, which is flashed into vapours. Crude oil is a mixture of different types of hydrocarbons, all having different boiling points. The vapours of the heavier hydrocarbons condense at a higher temperature near the bottom of the fractionating column. Those of the lighter hydrocarbons, such as kerosene and gasoline, bubble up through a series of trays until they condense at the relatively low temperatures at the top. Thus, a process of distillation separates the crude oil into various "fractions". Each fraction in turn must be refined before it is ready for the market. Fuel oil accounts for about half the production of the Ras Tannurah refinery, which refines more than 300,000 barrels of crude oil daily.

Beginning in 1939, Saudi Arabia has become the world's largest exporter of crude and refined oil.

Ras Tannurah to the Jiddah refinery. The Jiddah refinery itself is owned and operated by Petromin with a production capacity of 45,000 barrels a day. In 1974, Petromin completed construction of another refinery in Riyadh, with an initial capacity of 15,000 barrels a day, to supply refined products to the central areas of the Kingdom. Petromin also lays marine pipelines and supplies sea terminals and drilling rigs through its Arabian Marine Petroleum Construction Company (Marinco).

In the late 1950s, two Saudi officials joined Aramco's Board of Directors, and this number was later increased to three. In 1968, the Kingdom's interest turned to participation and ownership as well as management. In 1972, the Saudi Government acquired a twenty-five per cent interest in Aramco's crude oil concession rights. On 5 June 1974 this share was increased to sixty per cent. Negotiations were then initiated to bring the Government's participation up to one hundred per cent while preserving the role of the American companies in providing expertise.

Saudi Arabia's leaders realized early that technicians and trained personnel would be needed. The College of Petroleum and Minerals was therefore established in 1963 in Dhahran (see also Education). From an initial enrolment of sixty-seven in 1964, the College's student body grew to about 1,500 in 1974–75, and was expected to reach the 3,000 level by 1985. In 1974 the College moved to a new campus with the most up-to-date classroom, laboratory and workshop facilities and a computer centre. In 1975 the College became a University, offering programmes for a Master's Degree in Industrial Management and Petroleum Engineering.

Saudi Arabia realized that its petroleum resources were not infinite. Part of the resulting industrialization effort was directed to developing petrochemical industries so as to maximise profits on each barrel of crude oil produced while importing new technologies into the Kingdom. Hence Saudi Arabia also planned huge increases in its refining capacity (see also Development).

To support large scale industrializ-

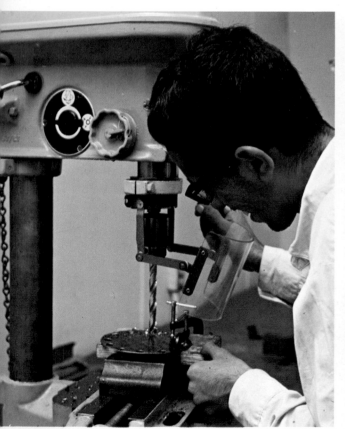

Oil production requires shortwave radio transmission between staff (above) *and a high technical precision* (below).

Aramco brings out over 95 per cent – the (Japanese) Arabian Oil Co. and Getty share the rest.

ation, a gas grid system was planned to provide just under 2,000 million cubic feet per day of methane and ethane gas. Under this plan, which was developed by Petromin, Aramco was to design, construct and operate a gas system enabling Saudi Arabia to utilize virtually all the gas produced in association with crude oil. This gas would be used to fuel the industrial complexes which were planned for both the Arabian Gulf and Red Sea coasts of Saudi Arabia, to

desalinate large quantities of sea-water, to generate several thousand megawatts of electric power, and to fuel Aramco's own operations. Such gas as could not be used locally was to be exported in the form of gas liquids.

For years, immense quantities of gas were wasted, for some 3,400 million cubic feet of gas were being produced daily, most of which it was necessary to flare off, a familiar sight in the Eastern Province to air or ground travellers.

Principal Petroleum Products

PROCESSED AT RAS TANNURAH REFINERY 1974
QUANTITY IN BARRELS

TOTAL 217,096,927

Product	Barrels
ASPHALT & MISCELLANEOUS	1,916,075
GASOLINE	6,822,961
KEROSENE	7,371,920
JET FUEL	7,815,765
NAPTHA	24,338,323
DIESEL OIL	27,147,523
NATURAL GAS LIQUIDS	50,235,620
FUEL OIL	91,448,740

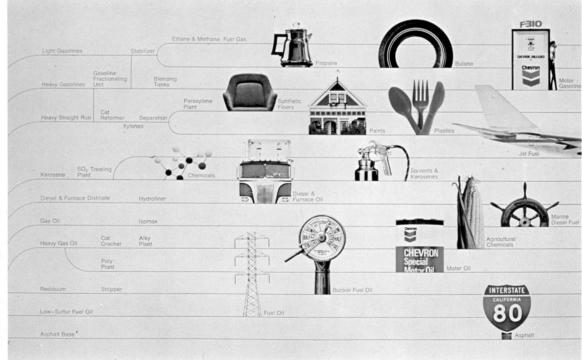

Massive tankers plying the Gulf route (including the world's largest, such as Globtek II) are fed their crude oil by pipeline direct from the Saudi oil fields. The reopened Suez canal shortened western routes but some tankers were too large.

Policy for Youth

THE youth of Saudi Arabia is growing up in a period of dramatic expansion. They are living at the centre of this drama: it is widely recognized that their innate abilities and talents should be as fully developed as possible. Luqman's proverb "A father's blows upon his son's back are like manure upon a field" could not be more outdated. Education is seen as the true means to build the personality of society's individual members, in order to enable them to continue developing their society. Education is free, but is regarded as imposing a debt on the student which he should repay by his service to the state.

In a Kingdom with a high level of illiteracy in the early 1960s a policy decision had to be made between opting for quality or opting for quantity of education. The urgent need for education led to the rapid expansion of primary and intermediate schooling. This emphasis resulted in a relatively small proportion of students passing on to secondary education. Perhaps the most worrying aspect during the period of the early 1970s was that substantially fewer pupils who qualified for secondary education actually availed themselves of the opportunity.

At the secondary stage the policy prevails of not allowing pupils to specialize too rigorously.

Although many educational books and syllabuses were initially imported from abroad, the aim of the Government has been to keep the study of Islamic beliefs as a basis of the educational system, so that new generations should not only achieve intellectual and practical skills, but should acquire them in the context of an awareness of their duties towards God and man.

Education is seen as a process which develops, controls and guides the life of a community towards its ideal, and awakens individual students to an awareness of their responsibilities towards their country. Different pupils with different aptitudes now have open to them a wide range of establishments in which they can gain practical and theoretical learning: at the secondary level

they can opt for the industrial education programme in technical institutes and the Higher Industrial Institute. At a higher level plans are prepared for a layer of polytechnics.

Commercial and administrative education has attracted far more pupils than

was originally envisaged. Teacher training is being expanded at secondary level institutes, in particular through the establishment of a junior college system for teacher training.

Young people are being encouraged to participate actively not only in intellectual pursuits but also in community activities, such as those attached to Community Development Centres.

School health services are being massively expanded, with a particular emphasis on preventive medicine; and sports facilities are growing as well. During 1974 the General Presidency for Youth Welfare was formed to frame policies for youth welfare. Eight general objectives have been formulated, and in achieving these objectives it will be the policy to ensure that services are comprehensive, integrated and justly distributed, and that the services are in harmony with both the Islamic code for rearing youth and modern knowledge of handling young people. A balanced education is looked for, such as will organize creative capabilities so that they both make an effective contribution to the nation's development, and support the family structure, by which great store is set in the Kingdom.

At the same time it is hoped to encourage young people to invest their free time in sporting and recreational activities that both enhance the enjoyment of living and improve physical fitness, so that the nation may raise the

standard of excellence in sports to an international level.

The Supreme Council for Youth Welfare provides programmes of activities in cultural, scientific, athletic and social fields. There are fifty-three sports clubs officially registered and nine national societies covering the following sports: football, basketball, volleyball, bicycling, handball, table-tennis, swimming, weaponry and athletics. (*See also* Sport.)

An Institute of Youth Leaders has been set up and youths are being encouraged to devote their energy and talents in public service at the local level – for example helping to eradicate illiteracy, repairing mosques and filling in swamps.

For children with a scientific bent, model science clubs are planned to start in 1977, with area competitions and annual exhibitions.

In 1976 television coverage of club athletics competitions was broadening that appeal. Seven new tough hostels and nine permanent youth camps are due to open in 1977.

By 1980 the Kingdom will be devoting twenty-five per cent of its resources to education. There are bound to be problems; yet the frustration of youth which has been a feature of Western societies and which at times has erupted in antisocial ways is considered unlikely to appear since the roots of that frustration lie in lack of facilities, educational and recreational, and in lack of opportunities.

Saudi Arabia is committed to the provision of superb facilities; few countries have experienced such a proliferation of opportunities for young people, whether male or female, to fulfil themselves as individuals, and as members of a nation.

A policy for youth, in a country where family ties are so strong, must take account of parental attitudes. It is seen as important that parents are themselves involved in the education and wider social activities of the young, and that a living relationship exists between home and school. The "generation gap" so evident outside the Kingdom, and which one would expect to be caused by so rapid a growth of change, may well thus be avoided.

Both the young and the old are enjoined to bear in mind the Prophet's recommendation for the adult to forgive the young and for the young to respect the adult.

Schools

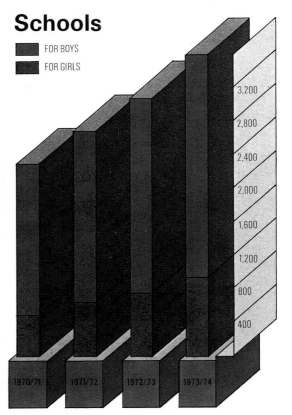

- FOR BOYS
- FOR GIRLS

3,200
2,800
2,400
2,000
1,600
1,200
800
400

1970/71 1971/72 1972/73 1973/74

From a literacy level of under 20 per cent two generations ago, Saudi Arabia already sends virtually every male child to primary school. By the 1980s, well over half the population will have secondary education.

Students

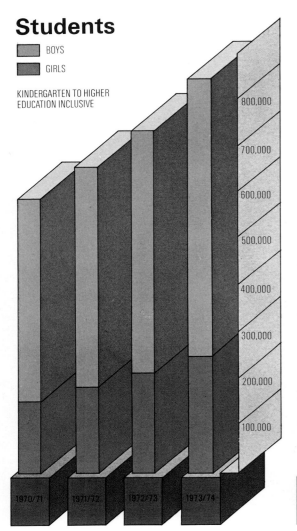

- BOYS
- GIRLS

KINDERGARTEN TO HIGHER
EDUCATION INCLUSIVE

800,000
700,000
600,000
500,000
400,000
300,000
200,000
100,000

1970/71 1971/72 1972/73 1973/74

Teachers

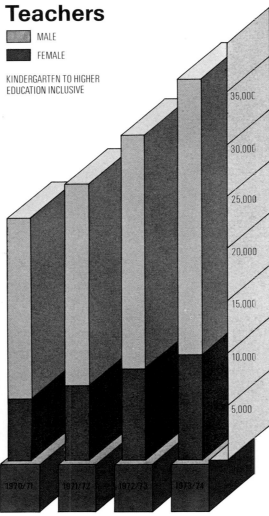

- MALE
- FEMALE

KINDERGARTEN TO HIGHER
EDUCATION INCLUSIVE

35,000
30,000
25,000
20,000
15,000
10,000
5,000

1970/71 1971/72 1972/73 1973/74

Higher Education

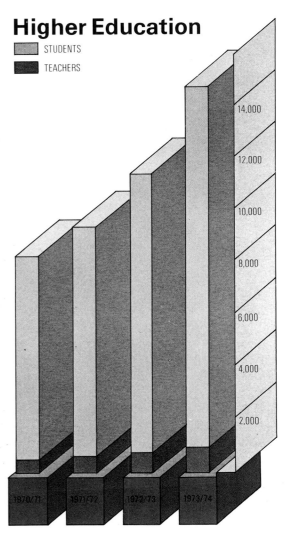

- STUDENTS
- TEACHERS

14,000
12,000
10,000
8,000
6,000
4,000
2,000

1970/71 1971/72 1972/73 1973/74

187

Pupils are happy amid the familiarity of local architecture, as in the south-western school (above), *or being taught in the open air as* (opposite) *in the Eastern Province.*

At Khaibar a modern school is tastefully decorated.

The principal boys' school at Ta'if is one of the most successful in the country.

Boys' Schooling

BEFORE the establishment of a Department of Education in 1924 there were few schools, all of them private institutions in the Hijaz concentrating on Qur'anic instruction and the rudiments of reading and writing. Even in the early years of the Department, growth was hampered by lack of money. At the same time there were many who feared that a modern educational system would damage the fabric of a profoundly religious society. Expansion was therefore confined to the few large towns and it was only in 1954, when the Department became a Ministry, supported by increased funds and headed by HRH Prince Fahd ibn Abdul Aziz, that school education began to spread systematically throughout the Kingdom.

The Ministry of Education is not the sole agency concerned with boys' education. The Ministry of Defence and the Religious Colleges and Institutes Administration each account for approximately 1.5 per cent of the total enrolment of boys at school, while private schools take care of some 4.5 per cent.

What the Ministry calls general education closely follows the pattern found in most other Arab countries and comprises four stages: kindergarten (*rawda*), primary (*ibtida'i*), intermediate (*mutawassit*) and secondary (*thanawi*). Government kindergartens are very few and most children start with primary school at the age of six. They stay there for six years and then take the Primary Certificate before going on to intermediate school. Three years and another exam, the *Kafa'ah*, then another three years at secondary school and the Saudi Baccalaureat, the *tawjihiyyah* – key to the tertiary stage. After one year at secondary school there is a choice of streams, scientific (*ilmi*) or literary (*adabi*). Progression is rigidly controlled by end of year exams, which take place in May–June with re-sits in September.

There is also a small but significant grouping of schools which come under the heading of technical education. Most important of these are the vocational secondary schools, which are at present the only local source of Saudi technicians

and middle management. The Royal Technical Institute in Riyadh takes graduates of the vocational secondary schools and gives them two years' higher technical training. The vocational secondary schools run by the Ministry of Education should not be confused with the vocational training centres run by the Ministry of Labour and Social Affairs, which take students of low educational level and turn them into craftsmen and artisans. There were to be thirteen of these centres by 1980, and the Ministry of Labour plans several more.

The Special Education Department of the Ministry of Education also runs schools for the blind, the deaf and dumb and the mentally retarded. In the mid-1970s the Ministry expressed interest in establishing a village for the handicapped near Riyadh, and this could be followed by similar villages in the Hijaz and the Eastern Province.

The following table shows the number of students and the number of Ministry schools at each level.

	1974–75	1979–80
Primary Education		
Students	401,348	677,458
Schools	2,063	2,908
Intermediate Education		
Students	70,270	127,136
Schools	372	596
Secondary Education		
Students	19,892	39,875
Schools	65	102

For administrative purposes the country is divided into zones. These vary enormously in size and importance – the Riyadh zone has more than 4,000 teachers, the rural Aflaj zone a mere 150 or so – but each one is a complete entity, with its own health unit, educational aids unit and so forth. The headmaster of each school reports to the zone director, who is in turn answerable to the Assistant Deputy Minister; the latter reports to the Deputy Minister for Educational and Administrative Affairs, who, under the Minister, is the *de facto* chief executive for most matters concerning boys' school education. Within the Ministry there are departments for primary, intermediate, secondary and technical education, each headed by a director-general. Attached to each department are a number of subject-specialized inspectors-general, who ensure that the centralized *curriculum* laid down by the Ministry is properly worked through in the schools. The inspectors-general are assisted by cadres of inspectors based in the larger towns.

The administration of school education is still highly centralized though there have been recent attempts to decentralize and eliminate bureaucratic procedures. There is a great need to train and retrain large numbers of lower grade officials, many of whom may have had only a very basic education them-

At Unayzah's secondary school, pupils display their work, including a maquette of a mosque. The teaching of English is imaginative (below). Right, *Riyadh pupils observe the pull of surface tension.*

selves. However, the institutes of public administration and the Ministry itself have done much to improve the situation over the last few years. On a higher plane, the results of the Ministry's scheme to send large numbers of headmasters and middle-grade zone and Ministry officials abroad on courses in educational administration are beginning to be seen, and at the middle management level there is a much greater willingness to take decisions and look for solutions than there would have been a few years ago.

In education particularly, the Saudi tradition of right of access at any level by members of the public militates against devolutionary procedures. But this time-consuming contact with members of the public is both an essential part of the Saudi democratic tradition and also a practical way for senior education officials to monitor the needs of the people and the public mood. Nevertheless the load of many officials is extremely heavy.

Formal centralization is most apparent in the financial and supply systems. The zone director has comparatively little say in financial matters, controls only a very small budget for local expenditure and is entirely dependent on the central authority for the supply of all equipment. If such a system is to work well, efficient supply and distribution services are prerequisites; but in a country where most supplies are imported and have to

As young minds are put in reach of knowledge, the fever to learn grows. Scientific disciplines carry the greatest allure – but not at the expense of respect for the country's special role in Islam.

191

Girls' Schooling

The education of girls was championed by the late King Faisal's wife, and from a relatively late start education is now in reach of most of the population. A number of outstanding schools, like Dar el-Hanan School in Jiddah (pictured below and opposite) lead the way.

SINCE the establishment of the first girls' school in Saudi Arabia in 1956 female education has become one of its fastest growing areas of social development. By 1974, not two decades since the foundation of the pioneering Dar el-Hanan Institute for orphans there were a quarter of a million girls in full-time education, many of whom will pursue careers closed to women only a generation previously.

Before 1960 girls' education was generally limited in scope and haphazard in organization, available only in the larger cities such as Jiddah, Mecca, Medina and Riyadh. As it was not socially acceptable for a girl to go out of the house on her own she would receive lessons from a private tutor or in a small group known as a *Kutab*.

Sufficiently wealthy families would employ for their daughters private teachers who lived with the family and in many cases acted not only as tutor and adviser, but also as nurse and companion to the children. Sometimes the tutor would be asked also to instruct the mother of the family in reading and writing.

The *Kutab* was the first method of group teaching for girls. A small number would attend classes given by a woman who had been fortunate enough herself to receive tuition from her father or a private tutor. This early form of education was religious rather than technical, but it was usual for pupils to learn to solve simple mathematical problems as well as read and memorize parts of the Qur'an.

In the late 1950s more organized teaching groups started to appear and private schools spread to other cities. The girls who learned at these schools or privately in their homes took the same exams and received the same certificate as boys, but mixed education has not been adopted in Saudi Arabia.

The history of the Dar el-Hanan Educational Institute for Girls gives an interesting example of the expansion of education in its early stages. Dar el-Hanan was founded in 1956 as a small home and school for orphans by H. M. Queen Iffat al Faisal, widow of the late

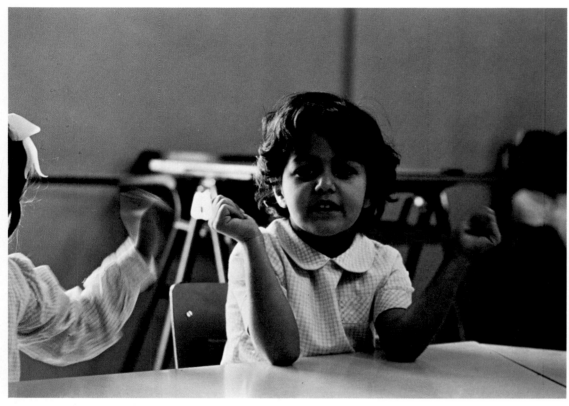

King Faisal. It was intended to be a home for needy girls, giving them an opportunity to learn and to acquire a better standard of living later on. In 1957 the Queen, realizing the pressing need for a girls' school, opened some classes at the upper nursery and primary education level, and thus the small institution started its work.

In 1959–60 the first group of girls studying at the school were able to present their primary school certificates. As the Saudi Government approved girls' education in the same year and opened some of the first state primary schools, the need then arose for intermediate (junior high) schools. In 1960 classes for teaching students at intermediate level were opened. In 1963 the first group of girls graduated from the intermediate school (the equivalent of the 9th grade in the American system). This brought Dar el-Hanan to its most challenging step – adding a secondary school (high school) for a small group of girls who wanted to further their studies. Despite the lack of qualified female teachers and equipment and a shortage of space, secondary stage classes were opened with eighteen girls in the first year (10th grade) and

nine girls in the second year (11th grade). The nine senior girls had already studied in other Arab cities such as Cairo, Beirut, or Damascus, or at home, and were now able to devote their attention to the sciences.

Intermediate education was taken over by the Government for the first year and the school followed the programme of the Ministry of Education with the help of a very small staff, most of whom were not adequately qualified. At the end of the school year 1964–65 the first group of secondary school pupils graduated from Dar el-Hanan, seven in sciences and one in arts subjects. They were the first group of girls to graduate from any regular school in the Kingdom. At that point the need for a better building was urgent and work started on the new school which now exists. By 1966, the year in which the school moved to its new location, the intake of students had risen to 620, rising further to 1,050 in 1973.

In 1969–1970 the Administration of Girls' Education opened a Teachers' Training College in Riyadh, relying on graduates from Dar el-Hanan and the Riyadh Secondary School for the re-

cruitment of their students. By that time a fully developed administrative staff had been established and girls were able to follow a well planned educational programme at all levels.

Dar el-Hanan will continue to forge ahead, opening up new lines of study and developing modern teaching techniques. These will be apparent, for example, in the learning of languages, where some schools are already making use of audio-visual 'language laboratory' methods to teach English and French. Those girls who are unable to move on to university but would like to work after completing their secondary education will be able to take one- or two-year courses in accountancy, arts and crafts, administration, child psychology or secretarial studies. Exchange schemes with schools or colleges abroad are under consideration.

Dar el-Hanan, although a typical Saudi Arabian girls' school in many ways, also exists to fill certain specialized functions. It provides a boarding school for girls whose parents do not live in Jiddah and for the daughters of those employed in the Foreign Service, who may already have started their education abroad. The institution has become an educational centre and laboratory for women's education in the Kingdom, with well-equipped laboratories, audio facilities and other modern aids. It already attracts women lecturers from a wide range of academic backgrounds and will always be an innovator in the academic world.

In 1960 the Government invested responsibility for girls' education in a group of religious leaders who formed what is now known as the Administration of Girls' Education. This body is effectively a Ministry but remains independent of the Ministry of Education. It is governed by a sheikh with the same powers, privileges and status as a Minister and an equal vote in the Seat of Ministers.

Education for women is now available in every village, town and city. There are 500 communities with schools for girls, well over the target of 300 set by the five

year plan ending in 1975. School construction projects in hand by 1975 would, when completed, provide the government school system with 129 elementary schools, 30 intermediate schools and 10 secondary schools.

In the elementary sector, nearly half the Saudi girls between the ages of six and twelve had school places in 1976, and elementary school enrolment was to be increased to about one hundred per cent by 1400 AH (1980), with a parallel reduction in overcrowding.

Intermediate education was to be brought to more small communities and rural areas and would continue to absorb eighty per cent of elementary school leavers. At this level it was hoped that the average number of students per class would fall to twenty-seven by the end of the 1395 AH (1975) five-year plan. (*See also* Boys' Schooling.)

Half of those who complete the intermediary stage progress to secondary education; here, the average number of

Following the precepts of the ancient Greeks, physical education is playing an increasing part (opposite page). *Modern language-teaching devices* (left and below) *are inevitably bringing an unprecedented cultural diversity within reach of the next generation of Saudi womanhood.*

The Prophet Muhammad is reported to have said, "To seek knowledge is obligatory on every Muslim, male and female." Basic education today is in reach of girls in every part of the Kingdom, and many go on to secondary schools.

students per class was to be reduced to twenty-three by 1400 AH (1980).

One of the difficulties involved in the rapid expansion of education is the recruitment of enough people with sufficient academic qualifications willing to become teachers. In the initial years a considerable number of non-Saudi teaching staff had to be employed; during the next decade these are to be replaced gradually by local staff. Participation in teacher training programmes by students from rural areas is to be encouraged through the provision of housing and special financial incentives, and the course of study in the secondary level teacher training institute programme will be increased from two to three years.

In keeping with the emergence of the Kingdom as a developed nation, and with a changing attitude towards the role of women in society, school *curricula* have expanded to embrace sciences and languages as well as Islamic studies. Although some careers taken up by Western women are still not considered suitable for Saudi females, there is a

wide variety of occupations for which technical training can be received. Enrolment in the four technical training centres in Riyadh, Jiddah, Mecca and Hasa was expected to double between 1975 and 1980 from 550 students to 1,200 and new departments would be created to provide skills such as those taught at Dar el-Hanan.

As an alternative to technical training, girls also have the opportunity of continuing their academic studies at a university. At Riyadh University undergraduates may study at home and take their degrees in Arts or Social Science subjects without compulsory regular attendance. There is also a School of Medicine and a teacher training college in the capital. Abdul Aziz University in Jiddah offers arts and science courses and the university of the same name in Mecca has degree courses in Arts, Education or Social Sciences as well as Shari'ah (Islamic law).

Social services required by school education are also being expanded. School meal programmes are being

It is an era of widening horizons for Saudi girlhood. Many girls advancing into higher education will grow up to travel and to accompany husbands whose professions take them abroad. Some will themselves take up professions demanding high skills.

started in selected elementary schools in rural locations and the service will expand as dictated by experience and need. The present nucleus of school health units with around forty-four doctors and medical specialists is being added to and all remote schools will enjoy visiting medical services. Medical laboratories and dental and ophthalmic clinics are to be established in school health units at Dammam, Jiddah and Riyadh.

To attract staff, housing will be provided for them and for students at intermediate and secondary schools and institutes that serve rural areas. The enlargement of bus fleets and replacement of outdated vehicles will also make school transport more efficient.

With a large proportion of older women still unable to read or write, an extensive adult literacy campaign is being conducted. Ninety-nine schools have been built to carry out adult literacy programmes and the present enrolment of some 29,000 women was to

be increased to 393,000 in 1399–1400 AH (1979–1980 CE), producing a total of 89,000 graduates during this period. The current syllabus is to be modified to make the basic subject material more relevant to women's needs and in co-operation with the Ministry of Information programme material to supplement and reinforce classroom work will be transmitted by radio and television. Short-term training courses for literacy teachers and supervisors are to be organized to improve the effectiveness of the current literacy programme.

These different branches of female education together make up a vigorous programme of learning for the young Saudi woman. The Kingdom is well on the way at least to providing universal state education at primary level, and when this has spread to higher levels future generations will enjoy social, academic and professional opportunities which could not have been envisaged only twenty years ago.

A study of medical science – and hence of anatomy and associated subjects – is considered a natural extension of girls' education for brighter pupils. A number of Saudi girls have gone on to qualify as doctors. While modesty in public remains the accepted conduct for women of all ages, increasing educational and social emancipation is widening the opportunities for women in careers such as teaching and medicine.

Higher Education

THE rapid advance of Saudi Arabia is seen at its most startling in the field of education and, in particular, education at the university and post-school technical level.

The Educational Policy in the Saudi Arabian Kingdom, published in 1970, laid out on its first page a statement about the nature of educational policy. It gave as the basis of educational policy to meet the "duty of acquainting the individual with his God and religion and adjusting his conduct in accordance with the teaching of religion, the fulfilment of the need of society and in achievement of the nation's objectives."

Higher education is thus not beset by the confusion of intent that is encountered so widely in Western European countries concerning the ends of education, nor, so far, by problems of student politics. Indeed politics at uni-

versity are not permitted; the authorities' attitude is that, all education being free, the student owes it to the State, in return, not to attack the State.

Thus by Western standards higher education in Saudi Arabia is determinedly paternalistic at all levels. The political and religious authorities keep a careful watch on the Universities and the administrators keep a careful watch on the students. Thus, "Any regular student whose attendance at the lectures, exercises and practical work in each of the prescribed courses is less than seventy-five per cent may be prevented by the faculty board from presenting himself for the examination. In this case the student is considered as having failed in all subjects." (*General Rules for Students* from the University of Riyadh Calendar)

In a country where primary education began only in the late 1930s, and where a serious secondary educational programme was only conceived in 1953, it is natural that Higher Education was at first given a lower priority than general education. But with the programme of general education increasing at an accelerating pace, King Faisal directed that special attention should be given to education at university level.

The ideals set by King Faisal are continuing with his successor King Khalid, in the conviction that the benefits of modern industry and technology can be transferred from the West without importing the disadvantages. By the late 1970s higher education was receiving a higher proportion of the education budget than previously, and at a time when the overall education budget was growing at an unprecedented rate. In 1955 the education budget was 15 million Riyals. Between 1965 and 1970 the budget doubled to over 500 million Riyals, followed by a five-fold increase to 2,500 million Riyals (over $600 million) in 1975. When, in May 1975, the new five year plan was unveiled, education was seen as given the biggest portion of development allocation: a staggering 74,000 million Riyals.

The goals for development laid down at the beginning of the plan once more put "maintaining the religious and moral values of Islam" above "developing human resources". This very close re-

lation between religion and education, while not posing problems at primary or secondary level, could be expected in the longer run to pose some problems at the level of higher education. Understandably, higher education in the present phase is very largely orientated towards the acquisition of technical and professional skills, rather than to purely academic intellectual development in philosophy, politics or the arts. The pure academic in a non-scientific subject is likely to find himself at the country's main non-secular university–the Islamic University of Medina which was founded in 1961 and now has over 1,500 students. Here the teachers speak Arabic only, and the University serves as a centre of Islamic studies.

The aim presented in the five year plan was to provide the nation with 25,000 university graduates by 1980. The main secular institutions of higher education are Riyadh University, in the capital itself, Abdul Aziz University, with faculties both at Jiddah and Mecca, the Imam Muhammad bin Saud University, also at Riyadh, the University of Petroleum and Minerals, at Dhahran, and King Faisal University at Dammam

At Riyadh's Abdul Aziz Technical Institute, over 1,000 boys receive a broad grounding in the basic sciences, which can lead directly to jobs in industry or to further education either at Saudi universities or abroad.

and Hofuf. In 1975 the Ministry of Higher Education was established, which is now in charge of all policies concerning scholarships awarded to Saudi students for study abroad, universities, and all other aspects of higher education. Within the universities policy is controlled by a University Committee, which is directly responsible to the Ministry of Higher Education.

Riyadh University was the first uni-

Faculty of Science was opened with Departments of Physics, Mathematics, Chemistry, Botany, Zoology and Geology. The Faculties of Pharmacy and Commerce were opened in 1959, followed by a Faculty of Engineering in 1962, a Faculty of Agriculture in 1965 and the Faculty of Medicine (1969/70).

Courses of study for a first degree last four years in all faculties except those of Pharmacy and Medicine (four) and Engineering (five) and in most of the first

of Engineering. In these faculties the system, based on that used in Egypt, of lectures given to large numbers of pupils, is giving way to a system of more individualized instruction. This is partly due to the determination that these faculties should refuse to lower their entrance standards; consequently classes are smaller. To enter, all students must have achieved a grade of at least seventy-five per cent in their baccalaureat examination, taken when they

versity to be established in the Kingdom of Saudi Arabia. It started in 1957–1958 with the Faculty of Arts. In its first year it had twenty-one pupils and nine teachers. By 1964 there were 1,032 students; by 1974 this had increased to almost 6,000 students, and 300 lecturers and professors, making it the largest university in the Kingdom. The Faculty of Arts included Departments of Arabic language, English language, History and Geography and, more recently, of Mass Media and Sociology; and in 1958 a

year are treated as an intermediate stage between secondary and university education, and are occupied with studies of a general nature.

The University also includes a Faculty of Education (1967) offering a four-year course, and an Advanced Training Centre. This centre provides a one-year course for university graduates wishing to train as teachers.

Riyadh University is particularly advanced in its Faculties of Medicine and

are eighteen years old (*tawjihiyyah*). By 1985 Riyadh University, which hitherto has had different faculties operating from a number of buildings in different suburbs of Riyadh, with no single focal point, will have been moved out of the suburbs to a desert site on the edge of the city at Diriyah. Work has already started on this massive project which is estimated to cost well over $400 million, and the Faculty of Medicine is planned to be the first department to move there in 1978.

Teaching materials were initially imported from abroad, and were often outdated, but latterly a greater allocation of resources is resulting in the most modern techniques being made available and adapted for specifically Saudi use by the Research and Materials Department of the Ministry of Education. Thus, for example, the Faculty of Medicine at Riyadh has made a long-term agreement with London University under which the latter is providing

1:10. Over the same period it was aimed to increase the total enrolment from 5,600 students in 1974–75 to 10,500 students in 1980. The criteria for admission would remain the grades achieved in the secondary school certificate. One quarter of incoming students were to be allocated to the Faculty of Education. Naturally the greatest growth in university enrolments would be in education, from 3,823 in 1974–75 to an estimated 23,000 in 1980.

need for higher education and the part it would play in building the country, decided to found a university in the Western Province of the Kingdom in the thriving Red Sea port and commercial centre.

The University developed so rapidly that its founders petitioned the government to take it over, and this took place in 1971. At the same time, the Government gave the University administrative jurisdiction over two institutions in Mecca formerly administered by the Ministry of Education: the College of Education, and the College of the Shari'ah (Islamic Law), which were incorporated as faculties of the Uni-

Saudi students of technology – both in Riyadh (as here), *and elsewhere – have the advantage of the finest equipment available.*

technical advice and teaching staff. In view of the eventual relocation of the University near Diriyah, development of facilities in Riyadh was restricted to renovation work, with overcrowding both in classrooms and in the administrative quarters of the University. The University has also suffered from shortages of Saudi teachers, and of suitably qualified university administrators.

It was planned to increase the number of staff from 1,400 in 1975–76 to 2,300 in 1980, aiming at a staff-student ratio of

At the same time other faculties at Riyadh will follow the lead of the Faculty of Education in switching from the system of yearly examinations with all its attendant traumas, to an American-style credit system, allowing continuous evaluation of student progress. The Faculty of Education is planning to establish a Short-Course Centre on specialized topics.

King Abdul Aziz University was started in Jiddah in 1967 when a number of Saudi businessmen, convinced of the

versity. Both faculties concentrate on the preparation of qualified teachers, the latter specializing in the training of judges. Courses are four years long and one of the admission requirements, as in Riyadh University, is that "students must undertake to teach, after graduation, for a period equivalent to the time spent at the faculty at government expense".

There are three faculties in Jiddah, namely those of Economics and Administration (opened 1968–69), of Arts (opened

1969–70), and of Science (opened 1975), and other faculties are to be opened soon.

The University also plans to build two new campuses within close proximity, one for men and one for women. Women were first admitted in 1969.

The double campus highlights the problems in higher education for women. Paragraph 153 of the 1970 *Educational Policy* document reads:

"The object of educating a woman is to bring her up in a sound Islamic way so that she can fulfil her role in life as a successful housewife, ideal wife and good mother, and to prepare her for other activities that suit her nature such as teaching, nursing and medicine."

Paragraph 155 reads "Co-education is prohibited in all stages of education with the exception of nurseries and kindergarten."

In a country where the veil is still worn and women are not expected to speak to men other than of their own family, the number of women entering higher education is still low. The Saudi Government only approved education for women in 1959–60; but within sixteen years over half the Saudi girls between the ages of six and twelve had school places, and this soon brought increased pressure for places at universities.

At King Abdul Aziz University the rule until the mid-1970s was that: "Female students can use the Central Library on Thursday evenings under the supervision of female tutors." (*Admission Guidebook*, page 26). Recently Aramco have helped to finance a new library specially for women. "Realizing the special position of women," continues the *Guidebook*, "the University began in 1971–72 to use a closed circuit television system to broadcast a number of lectures, and when broadcast live this system enables female students to take part in the question and answer interchange in the lectures."

The problem with this television learning is that it is impossible to apply to practical subjects (such as dissection in the Medical College for Women at Riyadh).

The alternative is for equal but separate facilities. While expensive, it is the probable development, and the first

With three major comprehensive universities and three specialized universities, Saudi Arabia is now able to provide places for its most able youngsters.

university where women will have equal facilities may well be King Abdul Aziz University where the new female campus is planned. But women are also allowed affiliation to Riyadh University, and the University of Petroleum and Minerals.

Apart from the system of affiliation to male universities, women have their own institutes of further education. In 1970 the Girls' College of Education in Riyadh opened with a four-year undergraduate *curriculum*. By 1975 there were 1,147 students, and it was planned to increase their number by over 300 per cent by 1980; over the same period the number of staff would increase from 115 to 364.

The Riyadh College programme includes seven major fields of study, and it was planned to increase this to ten fields by promoting existing minor divisions in history, mathematics and biology to major subjects.

In 1975–76 a two-year Master's Degree programme was introduced. At the same time a model school was launched to provide students with opportunities for practical application of teaching methods and educational aids.

In 1974, although not anticipated in the first development plan, a second College of Education was opened in Jiddah. The College is in temporary quarters, using two old school buildings, and has classes for 219 students with a staff of sixty-five. It was planned to expand the Jiddah College along the same lines as the Riyadh College, with a structure of ten departments and a staff increased from sixty-four to 289 catering for 2,895 students.

The new development plan aims "to provide female students with a sound education that will prepare them for participation in the social, economic and cultural growth of the Kingdom".

It is also planned that a new College of Arts should be established in Riyadh. This college is to commence enrolment in 1978–79, and by 1980 will have forty teachers and twenty-six administrative staff.

The University of Petroleum and Minerals is situated at Dhahran in the Eastern Province. It was founded as a College in 1963 with under one hundred students; by 1974 it had increased its intake of students to 1,500, and in 1975 was raised to university status. Its intake then was rapidly increasing.

The University is not controlled by the Ministry of Education but is an autono-

In one of Saudi Arabia's oldest colleges of further education, the Abdul Aziz (or Royal) Technical Institute at Riyadh (above), a mature social life among students has evolved – including amateur theatricals. Far left, students on the stage of the Institute's theatre rehearse a skit depicting what occurs when Government inspectors arrive at a remote desert community to persuade an elderly "youth" to attend literacy classes.

mous institution, under the authority of the Ministry of Petroleum and Minerals. While "in principle Arabic is the language of Education in all its items and stages", here all teaching is in English.

The University reached or surpassed all the targets set for it in the first development plan, and has become firmly established as a provider of graduate manpower for the petroleum and mineral industry of the Kingdom.

The number of instructors in 1974–75 was 166. Although this exceeded the number foreseen in the first development plan, it was in fact sixty-nine fewer than were needed to cope with the increased student intake, and by 1980 it was aimed to increase the number of instructors to 350, students to over 2,500.

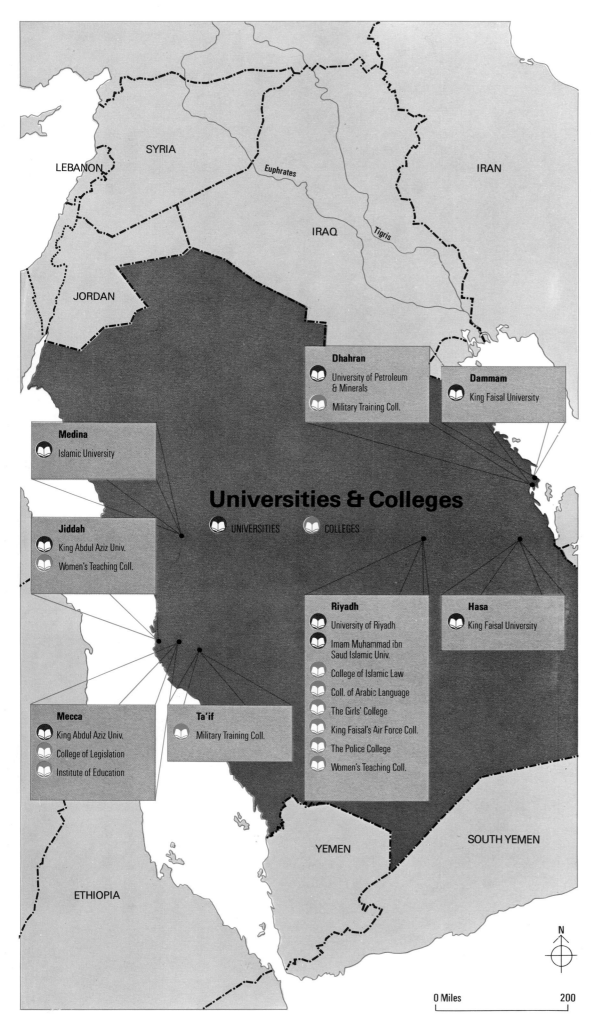

Universities & Colleges

📖 UNIVERSITIES   📖 COLLEGES

Dhahran
📖 University of Petroleum & Minerals
📖 Military Training Coll.

Dammam
📖 King Faisal University

Medina
📖 Islamic University

Jiddah
📖 King Abdul Aziz Univ.
📖 Women's Teaching Coll.

Mecca
📖 King Abdul Aziz Univ.
📖 College of Legislation
📖 Institute of Education

Ta'if
📖 Military Training Coll.

Riyadh
📖 University of Riyadh
📖 Imam Muhammad ibn Saud Islamic Univ.
📖 College of Islamic Law
📖 Coll. of Arabic Language
📖 The Girls' College
📖 King Faisal's Air Force Coll.
📖 The Police College
📖 Women's Teaching Coll.

Hasa
📖 King Faisal University

The continued development of the University into a Technical University of excellent international standard preparing students with the high degree of expertise necessary to fulfil the professional and managerial needs of the petroleum and minerals industry, will be achieved by correcting this staffing deficiency, and by widening its base through the addition of an atomic reactor. It is set fair to becoming a magnet for students from abroad seeking high training in petroleum technology and allied fields.

The King Faisal University opened the Faculties of Medicine, of Architecture and of Agriculture in 1975–76. Other faculties are planned to open soon.

Campus life for students in Saudi Arabia has its own special air of seriousness and commitment to learning. The pace of learning is certainly quickening, yet an atmosphere of conservatism prevails. Increasingly, of course, professors are drawn from Saudi Arabia itself. But the faculties attract staff from a very wide range of countries indeed. Professors and lecturers at the University of Petroleum and Minerals, for example, were drawn from Egypt, Jordan, Iraq, Syria, Canada, Pakistan, Morocco, France, Holland, Great Britain and the United States. While this remarkable eclecticism brings to university life a wide range of influences, and consequent stimulation, one result is that universities themselves are only slowly developing their own distinct characteristics and traditions.

Energy and enthusiasm for education prevail everywhere. And such is the commitment of young people in the country to its future, that the restlessness and rebelliousness that appear so often elsewhere to be a characteristic of youth have so far been harnessed by the sheer excitement of the acquisition of wider and new skills.

Technical training plays a major part in the structure of further education in the Kingdom. There are, for example, the technical school at Hofuf, and the vocational Higher Technical Institute, known as the Royal Institute, in Riyadh. Throughout the country, schools have been opened which all who have finished primary or intermediate school may enter for specialized training. In preparation for this manual work is taught for two periods weekly in primary and intermediate schools while several inter-

0 Miles   200

The Eastern Province's University of Petroleum and Minerals

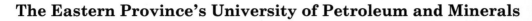

Perhaps the most dramatically successful architectural achievement of recent years anywhere in the Middle East, the Petromin University in Dhahran (pictured here) *has been a focus of world attention since its launching in 1972. Sited on a dominating bluff above Aramco's headquarters, it*

impresses the approaching visitor as a temple of learning. Its Texan architects provided it with a magnificent theatre/conference hall (top) and mosque; and enriched the natural stone of its water tower (right) with subtly tinted floodlighting. The original College began in 1963.

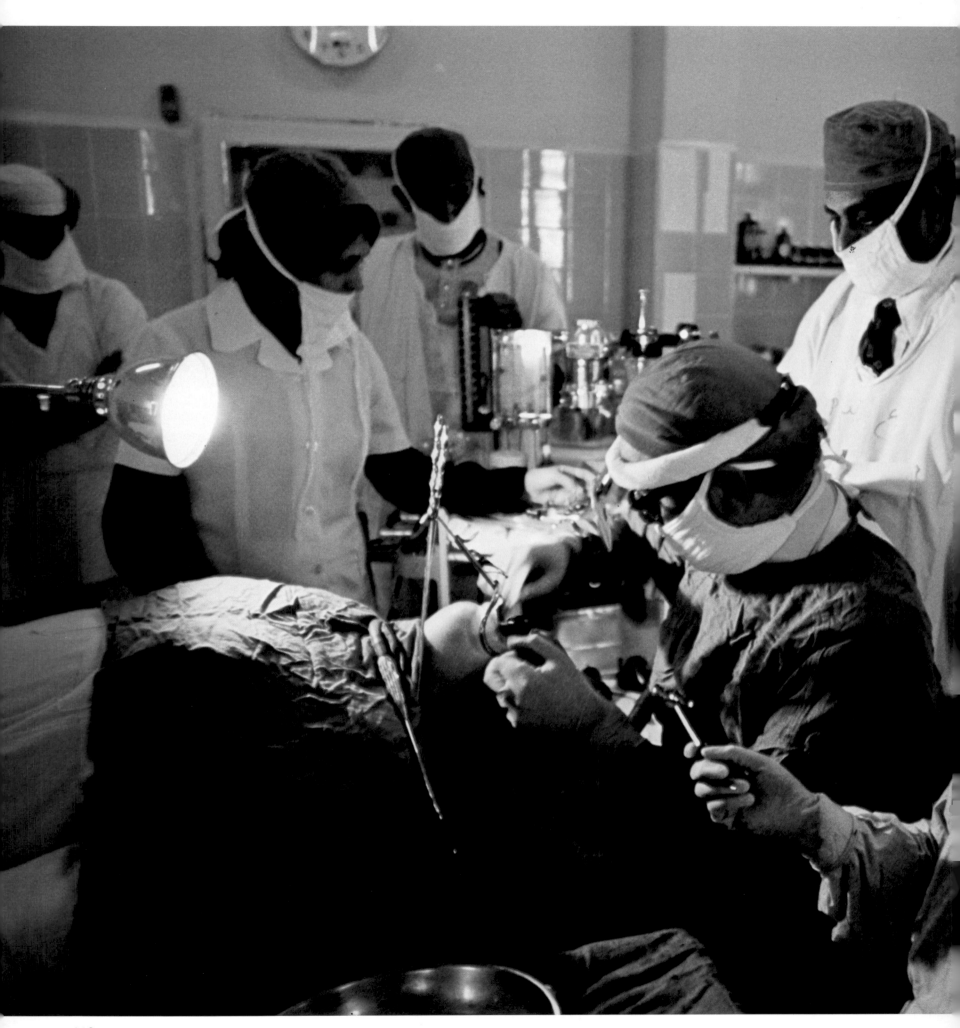

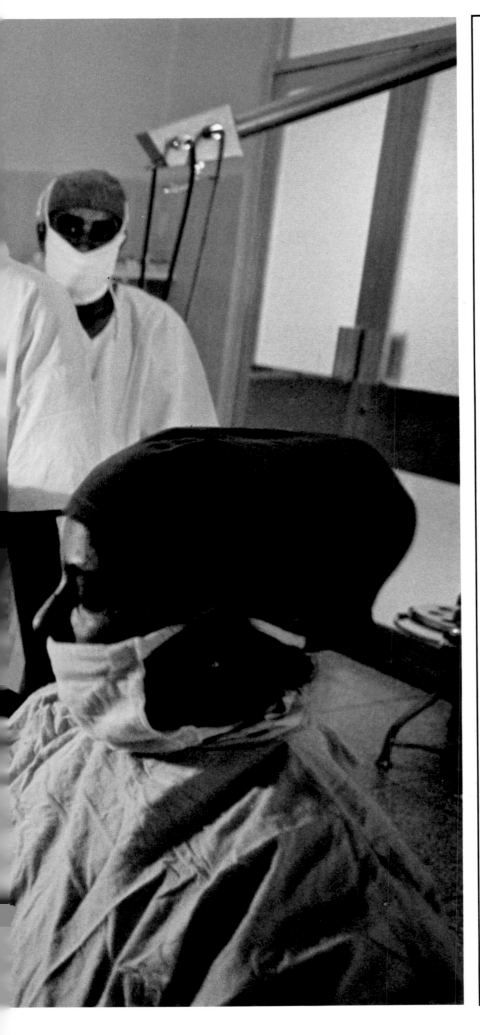

10 Social Development

The Holy Qur'an repeatedly enjoins on man responsibility for his fellows. The Government is the prime dispenser of the nation's wealth. High standards are set in social insurance and welfare for the needy – as high in terms of quality as in thoroughness of coverage.

Medicine, and care of the sick generally, has played a major role in Saudi Arabia's internal allocation of its massive resources. Newly equipped with some of the finest medical technology in the world, it is seeking to establish the human infrastructure of doctors, specialists, nurses and patient aftercare services to make the country self-sufficient in medical terms.

219

Riyadh's King Faisal Hospital

At a cost of over $300m the new King Faisal hospital and medical centre in Riyadh constitutes the best equipped medical centre that money can buy. It includes, for example, the hyperbaric unit illustrated (*below right*). With technically trained people at a premium, the cutting down of routine paperwork, avoiding delays in finding patients' records, speeding the process of laboratory tests and reducing nursing chores have been paramount factors. An elaborate computer and communications system – one of fourteen such systems (*below centre*) aims at fulfilling this function.

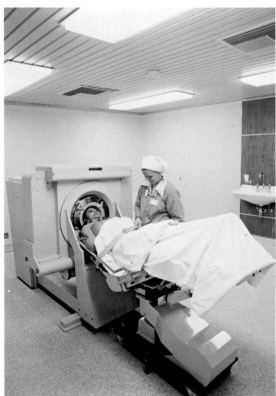

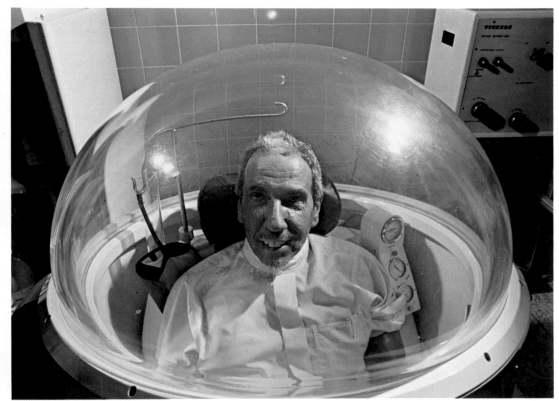

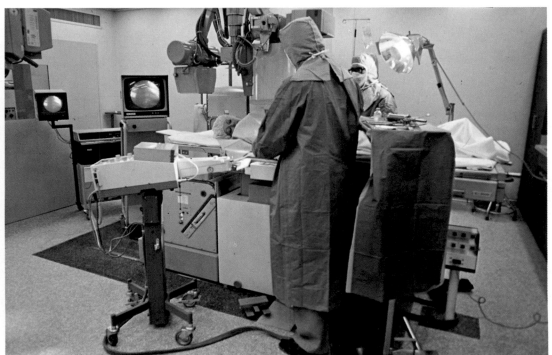

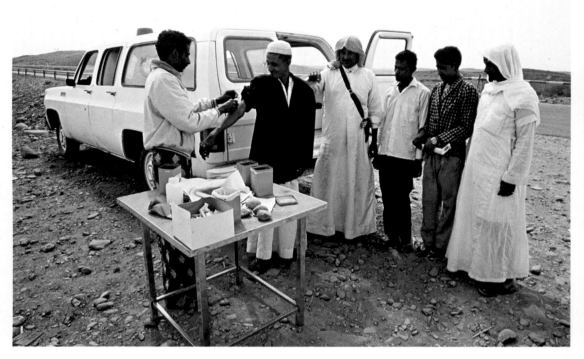

Preventive Medicine

Clinics cut infant mortality.

SAUDI ARABIA is, climatically, a healthy country. The arid atmosphere, the traditional hardihood of a desert people, sensible dietary customs and the rules of hygiene strictly observed by all good Muslims, combine to prevent the spread of sickness.

There is, for example, one of the lowest rates of heart disease *per capita* in the world. This is particularly true among those living the Beduin life.

Communal health hazards do exist, however, expecially in certain areas. In the south-western coastal regions bilharzia occurs; so does malaria – indeed, malaria is quite widespread, even where there is relatively little standing water. The trachoma virus, which attacks the eyes, is a common scourge, as in hot dry climates. And epidemics – of cholera, diphtheria and smallpox – are still a constant threat.

There is no settled community in Saudi Arabia beyond the reach of the network of medical care now provided. The urban areas are served by major general and specialist hospitals: elsewhere there are district dispensaries and health centres, and even the smallest and most remote desert community has access to mobile clinics and dispensaries, the "flying

doctor" and other emergency services.

At the same time, there is a continuous programme of vaccination, nutritional instruction, pre- and post-natal care for mothers, x-rays and dental care. Sources of carrier-bred disease, such as malaria and bilharzia, are systematically treated. Among the obstacles to be overcome is the over-readiness of unsophisticated people to accept disease as an inescapable fact of life.

One effect of the improvement in medical care has been a sharp upturn in life-expectancy. Infant mortality, which in some desert communities has been as high as twenty per cent, has fallen sharply. The linking up of road systems, especially in the northern and north-west parts of the country, should accelerate the process; so one of Saudi Arabia's chief obstacles to development – the lack of indigenous population – is being diminished in the most desirable way.

Meanwhile, Aramco and Harvard University have, for a long while, been engaged in joint trachoma research. In an effort to develop an effective vaccine, studies have been made of the natural immunity which occurs in some young people as they become adults. Other research units are planned, and there

will also be a network of mother and child care clinics; the immediate hope is to reduce the infant mortality rate to no more than 110 per 1,000 births.

Health education is itself a form of preventive medicine, and widespread efforts are being made to increase the public's awareness of health problems, their causes and how best to deal with them.

Mental Health

The Qur'an enjoins kindness.

Blood tests, quarantine and vaccination programmes all reach remote parts of the country. Below, the mentally sick – a relative rarity in Saudi Arabia – are cared for in a specially built hospital.

THE mentally defective or retarded constitute a special category of handicapped people, and one for which Islam has traditionally been particularly solicitous.

By and large the Kingdom has escaped the widespread mental health problems that afflict Western countries. This is ascribed to the strength of family ties and the security that the extended family provides: it is rare indeed for an Arabian infant or child to be deprived of the continuity of love and care within the family. The other factor that brings to society balm and balance is the depth and ubiquity of religious conviction. But there are, inevitably, a number of citizens suffering from mental defectiveness or brain damage.

An institute for retarded children was opened in 1968, offering full boarding facilities for fifty boys and fifty girls; and there are other institutes to care for the mentally retarded of all ages. Attached to each institute are social workers, whose responsibility it is to make a special case-study of every pupil. They visit homes and parents, and try to establish a relationship of trust.

Everything is done, as far as possible, on an individual basis. At the institute for retarded children, the maximum number of students in any house or class is five. A clinic is available for psychotherapy. Monthly meetings are held, to which both parents and pupils come. The discussion may be led by a visiting psychologist or social worker.

The Handicapped

Respect for Qur'anic principles lies behind Saudi Arabia's particular concern for the handicapped, the blind and the crippled. Many institutions and schools give work and education to the blind, seen working a loom (left and top), and (above) *reading Braille in Arabic. Opposite, right, a marvellous example of embroidery by blind patients in Jiddah shows a Saudi family tree.*

THE Saudi Arabian Government, in accordance with the principles of Islam, makes special provision for the care of handicapped people.

In 1958, the Ministry of Education was asked by Abdullah Al-Ghanem, who afterwards became Director of Special Education, to establish an evening institute for the blind. Within a year the institute had come into being. Based in an existing school in the suburbs of Riyadh, it provided classes for a hundred students. During the daytime they attended religious institutes; in the evening they came to this new Institute for the Blind, where they learned Braille and received vocational training.

When it was reorganized as a day school in 1960, the Ministry of Education accepted full responsibility for the academic and technical education of the students, whose number had now grown to 110.

Two years later, institutes for the blind were also established in Mecca and in Unayzah. Their teaching staff had been trained, and had acquired experience, at the Riyadh Institute. In the same year, 1962, the Ministry created its own Department of Special Education.

During the next few years several similar, or related, establishments were founded – institutes for the blind at Hofuf, Medina and Qatif; two institutes for the deaf and dumb at Riyadh (one for men, the other for women); and an institute at Riyadh to train women teachers of the handicapped.

The Department of Special Education provides everything necessary – buildings, audio-equipment, books in Braille and so on. The students are entitled to free transport from their homes to the institute; and they receive a small monthly grant throughout their training.

There are now several centres where teachers can learn how to care for, and work with, handicapped students; and the Department offers fellowships for advanced training abroad.

More institutes for the handicapped are being either built or planned and, in the light of experience, general policies have been evolved.

In the institutes for the blind, two courses – one academic, the other vocational – are normally provided. Pupils are admitted to the academic courses from the age of six to the age of eighteen, when they can sit the examination for a Secondary Education Certificate. Teaching methods are not dissimilar from those of ordinary schools, except for the use of Braille.

For pupils between the ages of six and twenty, vocational training courses are available in such subjects as basketwork, weaving and the manufacture of household equipment. These courses usually extend over six years, and culminate in the examination for a certificate in technology. Some general education is included as well, and all pupils are trained to read and write Braille. Amply

equipped workshops are available. The items which the pupils make – chairs, beds, baskets, cane tables, brushes, cloth, carpets – are usually of good quality, and sell quite readily on the open market.

The institutes for the deaf and dumb have to cope with even more difficult problems. A preparatory course is provided for young children aged four to six. Their exact degree of deafness has to be ascertained, and their ability tested. Deaf and dumb pupils are fed and clothed, as well as receiving their monthly grant and enjoying the medical and welfare services available to all handicapped people. They are taught in classes containing not more than ten, or fewer than five, pupils. For general supervision they are divided into houses of ten.

Every institute has social workers and a full-time nurse on the staff. The hope is that all students will acquire a trade. For the broader development of their personalities, and to give them satisfying lives, they are encouraged to take part in a full range of *extra-curricula* activities. It is wonderful to see them flower.

Deaf and dumb children are taught by skilled instructors with the assistance of electrical devices that produce perceptible vibrations (left).
Below: *playgrounds and special facilities in institutions are helping to enrich the lives of children crippled at birth or by accident.*

229

Social Insurance

NO major developing country has exceeded Saudi Arabia in its concern for its workers and their families.

Social Insurance is a system originally based on Islamic principles through which the State ensures the worker's safety and provides for a secure future in which he and his family can lead a decent stable life. The General Organization for Social Insurance (GOSI) began enforcement of the Social Insurance Law in 1393 AH (1973 CE). This Law lays down several types of protection for workers regardless of nationality or sex – disability, old age and death benefits (Annuities Branch), occupational injuries and occupational diseases (Occupational Hazards Branch), temporary disability due to sickness or maternity, and family grants in cases where the insured has several dependants. Unemployment compensations are made available and there is good protection for the self-employed.

The main parts to be applied so far have been the Annuities and Occupational Hazards provisions. By the end of 1394 AH (1974 CE) over 199,400 persons, employed in more than 770 private and public organizations, were covered under the Annuities programme.

The Annuities Branch includes: old-age annuity, non-occupational disability, payment of lump sums to insured persons who do not qualify for pensions, funeral expenses grant, heirs' annuity, marriage grant to widows, daughters and sisters, and voluntary insurance for old age.

When the insured worker retires at the age of sixty or more, the General Organization for Social Insurance pays him a monthly annuity for the rest of his life. The amount of the annuity depends on the contributory period and the average of his wage during the last twenty-four months of insurance. It is calculated on the basis of two per cent of his average monthly wages during the previous twenty-four months, multiplied by the number of years of his contribution in insurance. Added to the annuity is a dependants' allowance – ten per cent of the annuity for the first dependant, five per cent for the second dependant, and five per cent for the third dependant.

Annuities are paid monthly for the rest of his life, and the annuitant's heirs, after his death, are also entitled to monthly payments.

If the insured sustains a non-occupational disability and is crippled before he reaches retirement age, he is entitled to receive from GOSI a disability annuity payable to him monthly for the duration of his life. The amount of this annuity is computed in the same way as the old age annuity, at two per cent of the average monthly wage for the twenty-four months preceding the occurrence of the disability, multiplied by the number of years of his participation in insurance or forty per cent of such an average, whichever is the higher figure. A total disability allowance of fifty per cent of such annuity is added if the disabled person needs the assistance of others in the performance of his everyday activities. Both the annuity and the allowance is paid to the annuitant as long as he is incapacitated. If he is still disabled at the age of sixty, the annuity is then payable for life. After his death, the dependent members of his family are entitled to heirs' annuities.

The insured who has reached the age of sixty and who for at least six months has been without a job subject to insurance, and likewise the insured who is afflicted with a non-occupational disability before he reaches sixty, receives from GOSI a lump sum equivalent to his total contributions (five per cent of his wages) paid throughout the insurance period, plus a grant of five per cent of the total of such contributions, provided that he has completed a mimimum of twelve insur-

ance months and does not qualify for an old age disability annuity. If he dies, GOSI pays the lump sum to the widow or to the children, to the father and mother or, in the absence of any other person, to the brothers and sisters.

A grant of SR 400 is paid to the person who undertakes to pay the funeral expenses of an insured worker who dies in service after completing at least six insurance months during the last year before his death. A similar grant is available on the death of an aged or crippled annuitant. Upon the death of an insured person who received a non-occupational disability annuity, his dependants are entitled to the same annuity which used to be paid to their supporter (minus the dependants' allowance or total disability allowance). The heirs are entitled to the annuity if the deceased was not an annuitant, on the basis of the disability annuity to which he would have been entitled had he sustained the disability on the date of his death. If a son or daughter has lost both parents, the annuity is doubled.

The widow is given one half of the husband's annuity, and each of his other dependants receives twenty per cent of such annuity, provided that the total monthly amount payable does not exceed the original annuity; if the annuities exceed one hundred per cent of the deceased worker's entitlement, all the annuities are reduced in proportion. The widow is entitled to the annuity provided that the marriage took place at least six months before the death of the insured if he was in service, or at least twelve months before his death if he was an old

Typical of Saudi care for the unfortunate is this orphanage built in the Qasim area.

age pensioner or crippled annuitant. She continues to receive it until she remarries, in which case she is given a marriage grant. Male orphans under twenty years of age are also eligible for the annuity. The age limit is extended until they are twenty-five, if they are pursuing their studies in an educational or vocational institute. If they are unable to work by reason of a chronic disease or an infirmity, the annuity is paid to them as long as they are thus afflicted. Female orphans are supported until they marry, provided that they were supported by the deceased at the time of his death. Brothers and sisters of the deceased are provided for, subject to the same conditions applicable to orphans. Parents of the deceased who were supported by him at the time of his death, provided that the father is over sixty years of age and unable to work, are also entitled to the annuity. If an old age or disability annuitant's widow, daughter or sister marries, she is given a marriage grant equal to eighteen times the annuity she used to receive, and payment of the annuity ceases at the end of the month during which the marriage takes place. The allocation of this grant terminates any right derived from the insurance.

A worker who has been subject to the annuity insurance branch for at least five years and no longer qualifies, for any reason, to be subject to this branch, may continue his affiliation provided he submits an application to the General Organization for Social Insurance within six months after the date on which he ceased to be subject to insurance, and

undertakes to pay the contributions required both of him and of the employer (five per cent of his wages paid by the insured and eight per cent by the employer).

The Hazards Branch provides for insurance against employment injuries and occupational diseases. The accumulation of benefits in kind and cash is not conditional upon any qualifying period of insurance. The rate of contribution is fixed at two per cent of the wages of the insured and the employer alone is responsible for its payment.

The Social Insurance scheme operates on a contributory basis, that is, GOSI revenues comprise contributions from both employees and employers, as well as investment revenues and government subsidy. GOSI's annual revenues in 1394–95 AH (1974–75 CE) were estimated at SR 240.5 million.

GOSI is administered by a Board of Directors. The Directorate General in Riyadh supervises regional offices in Riyadh, Jiddah and Dammam, and a branch office in Abha. As with other government organizations, there is great difficulty in recruiting suitably qualified staff; only about sixty per cent of the 311 positions were filled at the end of 1394 AH (1974 CE).

GOSI has therefore concentrated on improving its efficiency. Steps taken include better availability and utilization of statistics, improved training for administrative and other personnel, planning for improved computer utilization, analysis of work methods, improved co-ordination with other government agencies and assessment of

new building requirements.

The primary objective is to provide a comprehensive range of insurance programmes for workers and their dependants, in accordance with the provisions of the Social Insurance Law. As the first priority, coverage of the Annuities programme will be completed for all workers in establishments employing five persons or more. Secondly, the Occupational Hazards programme will be extended to include all workers covered by the Annuities programme.

Insurance programmes will be developed to apply the remaining major provisions of the Social Insurance Law; temporary disability due to sickness or maternity, family grants for dependants of the insured, unemployment compensation and social insurance for the self-employed. The second major aim is to maintain GOSI on a financially self-sustaining basis without increasing the level of contributory payments. A high level of internal operating efficiency and a sound investment policy for GOSI's reserves will be adopted. Operations will be co-ordinated with those of other government agencies to avoid duplication of payments, data storage, and claims verification.

The Social Insurance Law is being expanded; it is expected that the increased coverage of the Annuities and Occupational Hazards programme will have covered 250,000 employees by 1400 AH (1980 CE). A new and larger computer is to be installed to meet GOSI's expanding data processing requirements as well as providing other agencies or ministries with a data processing service on a rental basis.

New branch and regional offices are being opened throughout the Kingdom. The productivity of employees should be increased by the introduction of a comprehensive series of measures relating to training with promotional incentives. For example, ten scholarships are to be awarded each year to senior Saudi personnel so that they may obtain training overseas; five of these scholarships will be devoted to academic courses and five to practical training.

Social Life

ALL over Saudi Arabia today traditional patterns of life are being affected both in their outward form and more intimately by swiftly rising levels of education, the dramatic impact of increased income, and the consequences of industrialization. Television, sound broadcasting, and the surge towards literacy are swiftly expanding the knowledge both of those living in cities and towns and of the peasantry and villagers. The new metalled roads and the internal airline system and railroad, linking rural areas with towns and cities, and the major centres with the outside world, have brought about an unprecedented flow of new ideas.

Simultaneously, the cities are attracting from the outlying areas, at an accelerating pace, people whose way of life in the desert has scarcely changed for centuries. They are brought into the towns and cities by the promise of work and are at once confronted by the complexities of modern urban life and the racket of a culture where technocracy rules. An industrial revolution which, in Europe, gathered pace over generations, is in Saudi Arabia being compressed into a matter of years. There is an advantage – to which those guiding the country have laid claim – that lessons can be learned from the experiences, both achievements and mistakes, of the already developed nations.

The strains and pressures within Saudi Arabian society today are recognized as inevitable. Yet the intent to preserve what is right and true in traditional values, while accepting the enlightenment of education and the challenge of so-called progress, wins the admiration of all who look at Saudi Arabia today closely.

The central point is that Saudi Arabians put first their role as guardians of the holy shrines of Islam and as the inheritors of the homeland of the Prophet. This role in their peninsula is their *raison d'être* as a people. They have standards to maintain on behalf of Islam. They grow up in the knowledge of this unique heritage. Whatever the temptations, they refuse to dispense with it.

The outsider is at once struck by the restraints which Saudi Arabians at all levels willingly accept. A devoutness, even an asceticism, prevails at all levels of society, even when luxury or great wealth is easily within reach. Young men and women who may have completed their education in the West' will return to Saudi Arabian society and, with apparent effortlessness, shed those aspects of indulgence and licence which the West takes for granted. The Qur'anic prohibition against alcohol is taken seriously. Modesty is indeed expected of womenfolk, and the segregation of the sexes in open society – while it is being modified in certain aspects – is widely accepted.

One of the central strengths of the Kingdom is that this subtle balance between traditional values and the modern world is struck by the Royal Family. By its vast network of relationships, it permeates almost all areas of authority in the Kingdom. Yet it has a subtly and determinately liberal attitude which is evident in general attitudes towards women. Up to the early 1960s there was no formal education for girls.

The central factor is the strength of the family. In a period of swift outward change, widely spread family links produce a complex of allegiances which ensure continuity and high standards of conduct.

Commerce (below, and opposite) *brings social intercourse. But the home is where friends meet, and homes – though sometimes given eye-appeal from without* (right, and above) *– are small fortresses of privacy.*

By the early 1970s, over 270,000 girls (probably one third of the girls in the country) were attending school, and the number and proportion were swiftly growing. The impulse for this remarkable development came directly from the top. By and large, this profound change has been achieved without ruction.

Similarly, for example, in the field of broadcasting and television the late King Faisal was alive to the educative potential of the medium. Some of his counsellors were not so persuaded. The King presented a closed circuit demonstration of readings from the Qur'an. The doubters soon became impressed. Today television plays a notable role in the religious life of the nation, indeed a role which reaches beyond that into general education and information, right into the home, where the women and children are to be found.

Traditionally in Saudi Arabia, the women's role centred exclusively on the home. Social contact with men outside the home was forbidden. While in the intimacy of the home a wife would play as full a part as her energy and intelligence and strength of character allowed her, the basic definition of a wife's role could be defined as that of serving her husband by obeying him, and serving her children by caring for them. If such a role has meant restrictions on the lives of women, it has nonetheless brought remarkable strength to the family unit in the country.

For womenfolk would meet womenfolk within the family, and family links have always been broad and often far-flung. Today the restrictions on the life and activity of women is often more apparent than real. The outsider can easily be deceived. In the streets women go veiled; in their homes, as in the schools and universities, they are unveiled. Indeed, they are unveiled when they enter the shops now selling expensive women's fashion in the major cities. The visitor from outside the country will not normally find himself in the company of women when taking a meal at the home of a Saudi friend. But this would not be so if he were a member of the extended family.

There is no woman in Saudi Arabia – of any nationality – to be seen behind the wheel of a car. On the other hand, Saudi women are taking university degrees in their own universities. The problem of listening to lectures given by male professors is overcome by the use of a closed circuit television. At the same time, more and more Saudi women are travelling abroad with their husbands, many of them executives in the modern structure of Saudi government or in Saudi-based international firms. Saudi women now carry their own passports, their unveiled faces appearing in their passport photographs.

Women may not yet take up jobs in industry and government, but they are readily accepted as doctors, teachers, nurses and social workers. For several years they have been employed as radio and television announcers and commentators.

Despite the singular moves towards the emancipation of women – many of them quietly instigated following the accession of the late King Faisal who was known to respect the relatively progressive views of his wife Iffat – there are few Saudi women who would not vigorously defend the virtues of the paramountcy of the woman's classic role of wife and mother. There is no wish among Saudi womanhood to rush headlong into the much vaunted emancipation of womanhood in the West which has been seen to have added not a whit to the happiness of mankind, to the strength of the family, or to social stability. The system of marriages being arranged between families is universally honoured as its success has long been proved. Westerners often forget that it is a system that prevailed successfully in the West itself until a few centuries ago.

Traditionally, it is the girl's parents who negotiate her marriage and the dowry which the future husband is expected to provide. Such is the basic system prevailing today. But an element of choice by the young people themselves is creeping in, especially among those girls who are beginning to become wage earners and therefore have more influence in their families. But this is not to imply that marriages take place against parental wishes. And if marriages in Saudi Arabia are seen by both families clearly not to work, the way in which married partners are separated is far less fraught than in, say, Western societies. Because divorce may not be a complicated process, it does not mean that it is excessively frequent. Qur'anic law provides quite clearly for marriages which do not work. Divorces take place privately, without fuss.

Privacy is a virtue of Saudi Arabian life. As elsewhere in the Islamic world, homes are built around an open centre. They do not look outwards. They are self-contained. Their freedoms are internal freedoms. Indeed, the liberality and ease of relationships within a family are well known.

Beyond the towns and cities, among the Beduin – perhaps ten per cent of the population – it is the tribal allegiances that still strongly prevail. The influence of the ancient, disciplined and dignified way of life markedly pervades all levels of Saudi Arabian society. And although the force of tribal loyalties is certainly diminished in town life, the loyalties are not forgotten. Among those from the families who hold the leadership of tribes and who have come to live in cities and to make their fortunes there, there is a widespread tendency to maintain the tribal links. The Beduin "wing" of the family or tribe is visited at festival times throughout the year. Conversely, tribesmen visiting cities or towns unfailingly find hospitality at the homes of relatives or tribal leaders who have taken up residence in the urban communities.

The Western visitor is frequently struck by the way in which drivers or servants may be ushered into the presence of the mighty along with distinguished visitors. The practice is exemplified by the accessibility of the Monarch himself, whom many subjects may visit at appropriate times and, in visiting, bend to kiss his cheek in welcome. Similarly – and in accordance with a Qur'anic principle – does the Saudi leadership eschew expressions of obeisance. All are equal in the sight of God; bowing and scraping do not take place in the Saudi court or in Saudi society.

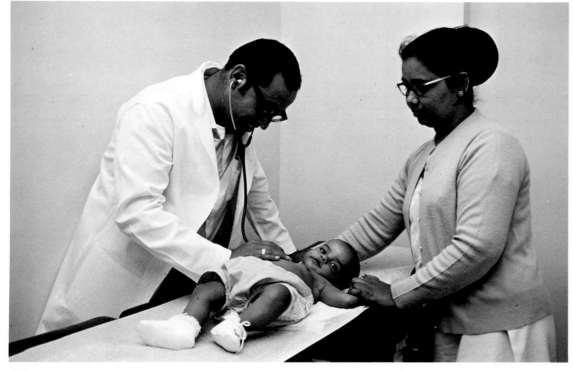

The strongest priority is given to care of the very young (above).

Even these foreign women find the black abaya, *which Saudi women customarily wear with a veil to cover the face in public, an elegant and suitably modest form of dress when shopping* (opposite).

In the desert, the life of the women is relatively less sequestered than in the cities. Veiling is largely unnecessary. There are no strangers in the group. Worship takes place within the group. In the Beduin encampment, there is no mosque – always a male preserve – to separate the sexes. Tasks of every kind must be performed jointly.

Despite the onslaught of technology, Saudi Arabians as a whole seem in no doubt as to where their values lie. Already a generation has passed and the structure of those values is largely intact. They are a people who have proved themselves unafraid of what technological progress can bring; at the same time they have proved themselves indifferent to the shallow carpings of those ignorant of the meaning of Saudi social traditions.

The Westerner in Saudi Arabia

FOR Western readers of this work, who may be visiting Saudi Arabia for the first time, the Publishers deferentially offer the following guidance on certain aspects of form in Arab society.

As providers of **hospitality**, Arabs are well renowned. There is a genuine delight in social interchange, and most Arabs take pride in the range and variety of their friendships.

The most familiar gesture of hospitality in Saudi Arabia, whether it is Arabians entertaining one another or foreign visitors, is the serving of coffee. The coffee is offered in small cups without handles, which are usually only half filled when offered. The coffee itself is strongly flavoured with cardamom, and sometimes with cloves and saffron. It is admirably refreshing in a hot climate. The server of coffee will refill the cup until the guest returns the cup to him giving it a little shake. To accept three such cups of such coffee is normal; more may be considered excessive. Sweet milkless tea often follows.

An invitation to dinner may prove to lead to the offering of a meal in the Western style. Alternatively, it may be a more grand affair in which Arab food is served in large dishes placed on a table-cloth on rugs on the floor, and the guests assemble seated on the floor, as round a table, to eat with the fingers of the right hand. The central dish could be a young camel, or a sheep – either boiled or roasted whole – served on a mound of steaming rice on large copper or brass trays. To eat with the left hand is not regarded as acceptable. Before and after such meals the right hand is washed.

Women do not mix with strangers in Arab society. Dinner engagements and more elaborate feasts are all-male affairs.

Westerners are often surprised at the ease of relationship between various **ranks in society**. This equality of men in the eyes of God derives from the teachings of the Holy Qur'an. Frequently, drivers or others in relatively humble capacities will accompany those in whose service they are employed into the presence of those of standing and high rank. There is little rigidity in social stratification, so far as it exists at all. The *sayyids* and *sharifs*, or descendants of the Prophet Muhammad, are accorded, however, special esteem.

It is customary to shake hands on meeting and parting. Hearty behaviour seldom impresses, and to give a sense of haste can cause affront. Those seeking to discuss matters with people in high

In a changing world, women have already made their mark in teaching (below: a Jiddah headmistress) and the medical profession (right). However, it is non-Saudi girls who fill the secretarial posts (left).

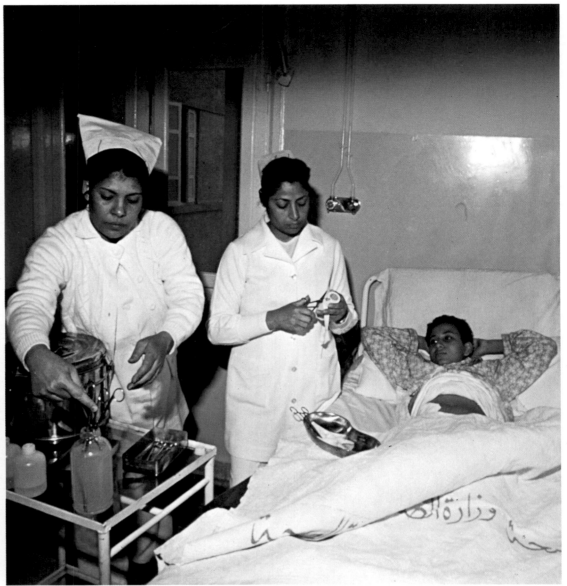

positions may find that when they are admitted there are several others present who have quite different business to discuss, or who are simply paying their respects. Conversations may thus overlap, and frequently be prolonged by interruptions. The reason is two-fold: Arab hosts strive to avoid abruptness and excessive briskness in social and business life; and those in authority like to be accessible.

It is customary for hosts to accompany visitors to the door of the house or of the office, or to an awaiting car. Such gestures should be reciprocated by Westerners receiving Arab guests; and a Western host should not be misled by the protests that his journey from desk to front door are hardly necessary.

As for **dress**, Saudi Arabians of virtually all ranks hold firmly to their traditional manner of dress in their own land, and may well prefer to keep the head covered indoors. To be less than well turned out is unacceptable.

Most Saudi Arabians rightly consider their own form of dress to be more appropriate to the climate of their country. Men wear the headcloth, *ghotra*, on the head, held in place by the *taqia* beneath, and the black woven circlet, *iqal*, above. The *ghotra* is usually of chequered red and white in the cooler months and of white in the hot months. The main body garment is the long white shirt, *thaub*, above which may be worn the loose and flowing gown, *mishlah*, not infrequently of a brown colour. Women wear the *abaya*.

The ubiquity of English among educated classes can easily mislead the visitor into overlooking the pleasure a knowledge of Arabic can bring to the Arabs with whom he may be associated. Even to be able to greet and to reply to a greeting in Arabic is regarded as a mark of some deference towards the society which the visitor is entering. Frequently **Arabic salutations** are extended. Here are a few of them:

Salutation	Response
is-salaam 'alaykum Peace be upon you	*wa-'alaykum is-salaam* And upon you be peace
sabaah il-khayr Good morning	*sabaah in-nuwr* "Morning of light"
masaa' il-khayr Good evening	*masaa' in-nuwr* "Evening of light"
kayf haalak? How are you?	*tayyib, il-hamdu lillaah!* Well, praise be to God!
fiy amaan illaah Good-bye – "in the care of God"	*fiy amaan il-kariym* "in the care of The Generous One"

The usual term for *please* when requesting something or a service is *min fadlak*; and when offering something *tafaddal*. Use of the term *shukran* is perhaps most common for the English *thank-you*, but *mashkuwr* and *askhurak* may also be used.

Growth of the economy under the Five-year plans

 INCREASE IN VALUE 1969/70 COMPARED WITH 1974/75

 INCREASE IN VALUE 1974/75 COMPARED WITH 1979/80

IN SR THOUSAND MILLIONS CONSTANT 1974 PRICES

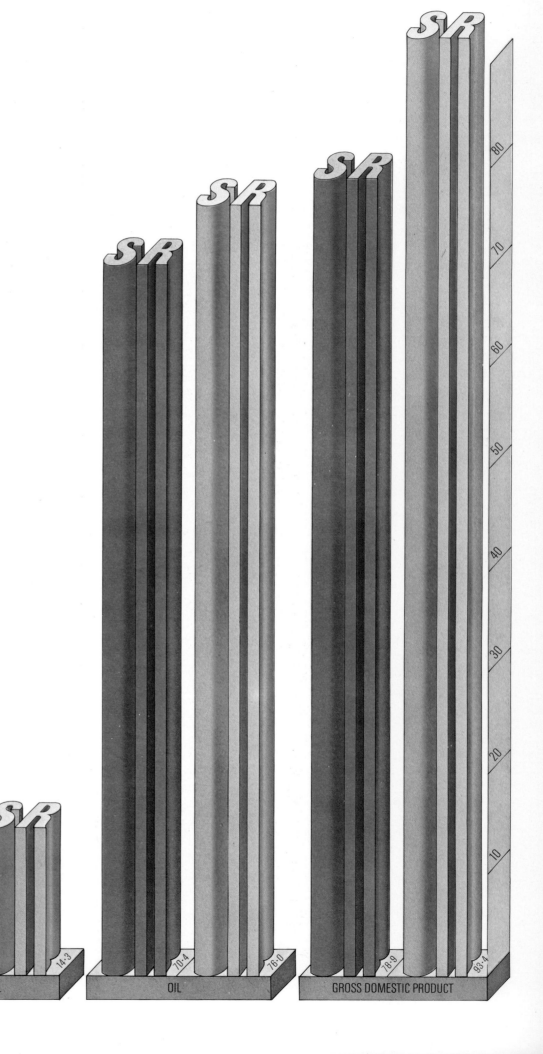

GOVERNMENT	PRIVATE NON-OIL	OIL	GROSS DOMESTIC PRODUCT
1·3 3·0	10·3 14·3	70·4 76·0	78·9 93·4

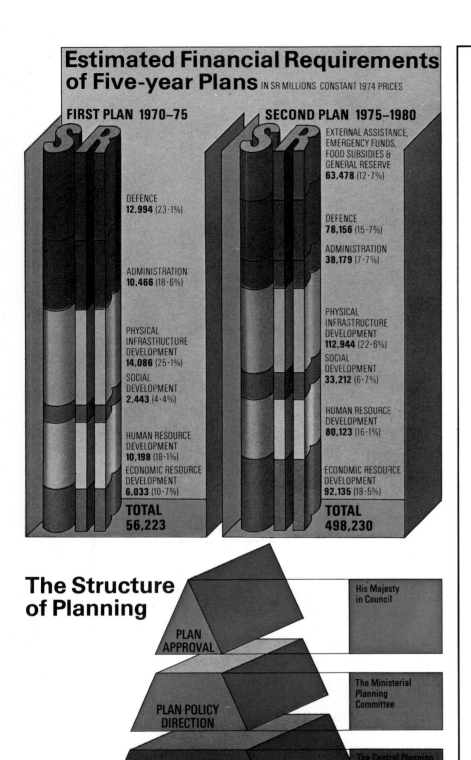

Estimated Financial Requirements of Five-year Plans IN SR MILLIONS CONSTANT 1974 PRICES

FIRST PLAN 1970–75

DEFENCE
12,994 (23·1%)

ADMINISTRATION
10,466 (18·6%)

PHYSICAL INFRASTRUCTURE DEVELOPMENT
14,086 (25·1%)

SOCIAL DEVELOPMENT
2,443 (4·4%)

HUMAN RESOURCE DEVELOPMENT
10,198 (18·1%)

ECONOMIC RESOURCE DEVELOPMENT
6,033 (10·7%)

TOTAL 56,223

SECOND PLAN 1975–1980

EXTERNAL ASSISTANCE, EMERGENCY FUNDS, FOOD SUBSIDIES & GENERAL RESERVE
63,478 (12·7%)

DEFENCE
78,156 (15·7%)

ADMINISTRATION
38,179 (7·7%)

PHYSICAL INFRASTRUCTURE DEVELOPMENT
112,944 (22·6%)

SOCIAL DEVELOPMENT
33,212 (6·7%)

HUMAN RESOURCE DEVELOPMENT
80,123 (16·1%)

ECONOMIC RESOURCE DEVELOPMENT
92,135 (18·5%)

TOTAL 498,230

The Structure of Planning

PLAN APPROVAL	His Majesty in Council
PLAN POLICY DIRECTION	The Ministerial Planning Committee
PLAN CO-ORDINATION	The Central Planning Organization in Consultation with Ministries & Agencies
MINISTRY & AGENCY PLANNING	Ministries & Agencies in Consultation with The Central Planning Organization
PROGRAMME & PROJECT PLANNING	Ministries & Agencies with some inputs from The Central Planning Organization
DATA COLLECTION & ANALYSIS	

11 The Future

Perhaps the first requirement is to have the resources. The next is to have the vision. But the resources and the vision are not in themselves enough for reality. The blueprint is the third requirement – an unrolling plan linking money, minds and hands, that month by month and year by year allows achievement to catch up with hope.

The first requirement: To maintain the values of Islam; the second: Assure the Kingdom's defence.

Planning the Future

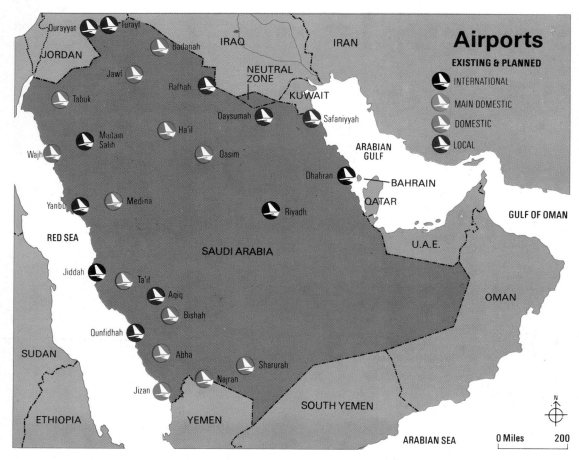

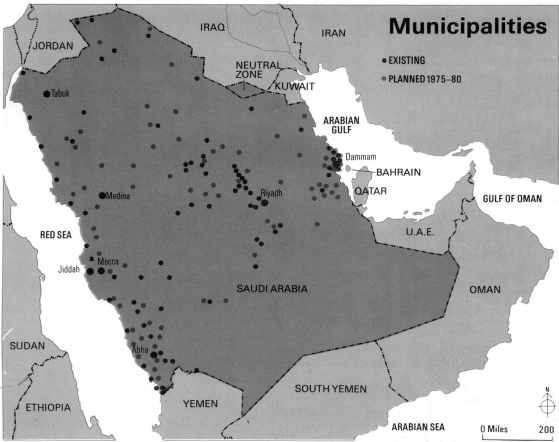

S AUDI ARABIA is, in one conspicuous way, unique – and it is a way which touches everything in the Kingdom. The spectacular increase in the revenue from oil has provided the financial resources to implement a development plan far larger, not only than could have been contemplated a few years earlier, but than has ever been possible for any country of comparable population at an early stage in its development into a modern industrial society.

This fortunate circumstance offered the Kingdom an unprecedented opportunity to improve the prosperity, security, health, education and general well-being of both present and future generations of its people. It also offered a challenge to demonstrate that abundant financial resources could be successfully used to produce, in a very short time, a modern nation capable of sustaining a high standard of living for all its people through the development of its human skills and material assets, without destroying its traditional values. Inherent in this opportunity and challenge was the risk that achievement would fall short of expectation.

On 1 Rajab 1395 AH (9 July 1975 CE), the second five year plan became operative, having been endorsed at a special session of the cabinet under the chairmanship of HM King Khalid ibn Abdul Aziz. Expenditure during this five year plan would run to SR 498 billion ($140 billion), which included SR 315 billion being spent on economic and social development projects. Sheikh Hisham Nazer, Minister of State and Chairman of the Central Planning Organization, presented the plan to the King and described it as reflecting "the effort and co-operation of all ministries, agencies and government departments concerned with the development of the economy and society of the Kingdom". It would bring about drastic changes in the living standards of the Saudi people, ensuring further prosperity and the highest levels of social security. It would also help combat illiteracy, providing free education at all levels to everyone in the Kingdom, thereby developing the nation's manpower.

Planning implies the efficient use of a

Average annual growth rate of the economy by sector

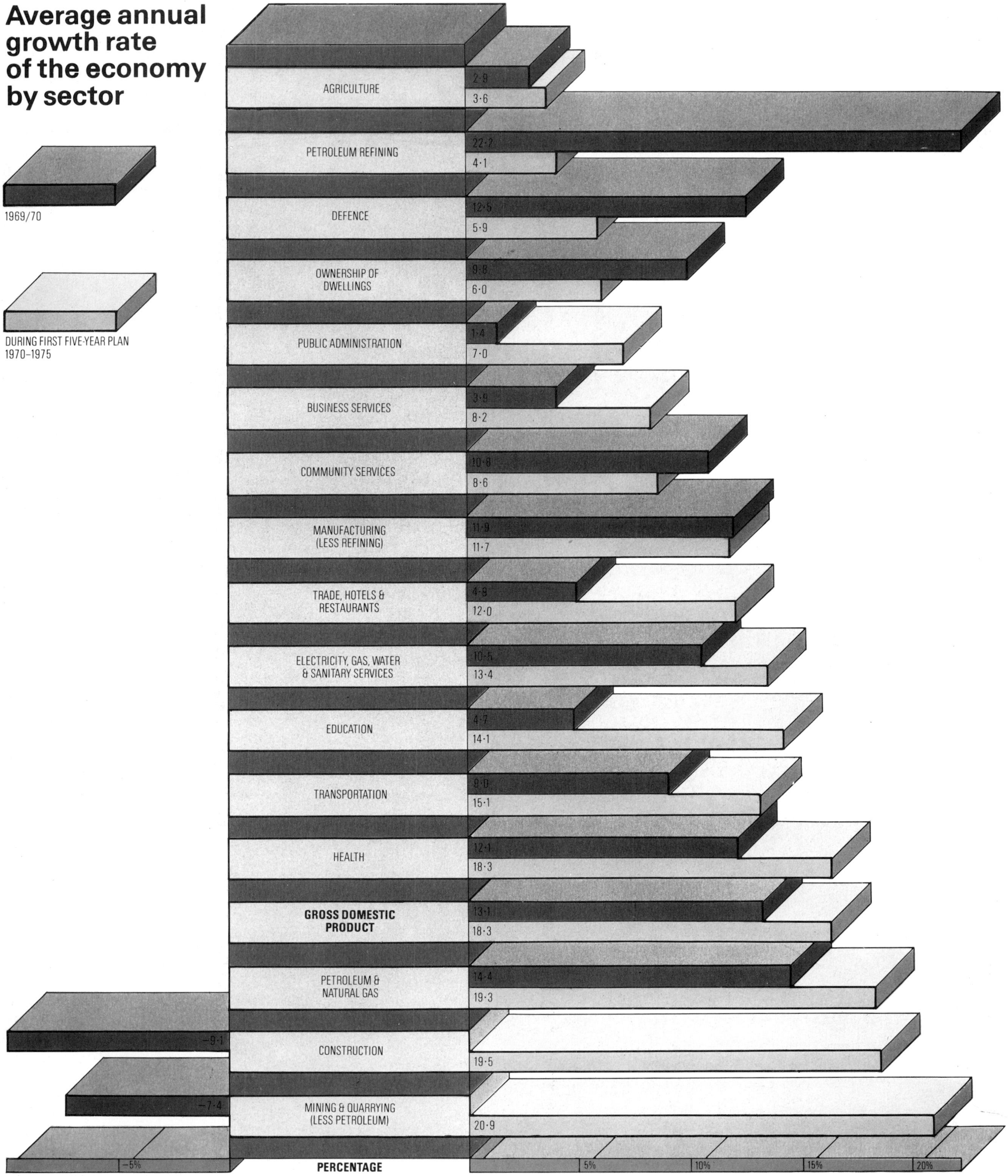

1969/70

DURING FIRST FIVE-YEAR PLAN
1970–1975

Sector	1969/70	1970–1975
AGRICULTURE	2·9	3·6
PETROLEUM REFINING	22·2	4·1
DEFENCE	12·5	5·9
OWNERSHIP OF DWELLINGS	9·8	6·0
PUBLIC ADMINISTRATION	1·4	7·0
BUSINESS SERVICES	3·8	8·2
COMMUNITY SERVICES	10·8	8·6
MANUFACTURING (LESS REFINING)	11·9	11·7
TRADE, HOTELS & RESTAURANTS	4·8	12·0
ELECTRICITY, GAS, WATER & SANITARY SERVICES	10·5	13·4
EDUCATION	4·7	14·1
TRANSPORTATION	8·0	15·1
HEALTH	12·1	18·3
GROSS DOMESTIC PRODUCT	13·1	18·3
PETROLEUM & NATURAL GAS	14·4	19·3
CONSTRUCTION	−9·1	19·5
MINING & QUARRYING (LESS PETROLEUM)	−7·4	20·9

PERCENTAGE −5% 5% 10% 15% 20%

Current Private Sector Recruitment by Region

NON-SAUDI LABOUR
TOTAL 13,880

SAUDI LABOUR
TOTAL 6,820

MID 1970's

'000

7

6

5

4

3

2

1

25·3%

33·1%

28·2%

55%

17%

21·7%

6·4%

7·0%

2·7%

3·6%

NORTHERN REGION

SOUTHERN REGION

CENTRAL REGION

WESTERN REGION

EASTERN REGION

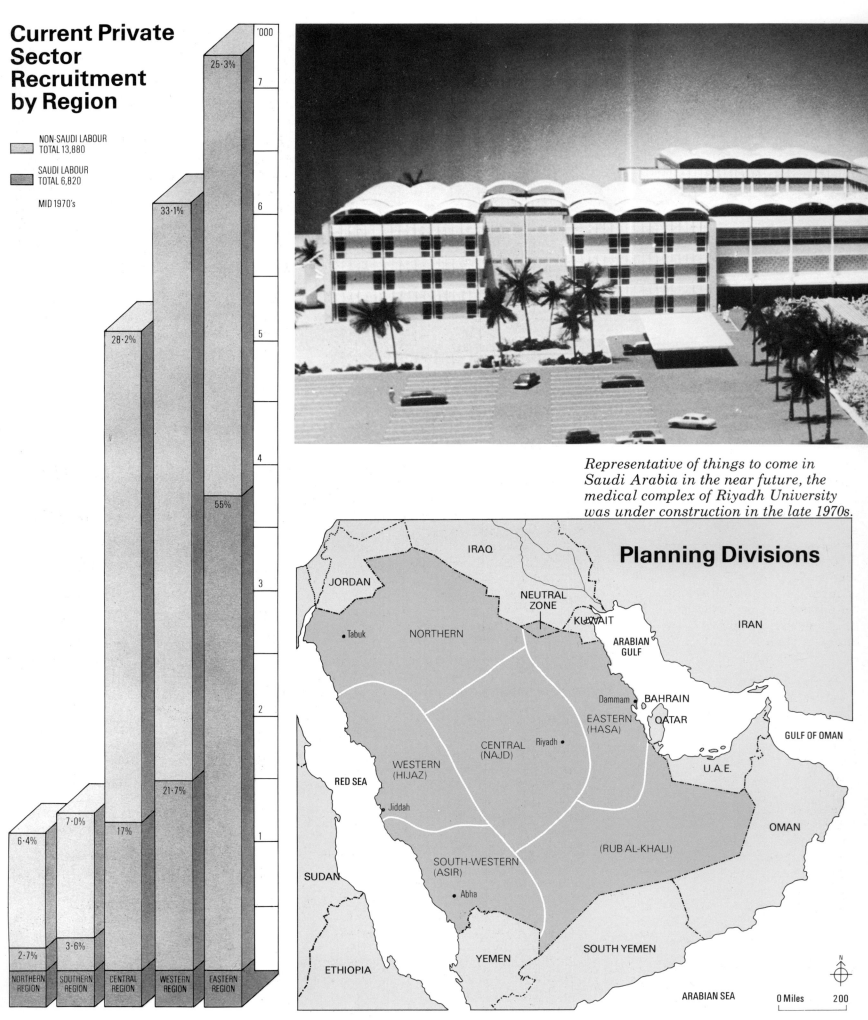

Representative of things to come in Saudi Arabia in the near future, the medical complex of Riyadh University was under construction in the late 1970s.

Planning Divisions

IRAQ

JORDAN

NEUTRAL ZONE

KUWAIT

IRAN

Tabuk

NORTHERN

ARABIAN GULF

Dammam

BAHRAIN

EASTERN (HASA)

QATAR

GULF OF OMAN

CENTRAL (NAJD)

Riyadh

U.A.E.

WESTERN (HIJAZ)

RED SEA

Jiddah

OMAN

(RUB AL-KHALI)

SOUTH-WESTERN (ASIR)

SUDAN

Abha

YEMEN

SOUTH YEMEN

ETHIOPIA

ARABIAN SEA

0 Miles   200

country's resources in accordance with certain rationally determined priorities for the attainment of national goals. A country's development plan essentially reflects its fundamental values and principles. The development plan 1395–1400 AH (1975–80 CE) provided for further advance towards social and economic goals, while maintaining the religious and moral values of Islam. The fundamental principles which guide Saudi Arabia's balanced development were set out in the plan:

To maintain the religious and moral values of Islam.

To assure the defence and internal security of the Kingdom.

To maintain a high rate of economic growth by developing economic resources, maximising earnings from oil over the long term, and conserving depletable resources.

To reduce economic dependence on the export of crude oil.

To develop human resources by education, training and raising standards of health.

To increase the well-being of all groups and to foster social stability under circumstances of rapid social change.

To develop the physical infrastructure to support achievement of these goals.

The plan especially aimed at diversify-ing the Kingdom's economic base, in order to lessen its dependence on oil, which constituted some seventy per cent of the gross national product and ninety-nine per cent of exports.

The country's natural resources – petroleum, mineral and gaseous riches – were to be fully exploited. At the same time there was to be a very high degree of industrial integration and co-ordination between the industries of various regions. The basic strategy inevitably depends on petroleum and natural gas in the Eastern Province and on launching similar industries in other parts of the country: but it was, of course, subject to economic feasibility studies.

There were to be two new major industrial centres; the first in Jubayl, in the Eastern Province, and the second in Yanbu, in the Western Province, linked together by two pipelines, one for the transport of oil, the other for natural gas. In Jubayl various industries were to be established – gas collection, a steel mill, an aluminium smelter, two refineries for petroleum products and three petro-chemical complexes. Ammonia and urea plants, grain silos, flour mills and a cement factory were to be set up in Dammam. As for Yanbu, it was to have an oil refinery for exports and a petro-chemicals complex, and a cement plant was to be built in Jiddah in addition to a lubricating oils plant and an expansion of the

The Kingdom's ability to absorb its vast revenues grows steadily. The goal requires diversification of the economy by spurring expansion in agriculture, industry and mining. Private rather than state industry is to carry the torch; the state is to provide the infrastructure and the incentives. Meanwhile the financial surplus is bound to grow during the immediate future, and a proportion of these funds will flow into private investment in the major Western financial centres.

243

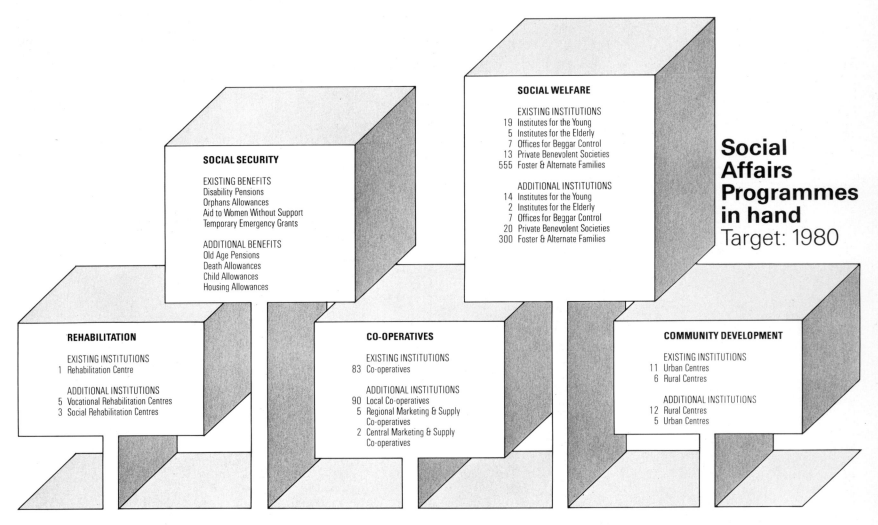

SOCIAL SECURITY

EXISTING BENEFITS
Disability Pensions
Orphans Allowances
Aid to Women Without Support
Temporary Emergency Grants

ADDITIONAL BENEFITS
Old Age Pensions
Death Allowances
Child Allowances
Housing Allowances

SOCIAL WELFARE

EXISTING INSTITUTIONS
19 Institutes for the Young
5 Institutes for the Elderly
7 Offices for Beggar Control
13 Private Benevolent Societies
555 Foster & Alternate Families

ADDITIONAL INSTITUTIONS
14 Institutes for the Young
2 Institutes for the Elderly
7 Offices for Beggar Control
20 Private Benevolent Societies
300 Foster & Alternate Families

Social Affairs Programmes in hand
Target: 1980

REHABILITATION

EXISTING INSTITUTIONS
1 Rehabilitation Centre

ADDITIONAL INSTITUTIONS
5 Vocational Rehabilitation Centres
3 Social Rehabilitation Centres

CO-OPERATIVES

EXISTING INSTITUTIONS
83 Co-operatives

ADDITIONAL INSTITUTIONS
90 Local Co-operatives
5 Regional Marketing & Supply Co-operatives
2 Central Marketing & Supply Co-operatives

COMMUNITY DEVELOPMENT

EXISTING INSTITUTIONS
11 Urban Centres
6 Rural Centres

ADDITIONAL INSTITUTIONS
12 Rural Centres
5 Urban Centres

The commitment to all the people of Saudi Arabia is that they will have access to education and training at all levels. Simultaneously, an economic climate is to be maintained enabling the citizen to fulfil his capabilities in gainful employment, to stand on his own feet, and make his contribution to the development of his country. The disadvantaged will be assured of a "dignified minimum" standard of living.

Jiddah oil refinery. Other industrial plants to be established elsewhere in the Kingdom included cement factories to step up the country's annual production of 10 billion tons. The plan entailed an expenditure of SR 60 billion on industrialization.

By the end of the second plan, demand for electric power would have reached 3,364 megawatts, while actual output was expected to be in excess of 4,538 megawatts, produced either by the private sector or through the desalination plants. The capacity of the desalination plants was to be increased during this period from 5 million gallons per day to 35 million in Jiddah, in Yanbu to 5 million, in Medina to 20 million, in Wajh to 5 million, in al-Khubar from 7.5 million to 57 million and in Jubayl to 20 million.

In the agricultural sector, the Kingdom's output of wheat should have risen from 42,000 tons per annum to 250,000 tons; its vegetable production from 276,000 tons to 300,000 tons, animal feeds from 180,000 tons to 250,000 tons, meat from 39,000 tons to 75,000 tons, and machinery from 185,000 tons to 280,000 tons.

Demand for unskilled manpower at the end of the first five year plan stood at 304,000, while the available manpower was 244,000. By the end of the second plan demand would have risen to 446,000 and available manpower would be 296,000. As for skilled labour, the demand would rise from 1,218,000 to 1,865,000, while available manpower would increase from 900,000 to 1,100,000. The plan laid emphasis on vocational training centres, where the number of graduates in 1980 will be about 28,000. Shortfalls of trained manpower were causing delay.

To help meet the demand, the plan envisaged an increase in schools – for males and females – from 3,335 in 1975 to 5,318, while the number of students was to be almost doubled from 791,000 to 1,400,000. As for college education, the number of students was to rise from 14,500 (including 1,000 females) to 49,000. The number of university graduates of both sexes would be around 25,000 by 1980.

In the field of health, there was to be a comprehensive health network all over the Kingdom. The number of hospital beds would rise from 4,000 to 11,400

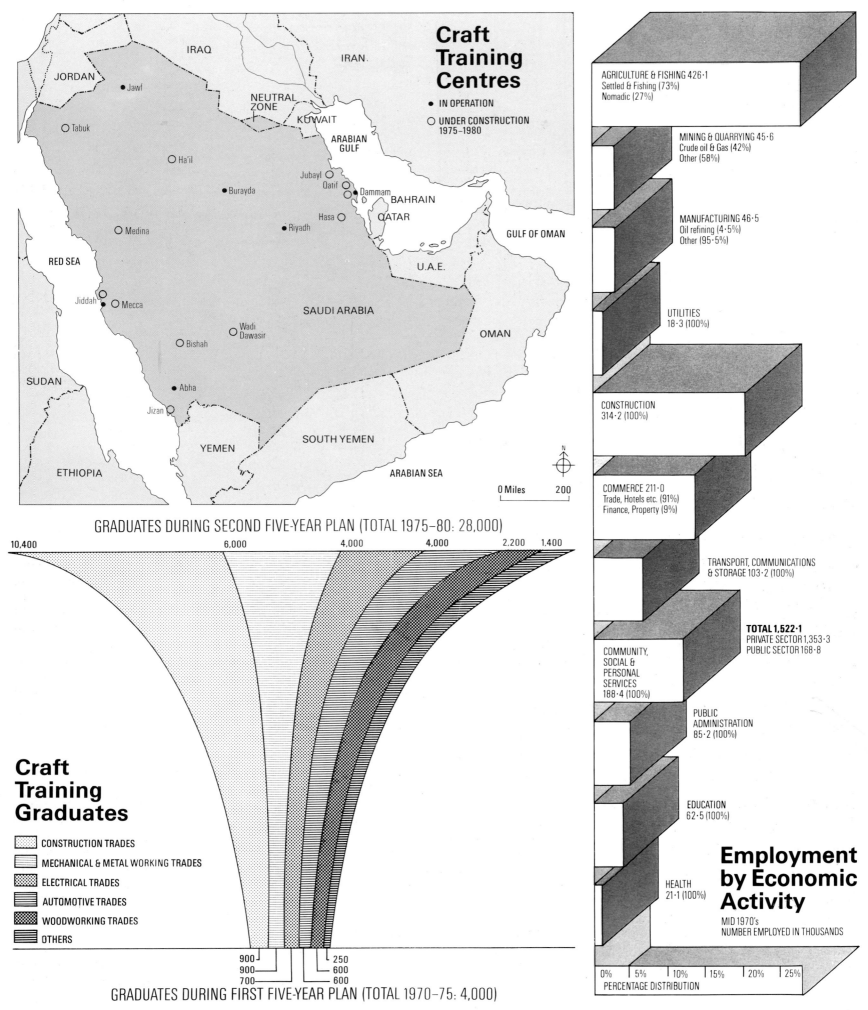

Craft Training Centres

- ● IN OPERATION
- ○ UNDER CONSTRUCTION 1975-1980

IRAQ

JORDAN

Jawf ●

NEUTRAL ZONE

IRAN.

KUWAIT

ARABIAN GULF

○ Tabuk

○ Ha'il

Jubayl ○
Qatif ○
Dammam ●
BAHRAIN
QATAR

● Burayda

Hasa ○

GULF OF OMAN

○ Medina

● Riyadh

RED SEA

Jiddah ○
● Mecca

SAUDI ARABIA

U.A.E.

Wadi ○
Dawasir

OMAN

● Bishah

SUDAN

● Abha

Jizan ●

YEMEN

SOUTH YEMEN

ETHIOPIA

ARABIAN SEA

0 Miles   200

Employment by Economic Activity

MID 1970's
NUMBER EMPLOYED IN THOUSANDS

AGRICULTURE & FISHING 426·1
Settled & Fishing (73%)
Nomadic (27%)

MINING & QUARRYING 45·6
Crude oil & Gas (42%)
Other (58%)

MANUFACTURING 46·5
Oil refining (4·5%)
Other (95·5%)

UTILITIES
18·3 (100%)

CONSTRUCTION
314·2 (100%)

COMMERCE 211·0
Trade, Hotels etc. (91%)
Finance, Property (9%)

TRANSPORT, COMMUNICATIONS & STORAGE 103·2 (100%)

TOTAL 1,522·1
PRIVATE SECTOR 1,353·3
PUBLIC SECTOR 168·8

COMMUNITY, SOCIAL & PERSONAL SERVICES 188·4 (100%)

PUBLIC ADMINISTRATION 85·2 (100%)

EDUCATION 62·5 (100%)

HEALTH 21·1 (100%)

0%   5%   10%   15%   20%   25%
PERCENTAGE DISTRIBUTION

GRADUATES DURING SECOND FIVE-YEAR PLAN (TOTAL 1975-80: 28,000)

10,400   6,000   4,000   4,000   2,200   1,400

Craft Training Graduates

- CONSTRUCTION TRADES
- MECHANICAL & METAL WORKING TRADES
- ELECTRICAL TRADES
- AUTOMOTIVE TRADES
- WOODWORKING TRADES
- OTHERS

900   250
900   600
700   600

GRADUATES DURING FIRST FIVE-YEAR PLAN (TOTAL 1970-75: 4,000)

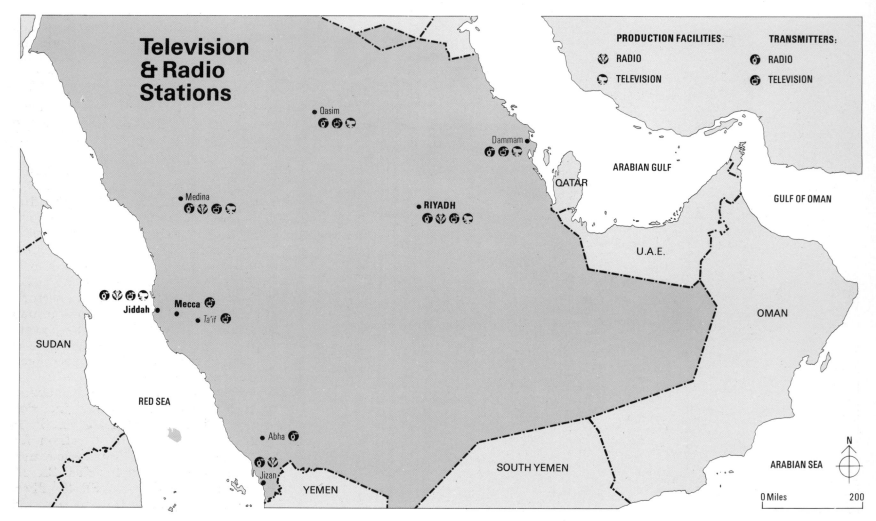

The expanding range and network of newspapers and broadcasting stations is building up the Kingdom's capacity to gather information nationally and worldwide, to produce and disseminate information on Islam, to enrich the spiritual life of Saudi citizens, to produce entertainment and news to stimulate and inform, and to encourage citizens to widen their horizons and fulfil their talents.

while those in specialised hospitals was to be doubled. Clinics would be increased from 215 to 452. The number of doctors was to be trebled from 1,900 to 4,200, to provide a ratio of twenty-eight doctors per 1,000 of the population, which compares favourably with twelve in Britain, seven in the Lebanon and two in India.

The mass media was also to be extended. The plan envisaged transmission of colour television programmes to ninety per cent of the population, with the hours of transmission increased from five to ten daily. The Ministry of Information's projects included the establishment of medium wave radio stations in Dhiba, Qurayah, Jiddah, Dammam and Jizan, in addition to the creation of twenty other radio stations. There were plans for the improvement of programmes and for training more technicians.

Another 117,000 housing units were needed, and an estimated 221,000 more would be required during this period, bringing the total number required to 338,000. About 270,000 could probably be built, leaving the country with a shortage of only about 68,000 units. In the municipalities, 2,337 kilometres of

streets were to be provided with permanent asphalting and lighting, while another 7,700 kilometres were to be given temporary lighting and asphalting. About 434,000 homes were to be connected to the main sewage networks. A total of 54 new shopping centres, 80 slaughterhouses, 628 public lavatories, 97 municipal buildings and warehouses, 13 health laboratories, 6·5 square kilometres of parking area, 100 kilometres of 'green belt' areas around major cities, 68 cultural centres, and 34 hostels were to be constructed. The development of over 39 square kilometres of new residential areas, and the preparation of 66 plans for various cities, were under way.

During the plan, 13,000 kilometres of main roads and 10,000 of secondary roads would be constructed, making Saudi Arabia's road network the best in the Middle East. Another twenty piers were to be built at Jiddah seaport, twelve in Dammam, three in Yanbu and two in Jizan, and a whole new port in Yanbu.

The number of telephones was to rise from 93,600 to 487,000, with an additional capacity for 667,000 lines. The objective was to have twenty telephones for every 100 persons in the major cities, and five

Ninety per cent of the population were to be in reach of television or radio by 1980.

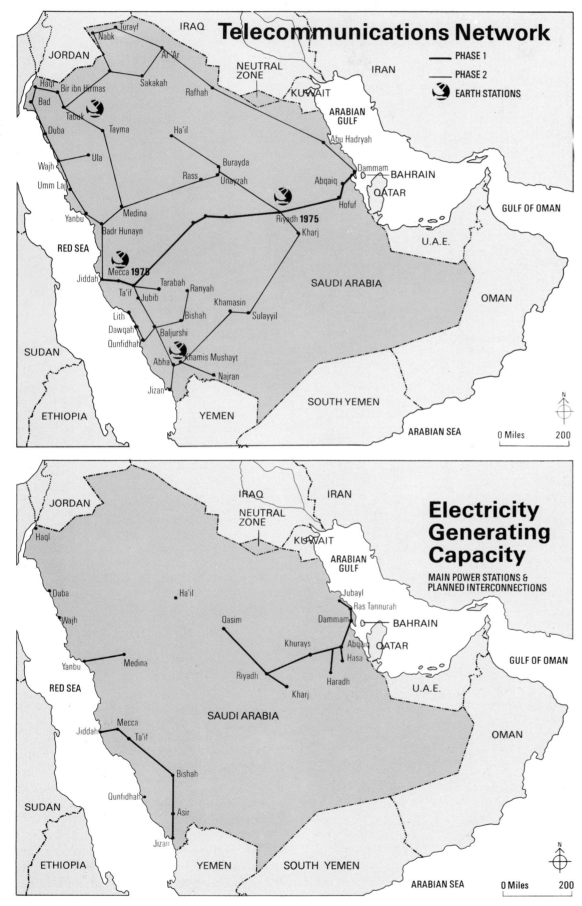

Over 3,000 megawatts were to be added to the electricity supply by 1975–80.

for every 100 in the small towns – which compared with twenty-five in Britain and two in Turkey. The postal service is being vastly improved. Three secondary schools for training in postal services were to be established with an enrolment of 720 students, and there were to be new training courses for 1,140 postal workers.

The gross national product at mid-1975 prices, excluding oil, amounted to SR 19,990 million at the end of the first plan. This figure was expected to rise to SR 57 billion by the end of the new plan. As for oil, the GNP stood at SR 128,700 million in 1975, which, it was hoped, would grow to SR 318,000 by 1980. During this period the public sector's contribution to the GNP was to be around three per cent and that of the private sector about fifteen per cent, while it was anticipated that that of petroleum would drop to eighty-two per cent.

The planned expenditure on government services and projects included SR 138 billion for administration, SR 88 billion for defence, SR 34 billion for water, SR 4.3 billion for agriculture, SR 62.6 billion for industries, SR 2.6 billion for electricity and SR 43 billion for education, amounting to a grand total of SR 315 billion.

The cost of particular projects in various cities of the Kingdom included SR 8,750 million in Riyadh, SR 8,800 million in Jiddah, SR 1,310 million in Ha'il, SR 2,100 million in Burayda, SR 4,000 million in Dammam and SR 900 million in Abha.

It was accepted that it might not, in practice, be possible to achieve all these targets within the time allowed. So much expenditure and so much activity tended to clog the existing infrastructure, both physical and administrative: and the social strains generated by rapid industrialization had to be absorbed. Some slowing down would not be a disaster. What mattered was that Saudi Arabia should move steadily towards its new goals while retaining its Islamic heritage.

His Majesty King Khalid told the nation: "After endorsing the five year economic plan, which we hope will realize the aspirations of the people in raising their living standards and contributing to the Kingdom's prosperity, I pray that you will work diligently and seriously to implement it and wish you all good luck and success." The response was swift.

247

Bibliography

This selected bibliography includes books covering a wide range of aspects of Saudi Arabia, but does not attempt to be definitive.

Abdel Wahab. *Education in Saudi Arabia*, Macmillan, London, 1971

Ali Abdullah Yusuf. *The Holy Quran*, Lahore, 1938

Aramco Handbook, The Arabian American Oil Company (Dhahran), revised edition, 1968

Armstrong, H. C. *Lord of Arabia*, Khayyat, Beirut, 1954

Asad Muhammad. *The Road to Mecca*, Simon and Schuster, New York, 1954

Assah, Ahmed. *Miracle of the Desert Kingdom*, Johnson, London, 1969

Azzam, Abdel Rahman. *The Eternal Message of Muhammad*, Devin-Adair, New York, 1964

Brémond, E. *Yemen et Saoudia*, Paris, 1937

Brockelmann, Carl. *History of the Islamic Peoples*, Putnam's, New York, 1947

Brown, W. R. *The Horse of the Desert*, Macmillan, New York, 1948

Bullard, Sir Reader. *The Camels Must Go*, Faber and Faber, London, 1961

Burckhardt, J. L. *Travels in Arabia*, 1826

Cheeseman, R. E. *In Unknown Arabia*, Macmillan, London, 1926

Collins, Robert O. (ed.). *An Arabian Diary: Sir Gilbert Clayton*, California, 1969

Cragg, Kenneth. *The Call of the Minaret*, Oxford University Press, 1956

De Gaury, Gerald. *Arabia Phoenix*, Harrap, London, 1946

De Gaury, Gerald. *Arabian Journey and Other Desert Travels*, Harrap, London, 1950

De Gaury, Gerald. *Faisal, King of Saudi Arabia*, Arthur Barker, London, 1966

Dickson, H. R. P. *The Arab of the Desert*, Hodder and Stoughton, London, 1957

Dimand, Maurice S. *A Handbook of Muhammadan Art*, The Metropolitan Museum of Art, New York, 1958

Doughty, C. M. *Travels in Arabia Deserta*, Jonathan Cape, London, 1964

Esin, Emel. *Mecca the Blessed, Madinah the Radiant*, Elek, London, 1963

Fisher, Sydney N. *The Middle East, A History*, Knopf, New York, 1969

Fisher, W. B. *The Middle East: A Physical, Social and Regional Geography*, 6th revised edition, Methuen, London, 1971

Gibb, Sir Hamilton A. R. *Mohammedanism*, Oxford University Press, London and New York, 1953

Glubb, Sir John Bagot. *The Life and Times of Muhammad*, Hodder and Stoughton, London, 1963

Graves, P. *Life of Sir Percy Cox*, London, 1941

Guillaume, A. *Islam*, 2nd edition, Penguin Books, Harmondsworth, England, 1956

Hartshorn, J. E. *Oil Companies and Governments*, 2nd revised edition, Faber and Faber, London, 1967

Hitti, P. K. *History of the Arabs*, 7th edition, Macmillan, London, 1961

Hogarth, D. G. *The Penetration of Arabia*, F. A. Stokes, New York, 1904

Hopwood, Derek (ed.). *The Arabian Peninsula*, Allen and Unwin, London, 1972

Howarth, David. *The Desert King*, Collins, London, 1964

Keiser, Hélène. *Arabia*, Silva, Zurich, 1971

Kiernan, R. H. *The Unveiling of Arabia*, Harrap, London, 1937

Lebkicker, Rentz and Steincke. *The Arabia of Ibn Saud*, Russell and Moore, USA

Le Bon, Gustave. *The World of Islamic Civilization*, Minerva, Geneva, 1974

Lenczowski, George. *Oil and State in the Middle East*, Cornell University Press, New York, 1960

Lenczowski, George. *The Middle East in World Affairs*, Cornell University Press, New York, 1962

Longrigg, S. *Oil in the Middle East*, 3rd edition, Oxford University Press, 1968

Meinertzhagen, Richard. *The Birds of Arabia*, Oliver and Boyd, Edinburgh, 1954

Meulen, D. van der. *Faces in Shem*, John Murray, London, 1961

Monroe, Elizabeth. *Philby of Arabia*, Faber and Faber, London, 1973

Musil, Alois. *The Northern Hejaz*, American Geographical Society, New York, 1926

Musil, Alois. *Arabia Deserta*, American Geographical Society, New York, 1927

Niebuhr, Carsten. *Description of Arabia*, various editions, 1774

Palgrave, William Gifford. *Narrative of a year's journey through Central and Eastern Arabia 1862–63*, 2 volumes, new edition, Macmillan, London, 1868

Pesce, Angelo. *Colours of the Arab Fatherland*, Riyadh, 1972

Pesce, Angelo. *Jiddah – Portrait of an Arabian City*, Falcon Press, 1974

Philby, H. St. John B. *The Heart of Arabia*, Constable, London, 1922

Philby, H. St. John B. *The Empty Quarter*, Henry Holt, New York, 1933

Philby, H. St. John B. *Arabian Jubilee*, Robert Hale, London, 1952

Philby, H. St. John B. *Saudi Arabia*, Ernest Benn, London, 1955

Philby, H. St. John B. *Arabian Oil Ventures*, Middle East Institute, Washington, 1964

Philips, C. H. (ed.). *Handbook of Oriental History*, Royal Historical Society, London, 1963

Pickthall, M. *The Meaning of the Glorious Qur'an*, New American Library, New York, 1953

Purdy, Anthony (ed.). *The Business Man's Guide to Saudi Arabia*, Arlington Books, London, 1976

Ryan, Sir A. *The Last of the Dragomans*, London, 1951

Sanger, Richard. *The Arabian Peninsula*, Cornell University Press, New York, 1954

Shroeder, Eric. *Muhammad's People: A Tale by Anthology*, Bond Wheelwright, Portland, Maine, 1955

Smith, Wilfred Cantwell. *Islam in Modern History*, Princeton University Press, Princeton, 1957

Thesiger, Wilfred. *Arabian Sands*, Book Club Associates, London, 1959

Thomas, Bertram. *Arabia Felix*, Scribner's, New York, 1932

Thomas, Bertram. *The Arabs*, Butterworth, London, 1937

Twitchell, K. S. *Saudi Arabia*, 3rd edition, Princeton University Press, Princeton, 1958

Vidal, F. S. *The Oasis of Al-Hasa*, Arabian American Oil Company, 1955

Wahba, Hafiz. *Arabian Days*, Arthur Barker, London, 1964

Wellsted, J. R. *Travels in Arabia*, John Murray, London, 1838

Winder, R. Bayly. *Saudi Arabia in the Nineteenth Century*, St. Martin's Press, New York, 1965

Yale, William. *The Near East: A Modern History*, University of Michigan Press, Ann Arbor, Michigan, 1958

Zirikli, Khair al Din. *Arabia under King Abdul Aziz*, 4 volumes (in Arabic), Beirut, 1970

Glossary

abal	scarlet-fruited shrub; eglantine	*Mataf*	parts of the pilgrimage area around the *Ka'bah*
abaya(h)	woollen outer cloak	*mihrab*	prayer niche in mosque (cf. qibla)
adabi	arts stream at secondary school	*mishlah*	loose outer cloak worn by Arab men
adat	customs	*muqallid*	lawyer who accepts as binding precedent in legal decisions
Ahadith	*see Hadith*		
alim, pl. ulama	Muslim scholar; scholar of Islamic law	*mutawassit*	intermediate stage of education
arfaj	yellow-flowered shrub	*mutawwif*	guide for pilgrims performing the *Hajj*
arikah	half-baked dough covered with honey	*nizam*	regulation
bayt Allah	house of God	*nomes*	(from Greek) provinces of ancient Egypt
dabb	plant-eating lizard	*qadi*	judge; ruler
Dhu 'l-Hijja(h)	the twelfth month in the Islamic calendar (in which the *Hajj* occurs)	*qibla*	recess in a mosque indicating the direction of the *Ka'bah* in Mecca; prayer niche
Diwan al-Mazalim	Board of Complaints	*Qiran*	combined performance of *Hajj* and *Umrah*
ghotra (ghutra)	headcloth worn by Arab men	*rababa(h)*	simple violin
hadh	prickly saltbush	*rajaz*	song with lines of four or six beats
Hadith, pl. Ahadith	traditions giving the sayings or acts of the Prophet Muhammad	*rawda(h)*	kindergarten school
		rimth	saltbush
Hajj	pilgrimage to Mecca and the other holy places obligatory for every Muslim	*sabkhah*	salt basins
		Sa'y	the running from as-Safa to al-Marwa in the *Hajj*
hajj, hajji	Muslim who has performed the *Hajj*		
hara	quarter of a city	*sayyid*	descendants of the Prophet
Haram	the holy *Ka'bah* sanctuary	*Shari'ah*	Islamic law derived from the Qur'an
Haramayn	the two holy cities of Mecca and Medina	*sharif*	the Prophet's descendants and their families (a wider meaning than *sayyid*)
harrah	extensive lava fields		
Hijra(h)	the migration of the Prophet from Mecca to Medina	*Suahil*	(Arabic: Sawahil) coasts of East Africa
		Sunnah	orthodox interpretation and commentary on the life of the Prophet Muhammad and on the Qur'an
hijrah	encampment; agricultural settlement		
hubara	MacQueen's bustard		
ibtida'i	primary stage of education	*suq*	space in town where the market is held
Ihram	pilgrim's dress	*Talbiyah*	words of acceptance of the pilgrimage duties chanted by the *hajj* pilgrims
ijma	consensus of non-specialist opinion on points of Islamic law		
		Tamattu	separate performance of *Hajj* and *Umrah*
Ikhwan	"the Brethren"; specifically a religious movement founded by King Abdul Aziz	*taqia (taqiyyah)*	cap worn under the *ghotra*
		Tawaf	circumambulation of the *Ka'bah*
ilmi	scientific stream at secondary school	*tawjihiyyah*	the Saudi baccalaureat, taken at end of secondary education
iqal	rope-like circlet holding *ghotra* in position		
jar Allah	God's neighbour	*thanawi*	secondary stage of education
jihad	holy war	*thaub (thawb)*	inner gown worn by Arab men
Ka'bah	venerated square stone building in Mecca, the house of God	*ulama*	*see alim*
		Umm Salim	"Salim's mother", hoopoe lark
kafa'ah	examination taken at end of intermediate school stage	*Umrah*	short form of pilgrimage to Mecca only
		uruq	crescent sand-dunes
Kiswah	black cloth covering the *Ka'bah*	*usul al-fiqh*	sources of Islamic legislation
kutab (kuttab)	small group of children to whom private tuition is given	*wadi*	former water course, now dry
		Wudu	ablutions before prayers
majlis	session for meetings and audiences	*Wuquf*	final prayer of the *Hajj* made standing on Mount Arafat
malpolon	(name first used in 1926) species of desert snake		
marsum	royal decree	*Zakah*	regular giving of fixed alms
mashrabiyya	lattice window in the Egyptian style	*ziggurat*	(from Assyrian ziqquratu) Sumerian brick tower
maslaha	welfare		

Note on transliteration

The system of transliteration employed in this work reflects the influence of two main aims which, to some extent, are in conflict with one another.

First, it was deemed important that the general reader should be spared the complexities of the elaborate system developed for scholarly purposes, and that transliterated forms should be similar to those encountered in the British and American press.

Second, it is clearly desirable that transliterated forms should represent the original as accurately as possible.

Where names have been in use in English and have achieved an accepted and established form,

the latter is employed even where this results in some inconsistency with the rest of the system, e.g. Medina rather than Madinah.

In accordance with the first-mentioned aim, the Arabic consonants *hamza* (glottal stop) and *'ayn* have been represented (as ' and ' respectively) only where their omission would have produced an unacceptable distortion of the original.

Arabic and vernacular words have been italicized except where words may be regarded as in common usage among non-Muslim people throughout the world – e.g. *ijma*, and *taqia*; but Qur'an, and sheikh.

Quotations from the Holy Qur'an

Unless otherwise indicated, the quotations from the Holy Qur'an have been taken from the rendering of Mohammed Marmaduke Pickthall The rendering by Arthur J. Arberry has been preferred where the requirement has been to indicate the tonal flavour of the original Arabic.

In deference to Muslim readers, the usage CE (Christian Era) has often been used in place of AD (Anno Domini), more familiar in Christendom.

Index

Mainly for reasons of regional variations in sound values, no generally accepted transliteration of Arabic nomenclature into Roman lettering has been established, nor indeed of Arabic usages in this volume (see note on transliteration on page 249). The difference in accepted usages in various contexts (e.g. historical, religious, commercial) is sometimes unavoidable.